DELINQUENT
Daughters

DELINQUENT
Daughters

PROTECTING AND
POLICING ADOLESCENT
FEMALE SEXUALITY IN
THE UNITED STATES,
1885–1920

Mary E. Odem

The University of North Carolina Press Chapel Hill & London

© 1995 The University of North Carolina Press
All rights reserved
Manufactured in the United States of America
The paper in this book meets the guidelines for permanence and
durability of the Committee on Production Guidelines for Book Longevity
of the Council on Library Resources.

Library of Congress Cataloging-in-Publication Data
Odem, Mary E.
Delinquent daughters: protecting and policing adolescent
female sexuality in the United States, 1885–1920 / Mary E. Odem.
     p. cm.—(Gender & American culture)
Includes bibliographical references and index.
ISBN 0-8078-2215-9 (cl.: alk. paper).—ISBN 0-8078-4528-0 (pbk.: alk. paper)
1. Teenage girls—United States—Sexual behavior—History. 2. Sexual ethics—
United States—History. 3. Social problems—United States—History. 4. Social control—
United States—History. 5. Middle class—United States— Sexual behavior—Attitudes—
History. 6. Working class—United States—Sexual behavior—History. I. Title. II. Series.
HQ27.5.O34 1995
306.7'0835—dc20   95-13185
CIP

9962A

Portions of Chapter 5 appeared earlier as "City Mothers and Delinquent
Daughters: Female Juvenile Justice Reform in Early Twentieth-Century Los Angeles."
In *California Progressivism Revisited*, edited by William Deverel and Thomas Sitton,
pp. 175–99. Berkeley: University of California Press, 1994.

Portions of Chapter 6 were published earlier as "Single Mothers,
Delinquent Daughters, and the Juvenile Court in Early Twentieth-Century Los Angeles,"
Journal of Social History 25 (September 1991): 27–43.

99 98 97 96 95   5 4 3 2 1

Winner of the 1994 President's Book Award,
Social Science History Association.

FOR MY PARENTS

CONTENTS

Acknowledgments, xiii

· · ·

Introduction, 1

· · ·

Chapter 1
"White Slaves" and "Vicious Men": The Age-of-Consent Campaign, 8

· · ·

Chapter 2
Teenage Girls, Sexuality, and Working-class Parents, 38

· · ·

Chapter 3
Statutory Rape Prosecutions in California, 63

· · ·

Chapter 4
The "Delinquent Girl" and Progressive Reform, 95

· · ·

Chapter 5
Maternal Justice in the Juvenile Court, 128

· · ·

Chapter 6
"This Terrible Freedom": Generational Conflicts in
Working-class Families, 157

· · ·

Conclusion, 185

Appendix: A Note on Court Records, 191
Notes, 193
Bibliography, 227
Index, 255

ILLUSTRATIONS

Frances Willard, 1895 83

· · ·

A "white slave" trapped inside a brothel, 1910 84

· · ·

A young woman being lured into a dance hall, 1910 85

· · ·

Women workers in a fruit-packing factory, ca. 1915 86

· · ·

Women office workers, ca. 1910 87

· · ·

Amusement park at Long Beach, California, 1920 88

· · ·

Promenade at Long Beach, 1909 89

· · ·

Young women in bathing costumes, 1910 90

· · ·

Mexican youths at Venice Beach, ca. 1925 91

· · ·

Alice Stebbins Wells, 1910 92

· · ·

Janie Porter Barrett, ca. 1884 93

· · ·

Juvenile Hall in Los Angeles County, 1914 93

· · ·

Miriam Van Waters, 1925 94

TABLES

· ·

1. Legal Ages of Consent in
the United States, 1885 and 1920
14

· · ·

2. Number and Proportion of Women in the
U.S. Labor Force, 1870–1920
22

· · ·

3. Percentage of Women Workers in
Nonagricultural Occupations, 1870–1920
23

· · ·

4. Disposition of Statutory Rape Cases in
Alameda County, California, 1910–1920
76

· · ·

5. Sentencing in Statutory Rape Cases,
Alameda County, California, 1910–1920
77

ACKNOWLEDGMENTS

This book has benefited from the support of many generous people and institutions. For financial assistance I am grateful to the American Council of Learned Societies, the Charles Warren Center for Studies in American History at Harvard University, the Huntington Library, the Woodrow Wilson National Fellowship Foundation, the Western Association of Women Historians, Emory University, and the University of California, Berkeley.

Numerous friends and colleagues have read and criticized various drafts of this book or portions of it. Linda Kerber's comments on several drafts were invaluable, as was her enthusiastic support of this project. I have also benefited from the insightful comments of Estelle Freedman, Lawrence Friedman, Linda Gordon, Robin Kelley, Joanne Meyerowitz, Peggy Pascoe, and Christina Simmons. Steven Schlossman has generously shared his time, resources, and knowledge of the juvenile justice system with me. Two close friends and fellow women's historians, Sherry Katz and Leslie Reagan, have given me emotional and intellectual support during the years of writing this book. I have benefited from their critical readings of my work and from our many conversations about women, reform, sexuality, and the law.

I owe a great debt to my teachers at the University of California, Berkeley, especially my adviser, Larry Levine, for his constant encouragement and intellectual guidance throughout this project. On many evenings, Larry and his wife Cornelia opened their home to me and other graduate students to enjoy lively discussions about our dissertations, much laughter, and delicious meals. Other teachers—Paula Fass, Kristin Luker, Michael Rogin, and Mary Ryan—have offered probing criticism and have continually challenged me to refine my ideas and analysis.

Numerous friends and colleagues in graduate school read various chapters of this study, and I am very grateful for their constructive comments and support during the years of research and writing. Many thanks to Laureen Asato, Stephen Aron, Michael Bess, Nancy Bristow, Robby Cohen, Bill Deverel, Larry Glickman, Paul Gorman, Anne Hyde, Lynn Johnson, Cathy Kudlick, Mark Meigs, Shirley Moore, Maura O'Connor, Michael O'Malley, Burt Peretti, Steven Petrow, Madelon Powers, Gerda Ray, Lucy Salyer, and Glennys Young.

xiv Acknowledgments ···

The History Department and Women's Studies Institute at Emory University have supported this project by offering me leave time and a stimulating community of scholars. I am especially grateful to Elizabeth Fox-Genovese and Jonathan Prude for their perceptive comments on the manuscript and sound advice about publishing. And special thanks to Margot Finn for her warm friendship, sharp criticism, and unfailing wit. I appreciate the comradely assistance of other Emory colleagues—Bill Beik, Michael Bellesiles, Tina Brownley, Geoff Clark, Cindy Patterson, Jim Roark, and Steve White. My graduate assistants, Lee Polansky and Patti Duncan, offered valuable help with the last stages of research. Thanks also go to Bradley Epps and Alan Taylor and to my former colleagues at the Charles Warren Center at Harvard University—Deborah Coon, Phil Ethington, Nancy Green, Susan Hunt, Peter Mancall, and Lisa Wilson—for the intellectual support and companionship they provided during a critical year of research and writing.

Kate Douglas Torrey, my editor at the University of North Carolina Press, has offered me encouragement and excellent advice at every stage. I am also indebted to Pam Upton at UNC Press for her excellent recommendations and skillful copyediting of the manuscript.

The staffs of numerous archives and libraries have greatly assisted me in carrying out the research for this book. In particular, I wish to thank the librarians and archivists at the Chicago Historical Society, the Huntington Library, the Los Angeles Public Library, the Newberry Library, the Oakland Public Library, the Schlesinger Library, the U.S. National Archives, UC-Berkeley's Bancroft Library, UCLA's Department of Special Collections, USC's Regional History Center, the Urban Archives Center at California State University, Northridge, and the interlibrary loan departments at UC-Berkeley's Doe Library and Emory University's Woodruff Library. My thanks to the archivists who helped me to locate photographs for the book—Carolyn Cole, Simon Elliot, Dace Taub, Tom Sitton, and Jenny Watts.

Finally, I would like to thank my parents, brothers, and sisters and my close friends Melanie, Ingrid, and Ralph, whose love and good humor have sustained me through the writing of this book.

DELINQUENT
Daughters

INTRODUCTION

· ·

*I*n the late nineteenth and early twentieth centuries, the sexuality of young single women became the focus of great public anxiety and the target of new policies of intervention and control by the state. Middle-class reformers and social experts expressed mounting concern about the sexual dangers and temptations that appeared to surround young working-class women in American cities. They conducted many investigations, produced a barrage of reports, and organized nationwide purity campaigns calling for government attention to the problem. Their demands resulted in an elaborate network of legal codes and institutions designed to control the sexuality of young women and girls. In particular, age-of-consent laws made sexual intercourse with teenage girls a criminal offense, and newly established juvenile courts, reformatories, and special police monitored and punished young females for sexual misconduct.

Campaigns for the moral protection of young women were not a new phenomenon in the late nineteenth century. Since the beginnings of urbanization and industrialization in the United States, middle-class Americans had worried about the impact of major social changes on the morality of young working women. In the period from 1820 to 1850, reformers in northeastern cities engaged in numerous efforts to prevent the corruption of morals among wage-earning women. Inspired by evangelical Protestantism, they ventured into working-class neighborhoods to set up missions, distribute Bibles, and establish rescue homes to convert wayward women to a Christian way of life.[1] What was new in the late nineteenth and early twentieth centuries, however, was the broadened scope of the campaigns and the mounting demands for state regulation of the problem. Public anxiety about the morality of young women greatly intensified and spread to all regions of the country during this period of rapid urban and industrial growth. Instead of the religious and voluntary efforts pursued earlier, moral reformers now began to insist on a forceful response from the state.

This book explores both the moral reform campaigns that produced new policies of sexual regulation and the actual enforcement of those policies at the local court level. It focuses on four sets of protagonists who had distinct, often competing goals and interests in this process: middle-class reformers who led moral campaigns; state officials (judges, police, probation officers) responsible for enforcing the new legal measures; working-class teenage girls who were the principal targets of sexual regulation; and working-class parents who became active participants within the legal system.

The expanded state regulation of adolescent female sexuality was part of a broad trend toward greater control of sexual behavior in general. Expressions of sexuality that did not conform to a marital, reproductive framework were increasingly subjected to government surveillance and control, as evidenced by a range of legal measures enacted during the period. These included legislation prohibiting the dissemination of obscene literature, the criminalization of abortion, stringent measures targeting prostitution, and heightened legal repression of homosexuality. Such developments reflected Americans' deep anxiety about the increased potential for sexual expression outside of marriage—a situation that threatened middle-class Victorian ideals of sexual restraint and marital, reproductive sex.[2]

The particular anxiety about adolescent female sexuality stemmed from profound changes in the lives of young working-class women and girls that increased their opportunities for social and sexual autonomy. Rapid urban growth and the expansion of industrial capitalism, which affected all aspects of national life, greatly altered the experience of adolescence for daughters in working-class families. New avenues of employment and recreation in American cities drew them increasingly out of the domestic sphere and into a public urban world where they experienced unprecedented freedom from family and neighborhood restrictions. Instead of being limited to domestic work or household manufacture, the main forms of female employment in the nineteenth century, young white women now had access to jobs in factories, department stores, and offices. These new prospects fundamentally altered the context of female labor as daughters worked in settings free of family supervision. Young African American women did not share in the new employment opportunities and were confined primarily to domestic service. But they too enjoyed greater social autonomy as they left farm households in the rural South to live and work in American cities.[3]

In the evenings after work, young women participated in a new world of commercialized leisure that further undermined familial control. The dance halls, movie theaters, and amusement parks opening in cities throughout the country catered to a young, mixed-sex crowd. In contrast to their mothers before them, young working women attended nightly entertainments with male and female peers instead of participating in family and neighborhood activities.[4] Within the youth culture that took shape in American cities, working-class daughters explored romantic relations and heterosexual pleasures outside of marriage. City streets, workplaces, and amusement centers all provided spaces for flirtation and intimate encounters with young men away from the watchful eyes of parents and neighbors.[5]

As they earned wages in stores, offices, and factories and spent their leisure hours in dance halls and movie theaters, young women were constructing a new social role for themselves. They were departing from a centuries-old pattern and ideal in which daughters had passed directly from the control and supervision of their parents to that of their husbands. An unprecedented number of young working-class women and girls now enjoyed a period of relative autonomy that lasted from the time they entered the paid labor force until they later settled into marriage. As they challenged traditional roles and expectations, working-class daughters became the focus of great social anxiety. Their move outside the home was linked to a host of social problems—prostitution and vice, venereal disease, family breakdown, and out-of-wedlock pregnancy. It was in response to these fears that middle-class reformers organized their nationwide campaigns to demand state regulation of female sexuality.

Delinquent Daughters traces two distinct stages of moral reform and regulation during this period that indicate an important shift in the way Americans conceived of and sought to control the sexual behavior of female youth. In the first stage, which began in the mid-1880s, white purity activists launched a national effort to make sex with teenage girls a criminal offense by raising the age of consent. Their demand was based on the belief that seduction by adult men was the major cause of moral ruin among young women and girls. Female reformers challenged a widespread perception of the "fallen woman" as depraved and dangerous by portraying her instead as a victim of male lust and exploitation. The way to protect young women from sexual harm, they argued, was to subject male seducers to criminal penalties.

The second stage took shape during the first two decades of the twentieth century under a new generation of Progressive reformers and social workers, who replaced the model of female victimization with one of female delinquency that acknowledged the sexual agency of young women. Instead of blaming evil men, Progressives looked to social and family environment to explain immorality among working-class female youth. Armed with this revised interpretation of the problem, reformers advocated new forms of sexual regulation that focused on controlling young women and their environments instead of their male partners. These measures included a reliance on special police officers, juvenile courts, detention centers, and reformatories to monitor and correct female sexual delinquency.

I make three main arguments about these crusades for sexual reform and regulation. First, moral campaigns to control teenage female sexuality were fueled by gender, class, and racial tensions in American society.[6] Middle-class white women stood at the forefront of such campaigns, and for them moral reform was part of a larger effort to overcome women's subordinate status in home and society. Age-of-consent reformers sought to address women's sexual vulnerability by challenging male sexual privilege and the double standard of morality. Progressives targeted poverty, low wages, and other social conditions that posed moral dangers to young women and girls. Both groups of reformers called on the state to address these issues, and at the same time they worked to expand female influence within the criminal justice system to ensure adequate legal protection for the members of their sex.

Moral reformers were motivated by concerns about class as well as gender relations. Even while they criticized male sexual behavior and attitudes, they were equally disturbed by assertions of sexual autonomy from young women wage-earners. Their campaigns for "protection" had a coercive aspect. Reformers assumed the authority to define an appropriate code of morality for female youth, one that was based on middle-class ideals of female sexual restraint and modesty. Young women who did not conform to these ideals were considered wayward and in need of control and rehabilitation by the state.

Moral campaigns were shaped, too, by the deep racial divisions in American society. Middle-class white women might reach across class boundaries, but they did not attempt to cross racial boundaries to address the sexual dangers facing African American women and girls. Racism was especially pronounced in the age-of-consent campaign. Reformers made it clear that their efforts were on behalf of the "white slaves" of male lust. Progressive women in the early twentieth century were more inclusive in their protective work as they addressed the needs of immigrant and, to a more limited extent, African American women and girls. But, for the most part, the moral protection of black female youth was ignored by white reformers and left in the hands African American women's clubs and organizations.

My second argument is that sexual regulation by the state had consequences that the reformers had not intended and could not necessarily control. They had succeeded in persuading legislators to enact criminal penalties for seducers and to establish juvenile courts and reformatories for wayward girls but could not ensure that the legal system would enforce these measures as they had planned. Male police and court officials responsible for enforcing age-of-consent legislation showed little concern for—and in some cases clear hostility toward—reformers' goals of ending the double standard and male sexual privilege.

In the second campaign for moral protection, reformers succeeded in gaining some influence over enforcement through the appointment of women police, women judges, and women probation officers in juvenile courts. Nevertheless, they could not always administer policies in accordance with their goals of protection and rehabilitation of female youth. As professionals within the larger criminal justice system, middle-class women became implicated in repressive and discriminatory policies directed against young working-class women who violated dominant codes of female respectability.

Finally, this book argues that the social and sexual autonomy of daughters was a major source of conflict in working-class families and led many of them into court. Reformers may have created the new policies of sexual control, but working-class parents actively used them for their own needs and purposes. The sexual culture of urban youth clashed not only with middle-class morality, but also with the moral codes of many working-class parents. As their traditional forms of sexual regulation eroded, numerous parents—immigrant and native-born, black and white—sought court intervention to restrain their rebellious daughters. This parental use of the courts to discipline daughters calls for a reassessment of a common view of courts and related institutions as instruments of social control that aimed to impose middle-class values on a resistant working class.[7] We need to conceive of the court system instead as a complex network of struggles and negotiations among working-class parents, teenage daughters, and court officials.

In recent years, several feminist scholars have presented a forceful critique of the social control interpretation by demonstrating that working-class women attempted to use state and welfare agencies to challenge male authority and abuse in the family. Their work demonstrates the importance of taking gender, as well as class, into account when assessing the role of state institutions in American society.[8] In addition, we need to consider to generational conflicts within working-class families that led them to seek state intervention. Parents, both fathers and mothers, sought the assistance of courts and public authorities to control disobedient daughters.

We also need to rethink our understanding of working-class family relations during the period studied here. Social historians have often portrayed the working-class family as a cohesive group, bound by ties of loyalty and obligation, with each member contributing to family maintenance and survival.[9] But this characterization cannot account for the serious generational conflicts that erupted between parents and daughters over questions of sexuality and social autonomy. Heidi Hartmann offers a more compelling view of the family as a "locus of struggle" wherein people with different activities and interests often came into conflict with one another.[10] I will explore in depth the disputes that brought working-class parents and daughters into court and elucidate their competing concepts of proper female behavior.

This book examines campaigns for moral protection from a national perspective, using newspapers, reform publications, and the personal papers of leading activists. It explores the actual enforcement of the new policies of sexual control through an analysis of criminal and juvenile court records from Alameda and Los Angeles Counties in California. The felony trial court records from the Alameda County Superior Court are particularly fruitful for analyzing statutory rape prosecutions. For the study of female delinquency cases, there is a very rich and detailed set of records from the Los Angeles County Juvenile Court, one of the few sets of juvenile court case files from the early twentieth century that have been opened to scholars. (See Appendix for more information on these case records.)

Like much of the rest of the country, these two counties and their principal cities, Oakland and Los Angeles, experienced dramatic social and economic changes that fueled anxieties about female morality: rapid urban growth, an influx of immigrants, the expansion of new employment opportunities for women and girls, and the emergence of mass commercialized amusements. California was also a major center of moral reform activity during the late nineteenth and early twentieth centuries, although this fact has received little attention from historians.[11] It is not surprising that reform flourished in the state, for along with immigrants and working-class laborers, many native-born, middle-class families also migrated to California during these years, bringing with them moral values and social reform traditions nurtured in the East and the Midwest.

The first three chapters focus on the age-of-consent movement and the last three on the Progressive campaign to control female sexual delinquency. Through an analysis of reformers, court officials, and working-class daughters and their parents, both sections explore the complex ways in which relations of family, gender, class, and race intersected on the terrain of adolescent female sexuality.

CHAPTER I

'WHITE SLAVES' AND 'VICIOUS MEN'

The Age-of-Consent Campaign

*I*n 1889 members of the California Woman's Christian Temperance Union (WCTU) lobbied legislators for a bill that was of great interest both to women in the state and also to the leaders of a national campaign. They aimed to amend the rape statute by raising the age of consent for women from ten to eighteen years. Under the proposed bill, men who had sexual intercourse with young women below that age would be guilty of statutory rape and subject to criminal penalties. The purpose of the law was to provide moral protection for young women and girls and to undermine the double standard of morality. For the previous two years WCTU members had circulated a petition throughout

California to gain support for the measure. The petition warned that "the increasing and alarming frequency of assaults upon women, and the frightful indignities to which even little girls are subject, have become the shame of our boasted civilization." It called on legislators to address this situation by enacting legislation "for the adequate punishment of crimes against women and girls."[1]

The reformers encountered stiff opposition to their efforts from male legislators who objected to women's participation in politics and claimed the proposed law would make men vulnerable to blackmail by immoral, designing young women. Undeterred, WCTU members continued to lobby vigorously for the measure and achieved a partial victory when the legislature raised the age of consent to fourteen. Still not satisfied that the law adequately protected young women, however, the WCTU continued to collect petitions and lobby legislators for the next eight years until state lawmakers voted in 1897 to raise the age of consent to sixteen.[2]

The effort to raise the age of consent in California was but one battle in a larger national campaign that originated in 1885 among a group of purity reformers in the Northeast and Midwest. At the time, the legal age of consent in most states was either ten or twelve years. This national reform campaign sought to protect young women and girls from moral ruin by subjecting their male seducers to criminal penalties. Within ten years the campaign had spread to all regions of the country, achieving impressive legislative changes and drawing enthusiastic support from suffragists, religious leaders, and labor organizations in addition to temperance advocates.

The campaign found its largest following and most forceful leaders among middle-class white women. Their vigorous activity in the cause stemmed from deep gender, class, and racial tensions over the issue of female sexuality. Most reformers advocated a higher age of consent because they believed that the moral downfall of young women was the direct result of male vice and exploitation. In speeches and campaign literature, they constructed a narrative of seduction that portrayed male seducers as outwardly respectable, middle-class men and their victims as innocent, white, working-class daughters. Through this narrative, women reformers challenged male privilege and the sexual double standard. At the same time, they promoted an image of female purity and passivity that demonstrated the vulnerability of young working-class women by denying their capacity for sexual agency and desire. Moral protection, however, did not automatically extend to all working-class female youth. Reflecting the racism of the dominant society, purity activists largely ignored the sexual dangers facing African American women and girls.

The age-of-consent campaign was part of a broad movement for social purity reform that developed in the United States in the last decades of the nineteenth century. The movement began in the 1870s as a response to attempts by physicians and public health authorities to institute a system of state-regulated prostitution in American cities. Social reformers, Protestant clergy, women's rights advocates, and former abolitionists joined forces to defeat such regulation bills in New York, Chicago, San Francisco, Philadelphia, and elsewhere. After their victory over the "regulationists," moral reformers expanded the scope of their activities. Moving beyond the defensive effort to end state licensing of prostitution, they now aimed to abolish prostitution altogether and to establish a single standard of morality for men and women. The organization at the heart of this movement was the New York Committee for the Prevention of State Regulation of Vice, whose leaders included, among others, Abby Hopper Gibbons, Aaron Macy Powell, Anna Rice Powell, Emily Blackwell, and Elizabeth Gay. Although its membership was small and concentrated in the Northeast, the organization helped to publicize and coordinate purity reform efforts throughout the country through its journal, the *Philanthropist*. In 1895 the New York committee joined with other moral reform groups to form a national organization, the American Purity Alliance.[3]

Another important bastion of purity reform was the Woman's Christian Temperance Union. Founded in 1874 by middle-class Protestant women, the WCTU aimed to end trafficking in liquor, which its members considered a serious threat to the home and family. They focused on moral suasion and the conversion of drunkards to achieve their goals, and they also engaged in political campaigns for local temperance laws. When Frances Willard became president of the WCTU in 1879 (a position she held for the remaining twenty years of her life), the organization embraced a much broader program of social reform. Under Willard's forceful and charismatic leadership, members campaigned for a wide range of issues in addition to temperance, including woman suffrage, prison reform, and the eight-hour day for workers. During this period of expansion, the WCTU also became a leader in the social purity crusade. In 1885 it established an official Social Purity Department whose purpose was to promote a single moral standard for both sexes. The WCTU brought great strength and experience to the social purity cause. With nearly 150,000 dues-paying members by 1892 and branches in every state, all major cities, and thousands of local communities, the WCTU was the largest women's organization in the United States in the late nineteenth century.[4]

The WCTU and other purity organizations initially relied on moral education and voluntary efforts to stop the spread of prostitution and immorality. They established shelters and rescue homes to lead "fallen women" to a moral way of life. They also carried out preventive and protective work with younger women and girls to keep them from going astray in the first place. They formed travelers' aid societies to direct young female migrants entering the cities to safe housing and employment. Various groups in cities throughout the country opened boarding homes to provide low-cost lodging and moral guidance for young women workers, and they organized social clubs such as the New Century Guild of Working Women in Philadelphia and the Working Girls' Society in New York to offer wholesome entertainment in place of morally suspect urban amusements.[5]

Just as important as protective work with girls was the goal of transforming male sexual behavior and attitudes. Toward this end, WCTU members sponsored mothers' meetings to teach women how to impart moral education to their children, particularly their sons. The mothers were urged to teach boys "that their virginity is as *priceless* as their sisters'." Reformers also organized purity societies for young men to encourage them to resist sexual temptation. In 1885 Episcopal clergymen established the White Cross Society, modeled after a similar organization in England, to promote social purity among young men. With the enthusiastic support of the WCTU, branches of the White Cross were soon established in nearly every state and territory.[6]

Social purity leaders considered voluntary efforts and moral education important, but they became convinced that these methods alone were not sufficient to protect young women and to control male vice in American cities. They began to demand state attention to the problem with the organization of the age-of-consent campaign in 1885, an effort to convince the government to enforce their vision of moral order by making sexual relations with young women a criminal offense.

American groups were first alerted to the age-of-consent issue by the British purity movement. British reformers believed that an underground system of "white slavery" existed in London whereby English girls were abducted off the streets by evil procurers and forced into a life of prostitution. Around this time, purity activists on both sides of the Atlantic began to use the term "white slavery" to describe the sexual exploitation and prostitution of young women. In so doing, they followed established conventions of female reform associated since the early nineteenth century with abolitionism and women's particular mission with regard to the end of slavery.[7] Yet the term also clearly exposes the limitations of the moral protection campaign, pointing to its racist dimensions. By identifying the abolition of "white slavery" as their goal, reformers implied that only young white women needed protection from sexual harm and that only white women's virtue was worth saving. This restricted ideological vision was fundamentally to shape the structure and the legal consequences of their movement.[8]

British purity activists sought to end the "white slave" traffic by demanding that Parliament raise the age of consent for females from thirteen to sixteen with the Criminal Law Amendment Act. When Parliament refused to pass the act, they enlisted the noted British journalist and reformer William T. Stead. Eager to use his pen to aid the purity cause, Stead published an exposé of the underground traffic in girls in the *Pall Mall Gazette* in the summer of 1885. Described by one historian as "one of the most successful pieces of scandal journalism published in Britain in the 19th century," "The Maiden Tribute to Modern Babylon" described in vivid detail the entrapment and ravishing of "five-pound" virgins by lecherous aristocrats. To expose the evil of this system, Stead arranged to purchase a white working-class girl, Eliza Armstrong, from her mother, ostensibly for the purpose of prostitution. After the publication of the exposé, the police arrested Stead for abducting Eliza. Although they knew she was safe in a Salvation Army home, the police were anxious to punish Stead for the embarrassment he had caused them. He was found guilty and sentenced to three months in prison. Despite his arrest and imprisonment, Stead had succeeded in stirring the British public into action. After publication of "The Maiden Tribute," a crowd estimated at 250,000 gathered at Hyde Park to demand legislation for the protection of young girls. Shortly thereafter, Parliament passed the Criminal Law Amendment Act, raising the age of consent to sixteen.[9]

Stead's exposé and subsequent arrest generated great interest and concern among purity reformers across the Atlantic. Although some disapproved of his methods, all praised his valiant effort to save young women and girls. In an article about Stead's trial and sentencing, one reformer called him the "John Brown" of the "white slaves."[10] Already disturbed by Stead's disclosures, American activists became even more alarmed when they discovered, several months later, that the legal age of consent in all

states in their own country was even lower than that in England before
the passage of the Criminal Law Amendment Act. A survey of the laws
conducted by WCTU member Georgia Mark revealed that in most states
the age of consent was ten, in several others it was twelve, and in the state
of Delaware the age was only seven (see Table 1). Mark presented her findings about American age-of-consent legislation in the *Union Signal*, the
official journal of the National WCTU. "Those English laws that we have
scarcely done condemning," she stated, "were far in advance of our own
legislation on this subject, and indeed, there never was a period in English
history, from the most ancient times to the present, when girlish innocence
was so early left undefended by the law as it is now in our own land."[11]

The age of consent in American law was based on previously established standards developed over the centuries in England. Under English
common law, the age of female discretion was held to be twelve years. A
parliamentary statute in 1576 lowered the age of consent in sexual relations to ten years and explicitly designated such relations with an underage female, without benefit of clergy, as a felony. According to William
Blackstone, the foremost British legal scholar in the eighteenth century,
this statute superseded the older common-law standard of female consent
in rape cases. Hence, any male over the age of fourteen who had intercourse with a female under twelve, with or without her consent, was guilty
of the crime of rape. But whereas, in England, purity reformers had succeeded in pressuring Parliament to raise the age of consent to thirteen in
1875 and to sixteen in 1885, in the United States the ages remained at ten
and twelve.[12]

The revelation of these low ages of consent galvanized the American
reform community into action. Members of the New York Committee for
the Prevention of State Regulation of Vice immediately embarked on a
campaign to raise the age of consent in New York. Leaders of the committee circulated a petition demanding that the age be legally raised from ten
to eighteen. Aaron Macy Powell and Emily Blackwell met with the chief
justice of the New York Supreme Court to draft a model law to be introduced in the state legislature.[13] The organization also used the pages of the
Philanthropist to incite public concern about the issue. One editorial that
appeared in January 1886 stated: "It will doubtless astonish many of our
readers, who have hitherto avoided the subject as indelicate, or painful, to
be told that the young girl of the Empire State is held by its criminal laws
to be legally capable of giving 'consent' to her own corruption at the tender
age of TEN YEARS!"[14]

TABLE 1. *Legal Ages of Consent in the United States, 1885 and 1920*

State	1885	1920
Alabama	10	16*
Arizona	10	18
Arkansas	12	16*
California	10	18
Colorado	10	18
Connecticut	10	16
Delaware	7	16*
District of Columbia	12	16
Florida	10	18*
Georgia	10	14*
Idaho	10	18
Illinois	10	16
Indiana	n.a.	16
Iowa	10	16
Kansas	10	18
Kentucky	12	16*
Louisiana	12	18*
Maine	10	16*
Maryland	10	16
Massachusetts	10	16
Michigan	10	16
Minnesota	10	18*
Mississippi	10	18*
Missouri	12	18*
Montana	10	18
Nebraska	10	18
Nevada	12	18
New Hampshire	10	16
New Jersey	10	16
New Mexico	10	16
New York	10	18
North Carolina	10	16*
North Dakota	10	18
Ohio	10	16*
Oregon	n.a.	16

TABLE 1. *Continued*

State	1885	1920
Pennsylvania	10	16
Rhode Island	10	16
South Carolina	10	16*
South Dakota	10	18
Tennessee	10	18*
Texas	10	18
Utah	10	18*
Vermont	10	16
Virginia	12	16
Washington	12	18*
West Virginia	12	16
Wisconsin	10	16
Wyoming	10	18

Sources: The official legal codes and statutes of the various states; Anthony and Harper, eds., state reports on legislative action and laws, in *History of Woman Suffrage*, 4:465–1011; Pivar, *Purity Crusade*, pp. 141–43; Benjamin DeCosta, "Age of Consent Laws—1886," *Philanthropist*, February 1886, p. 5; Leila Robinson, "Age of Consent Laws—1889," *Woman's Journal*, April 5, 1889, p. 105.

*The law in these states made sexual intercourse with underage females a criminal offense under a statute separate from the rape statute; the offense was typically referred to as "carnal knowledge of female child."

The low age of consent in the United States also stirred the Woman's Christian Temperance Union into action, and the political skills and tactics honed in the temperance movement allowed its members quickly to assume leading roles in the campaign. The WCTU drafted a petition demanding that "the age at which a girl can legally consent to her own ruin be raised to at least eighteen years." This petition circulated among many local WCTU branches throughout the country, provoking a flood of letters to state legislatures in support of more stringent consent laws. The WCTU also organized a national petition drive to institute a higher age of consent in the nation's capital and the territories. Because of its extensive political network, the WCTU was better able than any single organization to build a formidable national campaign that touched every state in the country.[15]

Purity reformers received strong support from white suffragists. The two competing national suffrage organizations—the American Woman Suffrage Association, headed by Lucy Stone and her husband Henry Blackwell, and the National Woman Suffrage Association, led by Elizabeth Cady Stanton and Susan B. Anthony—both considered the age-of-consent campaign an important battle in the larger struggle to overcome the subordination of women in home and society. Stanton denounced the low age of consent as an "invasion of the personal rights of woman, and the wholesale desecration of childhood." The major national suffrage publication of the period, the *Woman's Journal*, edited by Stone and Blackwell, kept its readers abreast of progress of the campaign and urged them to support age-of-consent efforts in their local communities.[16] The many state suffrage organizations joined purity groups in circulating petitions and lobbying legislators. They added the age of consent to their list of legislative priorities for the improvement of women's status, which included the right to vote, liberal divorce laws, married women's property rights, and equal guardianship rights over children.[17]

Age-of-consent reformers found another important source of support among white workingmen's groups. When the WCTU organized its national petition drive, Frances Willard sought the assistance of the Knights of Labor, the largest labor organization in the country at the time. After meeting with Willard, Knights president Terrence Powderly had copies of the petition sent to all local assemblies of the organization. When the petitions were presented to Congress in January 1888, the Knights of Labor had supplied half of the nearly 15,000 signatures.[18]

The great appeal that the age-of-consent campaign had for white workingmen, suffragists, and middle-class women stemmed in large part from purity reformers' particular conception of sexual danger. Influenced by the Victorian belief in inherent female purity and passionlessness, reformers charged that male vice and exploitation were responsible for the moral ruin of young women and girls. In their publications and speeches, reformers recounted numerous tales of seduction that followed a common pattern in which men of status and wealth took advantage of poor, innocent young women, using various forms of trickery and deception, and force if necessary. The fate of female victims was always disastrous; typically they were forced into prostitution or endured a cruel and lonely death. This narrative of seduction had long been popular in nineteenth-century melodrama and romance novels, but reformers adapted it to their own social context and political purposes.[19] The female victim was typically a white working-class daughter in the city, and her male predator a middle-class businessman. The seduction frequently occurred in one of the new places of work and recreation for young women that were emerging in urban areas in the late nineteenth century.

Purity activist and suffragist Helen Hamilton Gardener re-created this narrative in two novels she wrote to assist the age-of-consent campaign. Reformers read her works avidly and distributed them to legislators and citizens in order to build support for their cause. The first novel, *Is This Your Son, My Lord?*, sold over 25,000 copies in the first five months after its publication in 1890. With this book, Gardener said, she hoped to do for the "fallen woman" what Harriet Beecher Stowe had done for the black slave.[20]

A strong condemnation of the double standard and male vice, the novel describes in lurid detail the ruin of an innocent young woman by two outwardly respectable men. One of these men, Mr. Mansfield, a wealthy mill owner and highly regarded member of his church and community, decides that it is time for his seventeen-year-old son, Preston, to become a man by having his first sexual conquest. Looking for a suitable victim, Mr. Mansfield takes Preston to New York City, where they befriend a white working-class girl of fifteen, Minnie Kent, who lives with her poor widowed mother. Mr. Mansfield invites the unsuspecting girl for a buggy ride in the park but takes her instead to a rooming house. After locking the door, he coaxes her to yield to his advances. When the frightened Minnie refuses, Mr. Mansfield takes a revolver from his pocket, forces her submission, and threatens to kill her if she breathes a word to anyone. After ravishing the girl himself, Mr. Mansfield then turns her over to his son. As a result of this rape, Minnie bears an illegitimate child and is forced to become a prostitute; Preston and his father return to their comfortable bourgeois home and family. Mr. Mansfield lives a long and prosperous life, but Preston's fate is not such a happy one. He is tortured by guilt over his cruel treatment of Minnie and eventually commits suicide because his past immorality prevents him from marrying the virtuous girl he loves.

Gardener's second novel, *Pray You, Sir, Whose Daughter?*, published in 1892, offers a ringing condemnation of the low age of consent. This story begins just after New York legislators had voted to place the age of consent at twelve years. The law has terrible consequences for fourteen-year-old Ettie Berton, who works as a shop girl in a department store. Ettie's moral decline begins when she accepts an invitation to go to the amusement park at Coney Island one Sunday with the manager of the store, a forty-year-old married man with a daughter Ettie's age. The manager takes Ettie first to the amusement park, then to a café, where he gives her wine to drink; later he seduces her. Because Ettie is over the age of consent, the man is held guiltless before the law. Whereas he suffers no consequences for his actions, Ettie is fired from her position in the store, rejected by friends and family, and eventually dies a lonely and agonizing death. Another shop girl in the story, Frances King, is saved from a similar fate through the moral guidance of Gertrude Foster, the college-educated daughter of a respectable family in town. Instead of ignoring the issue, as women are expected to do, Gertrude tries to influence legislators to vote for a higher age of consent. In addition, she organizes a working girls' club to offer moral instruction and wholesome recreation for girls like Frances.[21]

Gardener's seduction narratives illuminate the gender, class, and racial conflicts that fueled the age-of-consent campaign. They express female reformers' deep anger about women's sexual vulnerability in a male-dominated society. These reformers challenged the commonly held view of the "fallen woman" as inherently depraved and dangerous, portraying her instead as a victim of male lust and exploitation. They shifted the blame for moral wrongdoing from the young woman to her male seducer, whom they described in various accounts as a "fiend," "devil," "wild beast," and "moral monstrosity." Middle-class women's greatest anger was directed toward men of their own class, who, like the seducers in Gardener's stories, used their status and influence to take advantage of working-class daughters.

Purity activists charged that although such men were the aggressors in illicit encounters, society punished only their female victims. They condemned this double standard, rooted in American law and custom, which held women to a high ideal of chastity yet tolerated sexual license on the part of men. Women who strayed from the ideal were considered permanently "ruined," whereas such behavior by men was at most a mild and pardonable offense. Sexual prowess could even enhance a man's reputation among his male peers.[22] Purity campaigners recounted numerous instances in which young women like those in Gardener's stories were cast out of society and forced to turn to prostitution, infanticide, or death, while their male seducers remained ensconced in respectable society. In an address before a large audience in the First Methodist Episcopal Church of Chicago, Frances Willard discussed a recent case of "betrayal and outrage of a young girl" in that city. Abandoned by her lover, the seventeen-year-old girl killed her newborn baby to escape the shame and disgrace of her situation. Willard protested the injustice of the legal system, which punished the girl for the crime of infanticide yet allowed her seducer to walk away free of blame: "He, strong and well; she, weak and tortured with pain; he, pillowed that night in comfort; she, shivering in cold and shame; he, her worse than murderer, yet unpunished; she, his helpless victim, yet a criminal."[23]

Reformers called for legislation that would undermine the double standard and male sexual privilege by making the seducers of underage women subject to criminal charges. The way to protect women and girls, Willard declared, was no longer to shelter and seclude them from the world. "It is rather by holding men to the same standard of morality which, happily for us, they long ago prescribed for the physically weaker ... and by punishing with extreme penalties such men as inflict upon women atrocities compared with which death would be infinitely welcome."[24] Men who in the past had walked away from illicit encounters unscathed should now be held accountable for their actions.

Women reformers, however, did not trust men to carry out this task. They charged that patriarchal authority, both in the government and at home, had failed miserably in its responsibility to protect young women and girls. The tragic ends of Minnie and Ettie in Gardener's novels demonstrated the dire consequences of leaving moral protection in the hands of men. Mr. Mansfield, the key patriarch in the first story, had caused the moral corruption of his own son and destroyed the life of an innocent working girl. In the second story, Ettie's own father had favored setting the age of consent at twelve years and thus had contributed to the downfall of his daughter. One purity activist charged that these "infamous" laws were "enacted by fathers, husbands and brothers for the furtherance of animal lust and moral degradation in men, and the destruction of maidenhood."[25]

The dismal failure of fathers convinced reformers that it was up to the mothers of the country to see that young women and girls were adequately protected. Frances Willard called on WCTU members to join the battle with the following declaration at the organization's annual meeting in 1885: "Women only can induce law-makers to furnish this most availing of all possible methods of protection to the physically weak. Men alone will never gain the courage thus to legislate against other men."[26]

Since the early nineteenth century, Victorian culture had assigned middle-class women responsibility for the moral guardianship of the home and the moral training of children. By instilling values of sobriety and purity in their children, mothers would help to ensure a safe, moral social order. But this domestic role, reformers believed, no longer sufficed in the face of mounting sexual dangers and temptations that surrounded young women in American cities and towns. Women needed to enter the political sphere in order to carry out their role as moral guardians and protectors of the home. Gertrude Foster in *Pray You, Sir, Whose Daughter?* served as an example for middle-class women, who, in order to control vice and protect girls from sexual danger, had to be willing to risk public censure and engage in political activities outside of the home.

Initially, female reformers sought to exert their moral influence in the political realm by organizing petition drives and lobbying male legislators for age-of-consent laws. Soon, however, many came to argue that women needed the vote if they were to gain adequate protection for girls. Helen Gardener expressed the belief of many reformers when she claimed the low age of consent would never have been enacted in the first place if women had been allowed to vote.[27]

Class tensions, as well as gender tensions, also fueled the age-of-consent campaign. In the seduction model that informed the campaign, reformers focused specifically on the sexual vulnerability of white, working-class daughters like the fictional Minnie and Ettie. In the words of purity activist Emily Blackwell: "There is no class in society so helpless, so surrounded by temptation, as young working girls just growing up." Among the well-to-do, Blackwell explained, "the daughters live at home, under the protection of parents and family connections, to mature age. . . . The case is entirely different with the majority of working girls where poverty obliges them to go to work as soon as they are capable of earning. Ignorant, inexperienced, impulsive, they enter the great world of work, usually in wearisome and ill-paid labor, under the control and direction of men."[28]

The standard narrative of seduction did not accurately depict the reality of most sexual encounters experienced by young working-class women during this period. They usually formed intimate relationships with young, unmarried men of their own class, not with older, middle-class employers.[29] Though not based on reality, the seduction narrative nevertheless had great power among nineteenth-century audiences because it captured the deep social anxiety about the fundamental changes taking place in the lives of white working-class female youth. Urbanization and the expansion of the industrial economy were drawing more and more young women out of domestic and family settings and into a public, urban world of work and recreation. In the small towns and agrarian communities of nineteenth-century America, most daughters had worked in a family context under the close supervision of parents in farm households or small workshops, or as domestic servants in other households. They helped with cooking, cleaning, child care, and the production of candles, soap, and other household goods, and they labored in the fields when needed. Daughters in artisans' households also worked primarily in a family setting, tending to domestic duties and helping in family-run shops or businesses. Young women sometimes brought in additional income by engaging in household manufacture or the "putting-out" system, in which they made hats, matches, stockings, and other piecework goods in their own homes for local merchants.[30]

As the nineteenth century advanced, economic pressures compelled some artisan and farm families to send their daughters out into the paid labor force. By midcentury, a number of young white women were employed in textile mills and shoe factories in northeastern cities and towns, but factory workers still constituted only a small portion of the female labor force. The vast majority of young women who worked outside of their homes were employed as domestic servants in the homes of others. As late as 1870, 61 percent of all women wage-earners worked as domestic servants or in related occupations, while only 18 percent were factory workers.[31]

The expansion of the economy in the late nineteenth century drew ever larger numbers of young women into the work force and fundamentally altered the context of female labor, a development that had profound consequences for their social lives. The ranks of female laborers grew rapidly as native-born daughters left depressed rural areas and immigrant daughters migrated with their families to American cities in search of work. The number of women in the paid labor force more than quadrupled between 1870 and 1910 (see Table 2). In 1870 there were 1.72 million women wage-earners (15 percent of the female population); in 1890 there were 3.6 million (19 percent of the female population); by 1910 that number had increased to 7.01 million (24 percent of the female population). Most female workers were young, single women who contributed their wages to the support of their families.[32]

Even more significant than the numerical increase of women wage-earners were the profound changes in the nature of white female employment. Instead of being limited largely to domestic work and household manufacture, they now had access to jobs in factories, department stores, offices, and restaurants. As a result, the percentage of working women employed as domestic servants decreased with every decade. Between 1870 and 1910, it dropped from 61 percent to 26 percent. During this same

TABLE 2. *Number and Proportion of Women in the U.S. Labor Force, 1870–1920*

Year	Total Labor Force (millions)	Working Women (millions)	Women as % of Labor Force	% of All Women in Labor Force
1870	12.16	1.72	14	15
1880	16.27	2.35	14	16
1890	21.81	3.60	16	19
1900	27.32	4.83	18	21
1910	35.75	7.01	20	24
1920	41.02	8.28	20	24

Source: U.S. Bureau of the Census, *Sixteenth Census of the United States, 1940: Comparative Occupation Statistics for the U.S., 1870–1940* (Washington, D.C.: Government Printing Office, 1943), p. 92, table xv.

period, the proportion of women employed in factories grew from 18 percent to 23 percent, and that of women employed as saleswomen, clerks, and stenographers increased from 1 percent to 15 percent (see Table 3).[33] In the workplaces newly opened to women, daughters now labored in settings free of family supervision and control.

In their leisure time outside of work, young women took part in new commercial amusements that further undermined family influence. Dance halls, movie theaters, cafés, and amusement parks opened in cities throughout the country, offering nightly entertainment to urban youth. These commercial ventures differed in important ways from earlier forms of recreation. Most leisure-time activity throughout the nineteenth century had taken place in family and neighborhood settings and involved all age groups. Small-town families had participated together in picnics, community entertainments, church socials, and dances. Urban workers, too, had enjoyed their leisure in familial and communal contexts as they gathered on street corners and stoops after a day's work, took weekend excursions to the park, or celebrated religious and ethnic holidays in community groups. The few forms of commercial recreation that existed were generally the preserve of men. Male friends and colleagues joined one another in saloons, pool halls, and sports clubs, while women stayed close to home and their local neighborhoods.[34]

TABLE 3. *Percentage of Women Workers in Nonagricultural Occupations,
1870–1920*

Year	Servants and Related Occupations	Clerks, Saleswomen, Stenographers	Professions	Mill and Factory Workers	All Other Nonagricultural Occupations
1870 (N=1.44 million)	61	1	6	18	15
1880 (N=2.05 million)	47	2	9	21	21
1890 (N=3.24 million)	40	5	10	20	25
1900 (N=4.34 million)	33	9	10	22	26
1910 (N=6.27 million)	26	15	12	23	25
1920 (N=7.47 million)	18	26	13	24	19

Source: Hill, *Women in Gainful Occupations*, p. 45.

The amusement resorts dotting the urban landscape in the late nineteenth and early twentieth centuries departed from these earlier forms of leisure activity by catering primarily to a young, mix-sexed crowd. Adolescent sons and daughters often spent their evenings with their peers at amusement parks, theaters, and dance halls instead of participating in family and neighborhood gatherings. Similar developments had taken place earlier in more developed urban areas, such as New York City, but they became widespread throughout the country during the rapid urban and economic growth of the late nineteenth century.[35]

Urban and economic growth extended new possibilities but also new sexual risks to young working-class women. Increased social autonomy in work and recreation could also expose them to sexual harassment and assault by male employers, coworkers, and companions. Relations with boyfriends sometimes resulted in pregnancy and abandonment. In large cities with highly mobile populations, families could not force a marriage between pregnant daughters and their male partners as effectively as they had in smaller towns and communities. An out-of-wedlock pregnancy was a difficult, often traumatic experience for young women at this time. They had to bear the economic burden of caring for the child and faced social ostracism and possible family rejection. To escape this shame and financial hardship, young women sometimes resorted to extreme measures, most notably infanticide or illegal and often dangerous abortions to end a pregnancy. The seduction narrative constructed by reformers expressed this sense of sexual vulnerability and danger that young women faced.[36]

Where middle-class reformers saw only sexual danger in the public world of work, however, working-class daughters also perceived new opportunities. As they engaged in new jobs and urban recreations in American cities, these young women explored romantic relations and heterosexual pleasures outside of marriage. City streets, workplaces, amusement centers, and parks all provided spaces for flirtation and intimate encounters with members of the opposite sex away from the watchful eyes of parents and neighbors. Working girls used their earnings for fancy dresses, hats, and makeup; they frequented dance halls and cafés unchaperoned; and they made acquaintances with men their parents did not know. Many working-class daughters also demonstrated a more open sexual ethic that tolerated premarital sexual intercourse in certain social contexts. Clearly, among some young women, particularly Catholics, traditional codes of female chastity prevailed. Even so, the increased rate of premarital pregnancy—which rose from approximately 10 percent in the mid–nineteenth century to 23 percent in the period between 1880 and 1910—indicates a growing incidence of sexual experimentation among young unmarried women.[37]

Such behavior conflicted sharply with the bourgeois conception of girlhood sexual purity and innocence. Middle-class women criticized male behavior, but they were equally troubled by the assertions of sexual and social autonomy on the part of female youth. Reformers assumed a position of moral authority toward white working-class daughters and sought to impose on them a code of morality based on middle-class ideals of female purity and modesty. They upheld the belief, shared by many conservatives, that the loss of sexual purity was the worst thing that could happen to a young woman. Colorado reformer Carrie Clyde Holly told legislators that a woman's virtue was more important to her than "life itself," and Frances Willard claimed the seducer was worse than a "murderer" to a young woman.[38] Such attitudes reinforced the idea that young women involved in illicit encounters were "ruined" for life.

Reformers further insisted that young women were passive and dependent in all illicit sexual encounters. Holly expressed a common view among purity activists when she asserted that "no virtuous woman of any age, in her right mind, fully conscious of the consequences, ever did, or ever can, consent freely and voluntarily, without either physical or mental coercion to give up the most precious jewel in the crown of her womanhood!"[39] The only acceptable role for young women within the seduction drama was that of helpless victim. Working-class daughters who departed from the ideals of purity and passivity—by flirting with men on the streets, going to dance halls, wearing fancy clothes and makeup, or engaging in sex outside of marriage—were deemed wayward and in need of strict control by the state. The moral protection offered by middle-class reformers, then, came at a high price. It demanded adherence to a rigid code of morality that denied women sexual desire and agency.

Reformers established a hierarchical and custodial relationship with white working-class daughters, but that relationship excluded African American women and girls entirely. Purity activists emphasized that their campaign was waged on behalf of the "white slaves" of male vice and exploitation, and they ignored altogether the serious problems faced by young African American women in American society. These girls, too, experienced out-of-wedlock pregnancy, abandonment, sexual harassment, and assault as they migrated from farms and small towns to urban areas in search of employment. Even worse, black women and girls faced severe forms of sexual exploitation on account of their race. The demise of slavery may have limited, but clearly did not eradicate, the sexual victimization of black women by white men in the South. In fact, some southern men responded to Emancipation and the granting of political rights to former slaves by assaulting African American women. They used rape as a tool of racial intimidation and control over freed blacks in the South. During the Memphis race riot of 1865, a white mob attacked and killed blacks, burned their homes and schools, and raped black women at gunpoint. In 1871 the wife of a black radical Republican in Columbia, South Carolina, reported to a Congressional committee that Ku Klux Klan members had beaten her husband and gang-raped her to punish them for supporting the Republican Party. Another woman from Meridian, Mississippi, told the committee that Klan members had forced their way into her home, thrown her to the ground, and raped her at gunpoint.[40]

It was also common practice—particularly, though not exclusively, in the South—for white men of all ages and classes to make sexual advances to black women. Domestic servants were most vulnerable to this type of harassment. In a letter that appeared in the *Independent* in 1912, a servant who worked for a white southern family described how she resisted the aggressive advances of her male employer and consequently was fired from her job. The servant concluded that "a colored woman's virtue in this part of the country had no protection. . . . I believe nearly all white men take, and expect to take, undue liberties with their colored female servants—not only the fathers, but in many cases the sons also."[41] Given the structure of relations between whites and blacks in the South, women who resisted such harassment could expect to be fired from their jobs or forcibly assaulted. African American men who attempted to prevent sexual assaults on their wives and daughters by white men found themselves subject to criminal arrest or physical attack. When the husband of the woman quoted above confronted the white employer for accosting his wife, the employer struck him and had him arrested. When the husband appeared in court, he was fined twenty-five dollars for his bold behavior.[42]

Before the Civil War, white abolitionists had addressed the sexual exploitation of black women under slavery. After the war, however, white reformers ignored this issue, particularly with the end of Reconstruction, when political control in the South was returned to southern white leaders. Suffragists and moral reformers, eager to win white southern support for their causes, did not address the sexual vulnerability of black women and girls in the South.

Even though the white purity movement ignored African American concerns, black clubwomen and suffragists actively engaged in moral protection work for the young women of their own race, but they did not take part in the age-of-consent campaign. African American purity reformers tended to be college educated; many worked as teachers and most were married to men of middle-class status such as ministers, educators, lawyers, and physicians. They shared with their white counterparts a belief in the values of morality for both sexes, wholesome marriage, and family life, and they assumed responsibility for instilling these values in the "lowly and fallen" of their race.[43] A number of African American clubwomen supported temperance and the social purity movement through the WCTU, usually working in separate black chapters. In the last two decades of the nineteenth century, black clubwomen Jane M. Kenney, Frances E. W. Harper, and Lucy Thurman served as superintendents of "colored work" for the temperance organization. The major national organizations of black women in the late nineteenth century also adopted social purity as an important goal. These organizations included the National Federation of Afro-American Women, the National League of Colored Women, and later the National Association of Colored Women (NACW), which was formed by a merger of the first two in 1896. Mary Church Terrell, the first president of the NACW, stated in 1899 that as "the more favored portion" of their communities, black clubwomen should "strive to illumine the minds and improve the morals of those who it is in their power to uplift." In pursuit of this mission, black women's organizations distributed pamphlets and delivered talks on social purity at annual meetings; they pursued rescue and protective work for young women and the moral education of both sexes.[44]

Moral reform, however, had a different set of meanings for black women reformers. It was an integral part of a broad program of racial uplift that included efforts to improve education and health care, promote economic self-sufficiency, and end racial discrimination and violence toward African Americans. Black women reformers aimed, in particular, to counter the prevalent stereotype of black female immorality and to combat the sexual exploitation of black women at the hands of white men that had been a central feature of slavery and continued as a form of racial domination after the Civil War.[45] Before a meeting of black clergymen in 1886, teacher and activist Anna Julia Cooper made a plea for the protection of "the Colored Girls of the South" who live "in the midst of pitfalls and snares, waylaid by the lower classes of white men with no shelter, no protection nearer than the great blue vault above."[46] Black clubwomen thus defined sexual danger differently than white moral reformers. They worried about the sexual vulnerability that black women and girls faced in a racist society in which they had little power or control.

Black women did not focus solely on the sexual aggression of white men. They also sought to reform the moral behavior and attitudes of the young men and women of their race through education and voluntary efforts within the black community. Local black women's organizations founded boarding homes, social clubs, and travelers' aid societies for working girls in their respective cities and towns. Led by Victoria Earle Mathews, the Woman's Loyal League of New York established the White Rose Home in 1897 to offer housing, training, and moral guidance to young black female migrants to the city. Clubwomen organized similar homes and societies in numerous other cities during this period, including the Sojourner Truth

Home for Working Girls in Washington, D.C., the Phillis Wheatley Clubs in New Orleans and Chicago, the Harriet Tubman House in Boston, and the Home for Working Girls in Kansas City.[47]

Clubwomen and black ministers aimed to build the moral character of young men as well as women. Like white reformers, they were staunchly committed to a single standard of morality and sought to impress the men of their race with the importance of moral purity. At the Atlanta Exposition in 1895, members of the National Colored Woman's Congress, including Fannie Barrier Williams, Frances E. W. Harper, Victoria Earle Mathews, and Josephine Ruffin, made the following pledge, which was printed in the *Woman's Era* (the publication of the Boston Woman's Era Club and the first monthly journal published by black women in the United States): "That we require the same standard of morality for men as for women and that the mothers teach their sons social purity as well as their daughters."[48] To accomplish this goal, women reformers held mothers' meetings to discuss the moral education of sons and established purity leagues, clubs, and recreational programs for young men.[49]

Although African American clubwomen supported the single standard and moral uplift, they did not embrace the campaign to impose criminal penalties on male sex offenders, nor was the issue taken up by the many local clubs throughout the country or the major national organizations of black women.[50] They feared, with good reason, that the law would be used to target black men and would do little to protect young black women. African Americans had learned all too well that the criminal justice system would not deal fairly with them, particularly regarding sexual crimes. Law enforcement authorities repeatedly failed to prosecute assaults on black women by white men yet sanctioned the punishment and even the lynching of black men in the South on false charges of interracial rape. After the end of Reconstruction, the lynching of African Americans increased in number and ferocity, reaching a peak average of 188 a year in the 1890s; between 1882 and 1930, 3,386 African Americans were killed by lynch mobs. Local white mobs carried out the burning, torture, and murder of blacks, but civic leaders and law enforcement officials did little to stop or punish mob leaders and often publicly sanctioned their actions. The standard justification for this brutal crime was the rape of white women by black men, but in reality few lynchings were associated with sexual assault. Only 23 percent of the known victims of lynch mobs between 1882 and 1946 were even accused of rape or attempted rape. The primary purpose of lynching was to instill terror in blacks and to maintain the system of white supremacy in the South.[51]

If African American women had any hope that white purity reformers would address the severe racial discrimination in the handling of sexual crimes, they were sorely disappointed. Throughout the purity campaign, white reformers steadfastly ignored the sexual exploitation that black women and girls faced on account of their race. Further, they failed to condemn the brutal treatment of African American men and the racist stereotype of them as dangerous rapists.

When black clubwomen launched a campaign against lynching in the early 1890s, they approached Frances Willard, as the leader of an important Christian organization, and requested that she issue a public statement against the crime.[52] Willard at first hesitated to do so for fear of alienating her white southern supporters. But when British temperance reformers took up the antilynching cause after black activist Ida B. Wells made a lecture tour in that country in 1893, Willard could hardly avoid taking a position. The WCTU passed an antilynching resolution at its annual convention that year, yet, in an effort to appease southern members of the organization, Willard made the following equivocal pronouncement in her presidential address: "Our duty to the colored people have [*sic*] never impressed me so solemnly as this year when the antagonism between them and the white race have seemed to be more vivid than at any previous time, and lurid vengeance has devoured the devourers of women and children."[53] This statement made only a vague reference to the problem of lynching. Even worse, by referring to lynch victims as "the devourers of women and children," Willard accepted the argument of southerners that the act was a response to assaults on white women by black men. The resolution passed by the WCTU the following year made a similar claim. The organization expressed its opposition to "all lawless acts" but at the same time also condemned "the unspeakable outrages which have so often provoked such lawlessness."[54]

The response of Willard and other white women reformers angered black clubwomen throughout the country. An editorial that appeared in the *Woman's Era* in July 1895 acknowledged that Willard had accomplished good work but lamented that "we have failed to hear from her or the Woman's Christian Temperance Union any honest, flat-footed denunciation of lynching and lynchers."[55] The following month, the Woman's Era Club of Boston criticized the temperance organization for what appeared to be its "condonation of lynching."[56] In an open letter printed in the *Woman's Era* in June 1894, black clubwoman Florida Ruffin Ridley chastised another white woman reformer, Mrs. Ormison Chant, for voting against an antilynching resolution at the National Conference of Unitarian Churches. Ridley defended the character of black men against the charges made by apologists for lynching: "We here solemnly deny that the black men are the foul fiends they are pictured; we demand that until at least one crime is proved upon them, judgement be suspended."[57]

Black women were further angered by the failure of the legal system to protect black women and girls from assaults by white men. In the same letter Ridley wrote, "We read with horror of two different colored girls who have recently been horribly assaulted by white men in the South. We should regret any lynchings of the offenders by black men, but we shall not have occasion; should these offenders receive any punishment at all it will be a marvel."[58] Given the extreme racial bias within both the legal system and the ranks of purity reformers, it is no wonder that black women did not join the age-of-consent movement and instead relied on education and self-help within their own communities to protect black girls from moral dangers.

Although white purity reformers did not seek or receive the support of African Americans, they did generate considerable public support for their cause. With the backing of religious leaders, labor organizations, and women's rights advocates, they achieved important legislative changes by 1890. At the federal level, Congress had voted to raise the age of consent from ten to sixteen in Washington, D.C., and the territories. Reformers also led numerous successful campaigns at the state level in the 1880s. Twenty-four states had amended their age-of-consent legislation by the end of the decade. In three states—New York, New Jersey, and Pennsylvania—lawmakers had raised the age of consent from ten to sixteen. Similar efforts met with more modest success in another twenty states, where lawmakers raised the age variously to fifteen, fourteen, or thirteen.[59]

The greatest victory in the first stage of the campaign occurred in Kansas, which was the first state in the country to raise the age of consent to eighteen. This came about through the combined efforts of the local WCTU and the state suffrage association. The two groups had just recently led a successful drive to win municipal suffrage for women early in 1887. One month later they convinced the legislature to raise the age of consent, thus lending credence to the belief of many suffragists and purity reformers that the enfranchisement of women would lead to better moral protection for girls.[60]

Although support for the campaign was growing, strong opposition to the new laws still existed. This opposition was evident in the intense battles over the issue that took place in most state legislatures and in efforts by some legislators to rescind the recent gains made in their states. In 1889 Kansas legislators introduced a bill to lower the age of consent from eighteen to twelve. A similar measure introduced by New York senators in 1890 aimed to reduce the age from sixteen to fourteen.[61]

These lawmakers voiced several objections to the age-of-consent movement. Many were deeply opposed to women's participation in the political arena. They dismissed the campaign as the product of meddling women who did not know their place in society. One Nebraska legislator and physician, Dr. McKeeby, declared that he was "opposed to upholding a measure built on sickly sentimentalism, advocated by women who have not the least idea of law-making." Such remarks only thinly veiled the great antipathy on the part of numerous legislators to women assuming a political role. One male legislator who supported the campaign explained that the opposition of his colleagues resulted from the "unuttered, but nevertheless felt prejudice against widening the sphere of woman's activity."[62]

The main objection legislators made to raising the age of consent was that young women would use the law to blackmail men. In contrast to the narrative of seduction elaborated by moral reformers, male legislators constructed an opposing narrative in which innocent young men were victimized by scheming, immoral young women.[63] An Iowa legislator warned that raising the age of consent to eighteen would "open the field for blackmailing and designing females, who will inveigle unsuspecting and susceptible youth into situations in which a yielding to an almost irresistible temptation will place them within the power of the female."[64] The fear of blackmail found expression not only in legislative halls, but among members of the medical community, who used the same argument to oppose the measure. An article that appeared in *Medical Age*, a medical journal published in Detroit, Michigan, argued that a higher age of consent would enable "the licentious, designing *demi mondaine*, many of whom are under the age of eighteen," to "entice an innocent ignorant schoolboy to her *bagnio* and after seducing him, institute criminal proceedings under protection of the law."[65]

Several legislators insisted that the age should be no higher than the

onset of puberty, by which time, they argued, girls should know the difference between right and wrong. According to the Judiciary Committee of
the Vermont Legislature, "It is conceded on all hands that girls reach the
age of physical and mental maturity earlier than boys." The committee
argued that raising the age of consent "wrongs the weak boy, who falls in
temptation thrown in his path by the more mature and often more wicked
girl."[66] Legislators found support from medical authorities on this issue.
One physician held that girls reached physical maturity three to four years
earlier than boys. He explained that "these physical changes in the body of
girls are associated with equally rapid changes in the mind and social
habits, changes which indicate greater maturity of girls within their own
sphere than in boys of corresponding ages." In light of this, he warned that
raising the age of consent would lead to "some disagreeable or unfair
litigation and punishment."[67] Another medical authority even denied that
it was possible to force a female who had reached puberty to have sexual
relations against her will. "It is my confident belief," he wrote, "that under
ordinary circumstances no female who has arrived at the age of understanding, be she never so weak, so long as consciousness remains, can be
forced against her will to participate in the act of copulation by a male be
he ever so strong."[68]

In the Victorian sexual ideology of the nineteenth century, an image of
female passionlessness had replaced an earlier image of women as sexually
aggressive. Yet beneath this belief in inherent female purity lay a double-
edged view of women's sexual nature that was manifested in the age-of-
consent campaign. The responses of male legislators indicate that the
fears of a manipulative, dangerous female sexuality persisted. Although
middle- and upper-class women were still perceived as pure and passionless, working-class and African American women came to embody the
dark, unruly, and promiscuous forces within women.

Such views are particularly evident in the arguments raised against a
higher age of consent in the South. In voicing their objections to the new
laws, southern legislators revived the racist myth of "bad black women,"
which assumed a different sexual nature for black and white women and
held that the former were naturally promiscuous. Representative A. C.
Tompkins of Kentucky complained that the proposed law placed the "negro female on the same plane as the white female." He relied on the authority of a Kentucky physician to assert that "negro girls" matured earlier
than "white girls," for they began menstruating at eleven years, while
most white girls did not menstruate until age fourteen. Tompkins further

claimed that it was impossible to rape black women, for due to their "natural complaisance," the male was "able to easily satisfy his desire without violence."[69] He warned, "We see at once what a terrible weapon for evil the elevating of the age of consent would be when placed in the hands of a lecherous, sensual negro woman, who for the sake of blackmail or revenge would not hesitate to bring criminal action even though she had been a prostitute since her eleventh year!"[70] The myth about the inherent promiscuity of black women grossly distorted the reality of interracial sexual relations in the South and served to justify the sexual exploitation of African American women by white men. Men would not be held accountable for sexual harassment and assault as long as black women were defined as sexually aggressive and depraved by nature.

Legislators in other parts of the country assigned the image of female depravity to working-class women, depicting working girls, servants, and prostitutes as licentious seducers of men. One legislator claimed that in Kansas, where the age of consent had recently been raised to eighteen, "several young men from highly respectable families" had been sent to the penitentiaries by such "immoral young women." Texas lawmakers protested that under the proposed legislation, "working girls, especially typewriters, would blackmail their employers."[71] Opponents of the new law clearly feared that raising the age of consent would imperil their sexual prerogatives with working-class and black women. In an effort to temper this threat, many legislators insisted that consent laws should only protect females of previously chaste character. Although purity reformers vigorously opposed this measure, several states included such clauses in their amended statutes.

Despite the strong objections to their political involvement, female reformers continued to lobby legislatures, collect petitions, and use the vote (where they had it) to press for higher consent laws. When legislators tried to revoke the gains made in Kansas and New York, women quickly organized to defeat their efforts. After senators in Kansas voted to lower the age of consent to twelve, the Kansas Equal Suffrage Association publicly condemned the action and organized a successful opposition to the bill. In response to a similar measure in New York, the local WCTU called on the citizens of the state to protest the "infamous bill." A WCTU representative, Mary Hunt, appeared before the legislature to warn lawmakers: "I represent 21,000 women and any man who dares to vote for this measure will be marked and held up to scorn."[72] A stream of protests followed, and the bill was eventually defeated.

Other attempts to rescind recent gains in several states motivated purity reformers to launch a broader and more forceful attack on the low age of consent in the early 1890s. As part of this effort, they enlisted Helen Gardener to write a series of articles about the issue in the *Arena*, a national journal devoted to social and political reform. Founded and edited by the zealous reformer Benjamin O. Flower, the *Arena* supported a number of other crusades, including the single tax, municipal government reform, free silver, and prohibition of the liquor traffic.[73] Between January and November 1895, Gardener published a series of five lengthy articles dealing with the age of consent. Entitled "The Shame of America," Gardener's first piece recounted the valiant efforts of purity reformers, especially the members of the WCTU and the New York Committee for the Prevention of State Regulation of Vice, to secure better protection for girlhood. Although many gains had been made, there remained much to be done. Gardener reported that in eight states the age of consent was still ten or twelve, and in twenty other states it was under fifteen years. She declared that "the need of a vigorous crusade, in behalf of exposed girlhood and in the interest of public morality, against such shameful legislation, should be obvious to all."[74] She called on the women and men of America to come to the defense of the country's daughters by demanding a higher age of consent.

The stepped-up campaign generated a new flurry of moral reform activity across the country in the 1890s. Members of the WCTU and the New York Committee still stood at the forefront of the campaign, but they drew additional support from a range of other individuals and organizations. National suffrage leaders and many local suffrage groups continued to lobby for higher consent laws. Protestant ministers and church organizations were now joined by Catholic clergymen. The General Federation of Women's Clubs and the Young Men's and Young Women's Christian Associations also added their voices to the chorus.[75]

As the campaign expanded, purity activists also began to win the endorsement of some physicians. Reformers considered this a significant achievement, for in the past the medical community had been indifferent, if not hostile, to their work. But during the 1890s, an increasing number of physicians expressed their support for the social purity campaign. State medical societies passed resolutions in favor of raising the age of consent to eighteen. In New York, Arizona, Michigan, and several other states, physicians helped to push age-of-consent bills through the state legislatures.[76] Most physicians, however, gave different reasons for supporting this measure; they did not necessarily share reformers' feminist concerns. Unlike female reformers, they did not focus on the sexual vulnerability of women but rather emphasized the health menace posed by illicit sexuality. The two state medical associations of New York supported age-of-consent legislation "in the interest of public health and clean heredity." Physicians warned that the state should not allow young women to engage in activity that threatened society with disease and insanity or with "defective" offspring.[77]

The age-of-consent campaign also developed a strong following among southern white women in the 1890s and began to make important inroads in the South. Reformers considered this a major accomplishment because the South had been the region most resistant to earlier reform efforts. As late as 1893, no southern state had raised the age of consent above ten or twelve years. The conservative gender and racial politics of the region explain the late response to the age-of-consent issue. Southern white women lived under a more restrictive system of male dominance and did not have the same access to education and public activism as their northern and midwestern sisters. Since the early nineteenth century, women in the North and Midwest had organized around a variety of causes, including antislavery, prison reform, suffrage, education for women, and temperance. Aside from church activities, Southern women had little experience with reform organizations until the WCTU began to organize in the South in the 1880s. Frances Willard's several southern tours during this decade stimulated the development of an active southern women's temperance movement. For the first time, numbers of southern women challenged their subordinate political role by speaking in public and petitioning legislative bodies about the temperance issue.[78]

Even as they began to participate in temperance reform, though, southern women initially shied away from the social purity program of the WCTU. When the national organization established a Social Purity Department, most local chapters in the country took up its work, but the southern chapters at first hesitated to ally themselves with the cause.[79] The reluctance of southern women to engage in purity reform stemmed not only from the general conservatism of the southern chapters (most also did not support suffrage for women), but also from the troubling racial issues it raised. To take on the double standard and male sexual license in the South could mean confronting the practice of interracial sex and the sexual vulnerability of black women and girls at the hands of white men. Southern women, however, were unwilling to challenge the system of white supremacy, even its tool of sexual control, which disrupted their own marital and family lives.

When they finally did adopt the cause of social purity in the 1890s, southern reformers, like their northern counterparts, avoided the racial side of the issue altogether. This avoidance required considerable effort particularly in the South, for southern legislators made clear and frequent references to interracial sexual relations in their arguments against the age-of-consent law. Like legislator A. C. Tompkins, they claimed the measure would subject white men to blackmail by "lecherous" black females.[80] As they did in their daily lives, southern white women chose to ignore these signs. Their campaign for social purity focused on the protection of white female chastity and did not challenge white men's sexual exploitation of black women.

During the 1890s, purity reformers throughout the South began to confront legislators with demands for higher age-of-consent laws.[81] Their efforts met with varying degrees of success. The WCTU, joined by local suffrage organizations, made important gains in Tennessee and Louisiana, where the age was raised to sixteen, and in Texas, where it was raised to fifteen. Another three states, Alabama, South Carolina, and Virginia, raised the age to fourteen during the 1890s. In other southern states, legislators proved more resistant to the purity cause. In 1895, when female reformers from Atlanta lobbied state lawmakers to raise the age of consent, the bill never made it out of committee. During this period purity activists in Florida and Kentucky also failed in their initial attempts to convince legislators to raise the age of consent.[82]

Despite some setbacks in the South, the age-of-consent campaign had achieved impressive legislative gains by the turn of the century. Reformers had succeeded in raising the age to eighteen in an additional eight states: Arizona, Colorado, Idaho, Missouri, New York, Nebraska, Utah, and Washington. Smaller gains had been made in another fifteen states, where legislators had raised the age to sixteen.[83] Although most of the intense debate and activity surrounding the age of consent took place in the 1880s and 1890s, reformers continued their efforts in many states well into the twentieth century. In California, for example, suffragists and temperance reformers lobbied lawmakers throughout the first decade of the twentieth century to raise the age of consent to eighteen. When California women acquired suffrage in 1911, they made the issue one of their central legislative goals. Finally, in 1913, under great pressure from recently enfranchised women, legislators and the governor finally agreed to increase the age to eighteen.[84] Numerous battles also took place in southern states during the early twentieth century. In 1901 purity reformers in Florida led a successful drive to raise the age of consent to eighteen when they presented petitions bearing more than 15,000 signatures to the legislature. And in 1918, suffragists and reformers in Georgia finally convinced legislators to raise the age of consent in their state. By 1920 nearly every state in the country had raised the age at which a woman could legally consent to sexual relations to either sixteen or eighteen years (see Table 1).[85]

Purity reformers and women's rights advocates celebrated this development as a great victory for the female sex, but the legacy of the age-of-consent campaign is more ambiguous. Reformers had persuaded legislators to enact a law that they thought would protect young working-class women from sexual harm. In the course of the campaign, they developed a forceful critique of the double standard of morality and male sexual privilege, but one that did not extend to the particularly severe forms of sexual exploitation faced by black women in a white-dominated society. Further, in their efforts to gain protection for young white women, reformers promoted an image of female passivity and victimization that appealed to conservatives who did not share the reformers' feminist concerns. The moral protection offered by reformers demanded the denial of young women's sexual desire and agency.

In order to assess the full impact of the age-of-consent campaign, we need to move beyond the reform movement to the actual enforcement of legislation. Moral reformers had persuaded the government to enact new laws, but they could not control how and by whom these laws would be used.

CHAPTER 2

TEENAGE GIRLS, SEXUALITY, AND WORKING-CLASS PARENTS

*R*aising the age of consent in the United States brought many young working-class men and women into criminal court for engaging in sex outside of marriage. One typical case heard in the superior court of Alameda County, California, in 1915 was that of a white couple, sixteen-year-old Ruth Hayes and Earl Morris, a young man who worked for the railroad. Ruth first met Earl at a dance in a town near San Francisco where she lived with her parents. The couple had visited each other regularly for almost two months when Earl asked her to live with him. Without her parents' permission, Ruth left home and moved in with Earl in a hotel in downtown Oakland, where they registered as husband and wife. Ruth's father, a skilled worker employed as a carpenter for the railroad, notified the police as soon as he discovered that his daughter had left home. Two weeks later the police found the couple in the hotel, arrested Earl on a charge of statutory rape, and placed Ruth in the girls' detention home in Oakland to await the trial.[1]

This case and other similar ones that came before California courts shed light on the enforcement of age-of-consent legislation within local communities. In particular, they tell us about the role that parents played in the enforcement process and about the types of sexual encounters regulated by the new law. Middle-class reformers may have been responsible for raising the age of consent, but once this legislation was in place, working-class parents like Mr. Hayes used it for their own needs and purposes. In the California counties of Alameda and Los Angeles, working-class parents initiated approximately half of the prosecutions for statutory rape under the age-of-consent law.[2] They, along with middle-class reformers, were greatly disturbed by their daughters' assertions of social and sexual autonomy. As traditional forms of sexual regulation proved less effective, some working-class parents turned to the courts to control teenage daughters and their male partners. This chapter explores parents' use of the legal system through an analysis of statutory rape prosecutions in the Alameda County Superior Court for the decade 1910–20 (112 cases) and in the Los Angeles County Juvenile Court for the years 1910 and 1920 (31 cases).[3] (See Appendix for more information on these case records.)

The chapter also examines the nature of the sexual encounters regulated by law and the meaning of sexuality for working-class daughters. Like Ruth Hayes, the young women and girls who appeared in the Alameda and Los Angeles courts did not fit the images of female victim or evil temptress constructed by middle-class reformers and male legislators in the age-of-consent campaign. Most young women (72 percent of the Alameda cases and 77 percent of the Los Angeles cases) had willingly engaged in sexual encounters with young men of the same class background.[4] They had entered these romantic relationships for a variety of reasons—companionship, pleasure, marriage, and economic support. Even those cases that did involve forcible assault (28 percent of the Alameda cases and 23 percent of the Los Angeles cases) present a different picture of sexual danger than that elaborated by purity reformers.[5] They suggest that young women were most vulnerable to sexual abuse, not in the public sphere of work and recreation, but in the home, where they faced assaults by male relatives.

The California counties of Alameda and Los Angeles provide an instructive setting for this exploration of the role of working-class families in the prosecution of statutory rape. Like many urban areas in the rest of the country, these counties witnessed tremendous population growth and economic development in the late nineteenth and early twentieth centuries. The principal cities of the two counties, Oakland and Los Angeles, grew at an especially rapid pace. Between 1880 and 1920, the population of Oakland increased from 34,555 to 216,261 and the population of Los Angeles grew from 11,183 to 576,673.[6] The expansion of transportation, trade, and industry in these cities contributed to their dramatic growth. In 1869 Oakland was selected as the western terminus of the country's first transcontinental railroad. The arrival of the Central Pacific (later Southern Pacific) Railroad, along with its fine harbor, made Oakland the transportation hub of the region. Over the next several decades, existing industries grew and dozens of new manufacturing and processing plants opened in and around the city to take advantage of the transportation facilities. The area boasted a diverse economy of lumber and cotton mills, breweries, brass and iron foundries, canneries, machine shops, shipbuilding plants, and textile and clothing factories. Even as manufacturing and trade flourished, agriculture remained an important part of the economy of Alameda County. Large-scale farms produced a variety of fruits, vegetables, and dairy products. Because of its transportation facilities, Oakland became a center for the canning, processing, and shipping of the agricultural products produced in Alameda County and northern California.[7]

The railroad also spurred population and economic changes in Los Angeles. With the arrival of the Southern Pacific Railroad in 1876 and the Santa Fe line in 1885, Los Angeles grew from a sleepy pueblo to the major metropolis of southern California. The transportation network, favorable climate, and availability of cheap labor (mostly from Mexico) contributed to the development of large-scale agriculture and the food-processing industry. By the early twentieth century, the region had become one of the leading agricultural producers in the country. In the 1890s and 1900s, Los Angeles experienced marked commercial and industrial growth with the expansion of the port and the establishment of many lumber mills, foundries, and slaughterhouses. Large canneries and food-processing plants were also built to handle much of the agricultural produce of the Southwest. And with the major oil strikes of the early twentieth century, Los Angeles became an important refining center and manufacturer of petroleum equipment.[8]

Economic opportunities drew a succession of native-born and foreign-born workers to Oakland and Los Angeles. In the late nineteenth century, native-born white Americans and northern Europeans made up the bulk of the working-class population in the two cities. Irish, German, British, Scandinavian, and Canadian immigrants formed the largest non-native groups. After the turn of the century, thousands of southern and eastern Europeans, Mexicans, and Asians joined these earlier migrants to California.[9] The immigrant communities of Oakland and Los Angeles, though smaller than those in some eastern and midwestern cities, were nonetheless substantial. In 1910, approximately 58 percent of the inhabitants in Oakland and 42 percent of those in Los Angeles were either foreign-born or had at least one foreign-born parent.[10]

The influx of various native and foreign-born groups created a diverse labor force in which race and ethnicity shaped occupational prospects for both male and female workers. Among male workers, native-born white Americans, Canadians, and northern Europeans and their descendants dominated the skilled trades in transportation and manufacturing. They worked as teamsters, longshoremen, metal workers, and carpenters. Native-born white women and those of northern European background predominated in the higher-status female jobs in offices and department stores and the better-paid factory positions.

The major southern and eastern European groups that moved into California were the Italians, Portuguese, and Russian and Polish Jews. Many Jewish immigrants made their way to California after living first in eastern and midwestern cities. They settled in the downtown neighborhoods of West Oakland and Los Angeles's Boyle Heights alongside other immigrant groups and found employment as factory workers, store clerks, peddlers, and shopkeepers.[11] Italian immigrants came from both northern and southern Italy, where most had worked in agriculture and a smaller number in fishing. Once in Alameda and Los Angeles Counties, some continued to follow the fishing and agricultural trades, but most worked as laborers in the railroad yards, lumber mills, construction sites, canneries, and shipyards. A number of families opened small commercial enterprises, such as fruit and vegetable stands, barbershops, and grocery stores.[12]

Alameda County was one of the major centers of Portuguese settlement in the country. Most Portuguese had migrated from rural communities in the Azore Islands, where they had worked as farm laborers or independent cultivators on small plots. In Alameda, they found jobs in canneries, shipyards, and cotton mills. Others engaged in agriculture, mostly as farm laborers or renters, but some managed to purchase small tracts of land for vegetable and dairy farming. Adolescent daughters and some wives took jobs in food-processing plants, clothing mills, and other factories to help support their families.[13]

The nonwhite groups who settled in Alameda and Los Angeles were restricted to the lowest rungs of the occupational structure, where most worked as unskilled laborers. Mexican, black, and Asian men were largely excluded from skilled jobs in transportation and manufacturing and from nonprofessional white-collar jobs as clerks and salesmen. Women of color were typically excluded from positions in department stores and offices, except for businesses run by members of their own racial and ethnic communities.

The massive immigration of Mexicans to southern California took place during the first three decades of the twentieth century. Between 1900 and 1930, approximately 1.5 million people had left small towns and villages in rural Mexico to move to the United States. Most of them settled in the Southwest, seeking work in the region's expanding economy. Many Mexican immigrants worked as farm laborers in the huge agricultural enterprises of southern California. In the city of Los Angeles, Mexican men were also employed as common laborers at construction sites and railroad yards, while women worked in canneries, packing houses, laundries, and clothing factories. A number of women, usually older ones, worked in private homes as domestics. Many Mexican families and their children in Los Angeles also engaged in migratory farm labor for part of the year.[14]

Oakland and Los Angeles were the major destinations of blacks migrating to California in the late nineteenth and early twentieth centuries. Thousands of African Americans, mostly from the southern states, headed west in hopes of finding better economic opportunities and a more hospitable racial climate. Many came to Oakland to work for the railroad as sleeping-car porters, section hands, cooks and waiters, baggage handlers, and car cleaners. A small community of African Americans resided in Los Angeles before 1900, but the population increased sevenfold between 1900 and 1920. In Los Angeles most black men worked as common laborers, janitors, porters, and waiters, and most women who worked outside of the home were employed as domestic servants or cooks. A small number of African American men and women in Oakland and Los Angeles worked as professionals or operated small businesses that served the black community, such as beauty salons, barbershops, bars, and restaurants.[15]

This diverse population of working people in Alameda and Los Angeles

Counties exhibited a range of sexual mores and practices. Many adhered to strict moral codes that placed great importance on the chastity of daughters. Some of these parents eventually turned to the legal system to enforce their moral order and to punish rebellious daughters and their male companions. Virtually all of the parents who filed statutory rape complaints in Alameda and Los Angeles were from the working class; that is, they and/or their spouses were employed as skilled, semiskilled, or unskilled workers. This group of parents reflected the diversity of the working-class populations in the two counties. They included native-born whites and blacks, skilled workers and common laborers, rural migrants and seasoned urban dwellers, and immigrants from Germany, Ireland, Italy, Portugal, Russia, Canada, and Mexico.

· · ·

Historians have usually associated the emphasis on female sexual purity with bourgeois Protestant culture and have drawn clear distinctions between the sexual behavior and norms of middle-class and working-class people. They have shown that middle-class Americans in the nineteenth century developed an ideology of sexual restraint that emphasized female purity and male continence and relied on individual self-control to regulate passions.[16] We know far less about the sexual mores of white, immigrant, and black working-class people during this period, but it is generally assumed that they were not bound by middle-class moral reticence. They supposedly had more fluid definitions of licit and illicit behavior, were more tolerant of sex outside of marriage, and did not stigmatize children born out of wedlock.[17]

Although there clearly were important differences between middle-class and working-class expressions of sexuality, one has to be careful not to overgeneralize about the working-class experience or to neglect the strict moral codes that operated within many working-class and immigrant communities. Concern with female chastity was not rooted in middle-class Protestant culture alone. It was also based in the patriarchal family structure of preindustrial societies, in various religious traditions, and in a code of honor that linked family reputation to the morality of wives and daughters. Many of the migrants to California came from rural communities and small towns in Europe, Mexico, and parts of the United States in which fathers had controlled both the labor and the sexual lives of their wives, children, and servants in ways that best supported the family economy. Sons could be required to delay marriage or sexual relations until fathers had parceled out land to them. The stability of the patriarchal household demanded particularly close control over the sexuality of wives and daughters. Out-of-wedlock births threatened the limited economic resources of the family and the need to ensure "legitimate" male heirs.[18]

Religious teachings reinforced the importance of premarital chastity in preindustrial communities. According to the Judeo-Christian ideal, sexual intercourse before marriage, and after marriage except with one's spouse, was sinful. The Catholic Church, in particular, placed great value on virginity. The church associated all carnal desire with the fall from grace and considered celibacy the highest state of godliness. Catholic doctrine forbade sex outside the bonds of marriage and held that sex between married partners was strictly for the purposes of procreation.[19]

In theory, religious strictures on chastity applied to both sexes, but religion competed with a popular ethos that expected moral purity in women, yet tolerated and even encouraged male sexual license. This double standard of morality was deeply rooted in Anglo-American culture and shaped both law and social custom in Britain and the United States.[20] The insistence on female chastity was just as pronounced in the Mediterranean societies from which Italian and Portuguese immigrants came and also in Mexico, where a code of honor linked a family's status and reputation to the sexual purity of its daughters and wives. Here again, though, the double standard was in operation, for whereas sexual promiscuity destroyed a woman's honor, it enhanced a man's prestige and status in society. It was the duty of male kin to guard the chastity of female relatives and to punish those who threatened the family name through promiscuous behavior. The loss of virginity had serious consequences for daughters, who might be ostracized by friends and villagers, abandoned by their families, or rejected as unsuitable for marriage. The code of honor was adhered to most strongly by the upper classes of society, but it also had considerable force among peasants and those who aspired to landholding status.[21]

Other working-class and immigrant groups came from communities that were somewhat less vigilant about guarding female chastity. In some small towns and rural villages of northern and western Europe and the United States, families tolerated sexual play and sometimes intercourse among young betrothed couples. Through the practice of "bundling," couples were permitted to sleep together in the same bed as long as they remained clothed or kept a bundling board between them. Young couples

also engaged in "nightcourting," in which they paired off in the evening
and spent the night together in barns or in the young woman's home. They
engaged in kissing and fondling, but were expected to refrain from intercourse, although, of course, not all did. Families and communities permitted such courting practices because it was expected that marriage
would follow, particularly if pregnancy resulted. Families and community
leaders could usually pressure a reluctant father to marry his pregnant
girlfriend.[22]

To regulate the sexual behavior of youths, preindustrial and rural societies relied on external methods of control that operated best in relatively
small, close-knit communities. Family, community, and church worked together to monitor young couples and to channel sexuality into marriage. In
the small towns and rural villages of the United States, Europe, and Mexico, most daughters worked in farm households or small workshops and
family businesses, under the close supervision of their parents or other
relatives. By the late nineteenth century, there was a small female factory
proletariat among Jewish women in eastern Europe and among American
women in the Northeast. But even within these groups, a home-based
putting-out system was the more usual form of female labor, rather than
factory production.[23] The familial context of such work not only ensured
that parents retained control over their daughters' labor and services, but
also enabled them to monitor the young women's social activities and relations with men. Families generally were well acquainted with the young
men who courted their daughters. Couples usually met at the young woman's home or at community events and celebrations under the watchful
eyes of neighbors. In southern European and Mexican villages, daughters
were usually chaperoned by family members whenever they left home to
go to the market, attend religious services, or take part in social events.[24]

Neighborhood gossip and various rituals of public shaming also served
as checks on sexual impropriety. In Mexican communities, single women
who engaged in illicit relations could be punished by having their braids
snipped off. Local youths in western European villages sang profane songs
under the window or placed a bad-smelling bush outside the door of any
young woman suspected of immoral conduct.[25] In various preindustrial
communities, groups of young men (known as *charivaris* in France) gathered together to harass community members who had violated sexual
norms by surrounding their homes and creating a racket with horns,
pots, cowbells, and the singing of profane songs. Some immigrant groups
brought this custom to the United States. In mid-nineteenth-century

Brooklyn, for example, an Irish mob gathered to condemn a minister who had been accused of seduction and adultery. The group visited the minister's house on his wedding day and shouted, groaned, and pounded drums and tin kettles for hours.[26]

Among African Americans in the rural South of the late nineteenth and early twentieth centuries, sexual mores and the methods used to regulate them resembled those of other preindustrial communities. Rural blacks accepted premarital sex as part of the courtship process. When a pregnancy occurred, it was generally expected that marriage would take place. But although marriage did follow most prenuptial pregnancies, African Americans generally did not ostracize unmarried mothers, but instead accepted and cared for them and their children as members of the community. In addition, communal and religious sanctions helped to enforce marital and sexual norms. For example, black churches might sometimes punish people who were guilty of fornication and adultery by suspending them from the church, with acceptance of the sinner back into the religious community requiring the approval of other church members.[27]

Even among experienced urban workers, as well as among migrants from rural areas and small towns, a preoccupation with female morality was evident. By the late nineteenth century, certain sectors of the American working class had embraced standards of sexual respectability that resembled those of the middle class. This was particularly true of the aristocracy of skilled laborers—made up primarily of native-born Americans and workers of Canadian and northern or western European backgrounds (German, English, Irish, and Scottish)—and of the small elite in African American society. However, this development should not be read as a passive acceptance of bourgeois values, the end result of decades of moralizing by middle-class reformers and ministers, but rather, according to Jeffrey Weeks, as "a negotiated redefinition on the part of the respectable working class." In other words, these white and African American workers reformulated dominant standards of respectability in response to their particular needs and social experiences. Many skilled workers and their wives embraced the values of female domesticity and moral purity yet at the same time mounted a radical attack on industrial capitalism, which, in their view, destroyed the home by forcing women and children to work for wages, thereby threatening their physical and moral well-being. These workers and their unions fought for a "family wage" that would enable them to keep their wives and young children out of the paid labor force. This strategy aimed both to protect male wages and the family's standard of living and also to preserve the moral respectability of wives and daughters.[28]

Skilled workers in black communities also demonstrated considerable concern for sexual respectability. African Americans did not idealize female domesticity as did some elite white workers; they continued to view employment and economic self-support as central to woman's role. But the small elite of black skilled workers and professionals did adopt similar values of moral respectability. During the late nineteenth and early twentieth centuries, paralleling the efforts of white purity reformers, black ministers and clubwomen organized to improve the home lives and sexual morals of their race through purity leagues, youth recreational programs, and homes and shelters for working girls. Moral respectability, however, had a distinct meaning for them. It was part of a broad program of racial uplift that also included efforts to improve health and education, promote economic self-sufficiency, and protest racial discrimination and violence. In stressing moral improvement, African American men and women were particularly concerned to combat the charges of immorality and end the sexual exploitation of black women by whites that had been central features both of slavery and of race relations after Emancipation.[29]

For a range of economic, cultural, and religious reasons, then, diverse groups of native-born and immigrant working people in Alameda and Los Angeles Counties placed a value on female chastity and used various means to enforce it. Traditional expectations of daughters and controls over their social interactions and relations with men, however, were seriously challenged in the rapidly growing and changing urban environments of Oakland and Los Angeles. In such large cities, earlier methods of regulating the sexuality of youth through family, community, and church were far less effective than they had been in villages and small towns. The great geographical mobility of workers, the crowded, ethnically diverse neighborhoods, and the growing number of young people living away from home made it difficult for parents or community leaders to ensure that marriage would automatically ensue when young women engaged in sex or got pregnant. Gossip and religious or communal sanctions did not have the same power to control deviant sexual behavior in large, heterogeneous cities as they had in small, face-to-face communities.

Compounding the problem, working-class daughters began to challenge familial expectations and roles as a result of new forms of work and recreation that drew them increasingly into the public sphere, where they experienced greater freedom from family constraints. Daughters continued to play a vital role in the family economy, for most working-class fathers did not earn enough to support the whole household on their wages alone. But the context of women's labor had changed dramatically. Instead of domestic work or industrial home work in family settings, the principal forms of female employment in the nineteenth century, daughters now worked in department stores, offices, factories, canneries, and restaurants. In Los Angeles some also had access to a variety of jobs in the burgeoning movie and entertainment industry.[30] Most of these changes in employment opportunities did not apply for African American women, who were barred from the higher-status female jobs and compelled to work mostly in domestic service. But even young black women experienced greater social autonomy during this period as they left their families and farm households in the rural South to live and work in new urban environments.[31]

Working out from under the supervision of family members, young women formed casual acquaintances with men they met on the streets or in the workplace. They used their status as wage-earners to assume privileges such as staying out late, going to dance halls, and using part their earnings to buy stylish clothes, makeup, or movie tickets. Some daughters took advantage of their new economic power to move away from home and live with friends or coworkers. Although most wage-earning daughters continued to live with parents or relatives, a growing number boarded in apartments and rooming houses with their peers.[32]

The expansion and commercialization of leisure activities in Oakland and Los Angeles at the turn of the century created a youth-oriented, mixed-sex world of amusement that altered courtship patterns and further undermined family control of daughters. Urban youths spent many of their leisure hours with peers in the dance halls, movie theaters, and cafés that sprang up in the downtown areas, and they also flocked to the amusement parks built in the early years of the twentieth century in both cities. Opened in 1903, Oakland's Idora Park covered seventeen acres and offered numerous attractions to the thousands who visited daily: a carousel, a roller coaster, a vaudeville theater, a dance pavilion, and a skating rink featuring a Tunnel of Love. In Los Angeles young men and women could ride the trolley from almost anywhere in the county to the beachside amusement parks at Venice and Long Beach, which featured roller coasters, merry-go-rounds, penny arcades, shooting galleries, and brightly lit promenades with cafés and dancing pavilions. These new recreational facilities provided social spaces for unsupervised flirtation and intimate encounters with members of the opposite sex.[33]

In response to these changes, immigrant and working-class families tried various strategies to monitor their adolescent daughters as they worked and played in American cities. Mexican and Italian families attempted to maintain a system of chaperonage by having a relative, often an older brother, accompany daughters when they left home. Some parents also tried to supervise their wage-earning daughters by having them work in establishments with other family members.[34] In the rapidly growing cities of Oakland and Los Angeles, however, such careful supervision was difficult to maintain. Over the objections of their families, daughters still went out in the evenings on their own, and they continued to form intimate relationships with young men they met at work, on the streets and beaches, and in the various amusement centers.

When familiar methods of sexual regulation proved ineffective in modern urban environments, some working-class parents turned to the courts for assistance. They used the age-of-consent law to restrain those daughters and their male partners who violated traditional moral codes. Numerous working-class parents sought legal intervention to end intimate relationships that their daughters had formed with male companions. In one case, a fifteen-year-old Portuguese girl left home and stayed in a hotel for several days with a young man she had been dating. When her father found out, he first confronted the man in his place of employment and then had him arrested for statutory rape. He explained to court officials, "You know how I felt towards him, what I wanted to do when he ruined my home."[35] One working-class mother called on the court when she learned that her fifteen-year-old daughter Louise was involved in a sexual relationship with a young man nineteen years of age. The couple first met at the Majestic Dance Hall in Oakland and had been seeing each other for several months without the mother's knowledge. When the older woman discovered a letter from the young man that revealed the nature of the relationship, she beat her daughter, reported her to juvenile authorities, and had the young man arrested for statutory rape.[36]

In a similar case, fifteen-year-old Edith Cook became sexually involved with her boyfriend, James, a nineteen-year-old who was training to be a mechanic. On several occasions, Edith invited James to sneak into her bedroom at night without her family's knowledge. On one of these occasions, Edith's brothers discovered James in her bedroom. They chased him with a revolver and threatened to kill him, but James escaped through the window. He was stopped by the police as he ran down the street and, at the brothers' insistence, was arrested for statutory rape.[37] The Martínez fam-

ily, immigrants from Mexico, also became very concerned when they
learned of the romantic relationship their teenage daughter, Eleanor, had
formed with a young Mexican man, Fernando Sandoval. Eleanor's older
brother warned Fernando to stay away from his sister when he discovered
a love note she had written to him. Several weeks later, Eleanor left home
after an argument with her mother and spent the night with Fernando.
When she returned home the next morning, her brother reported her to
juvenile authorities and filed charges against the young man.[38]

In numerous cases, parents used the law to retrieve runaway daughters
and their male companions. During the late nineteenth and early twentieth centuries, female runaways presented a serious problem to families
in Oakland and Los Angeles, as well as other urban areas in the country.
The local newspapers contained daily notices about teenage girls missing
from home. Parents and police often suspected that the girls had been
kidnapped or enticed by white slavers. A typical notice in the *Oakland
Tribune* read: "Grace Logan goes to pay a visit to friends in Alameda and
drops from sight. . . . It is the opinion of the girl's brother that she was
either 'spirited away or has been the victim of white slavers.'" According
to historian Mark Connelly, using white slavery abductions to account for
missing and runaway girls was common throughout the country.[39]

Court records and newspapers, however, reveal that the young women
and girls had more complex reasons for leaving home. Some were seeking
greater independence and freedom from strict parental supervision. The
Oakland Tribune reported that the mystery surrounding one seventeen-
year-old girl's disappearance was solved when her friend reported "she
was tired of restrictions placed on her by parents and planned to leave
home and seek employment to make her own way in the world."[40] There
was great conflict in many families over how late daughters remained out
at night, whom they dated, and where they spent their leisure time. Such a
dispute led to the case of two female cousins who, frustrated with strict
familial control of their behavior, ran away one Sunday afternoon. They
headed immediately for the dance pavilion in Oakland's Idora Park, where
they met a young man employed as a sales clerk at a local store. After
spending the evening with them at the amusement park, the man invited
the teenagers to stay in his room for the night. The next evening, as the
girls were on their way to another dance, they were apprehended by the
police.[41]

A number of other cases involved teenage girls who had run away to
escape unhappy or abusive home situations. One Russian Jewish girl left

her father's house because of his constant beatings. She moved in with her boyfriend, a young man who had previously boarded in her home until he was kicked out of the house because he tried to prevent the father from beating his daughter. The parents sent the police after the couple and had the young man arrested.[42] Other young women also left home without their parents' permission to live with their boyfriends. In one such case, sixteen-year-old Sara Gardner, who worked as a sales clerk, met a young French man, a musician, at a dance pavilion in San Francisco. Over the next few weeks, the man visited her home, met her parents, and took her out several times to the movie theater and ice-cream parlor. Then he persuaded her to leave home and live with him in his Oakland apartment, and he helped her find a job in the same theater where he worked. Within a week Sara's mother, uncle, and the police tracked down the couple at the theater and had the man arrested for statutory rape.[43]

Parents were particularly concerned about the sexual behavior of their daughters because of the threat of out-of-wedlock pregnancy, a problem that threatened both the economic stability and the social standing of many working-class families. Covering the costs of a daughter's pregnancy and the care of her child imposed a serious economic burden on those employed in a wage-labor economy. Additionally, parents lost their daughter's crucial contribution to the family income if she had been working. Faced with an unmarried, pregnant teenage daughter, some families turned to the courts to pressure the suspected fathers into marriage or at least to obtain financial support from them for medical and child care expenses. Nonmarital pregnancy was a factor in 15 percent of the Alameda cases and 15 percent of the Los Angeles cases studied here.

A single mother in Los Angeles, who was separated from her husband and no longer received financial support from him, faced an economic predicament when her teenage daughter got pregnant. She filed a rape complaint against the suspected father and explained to court officials that she thought the young man or his family should help pay for medical expenses.[44] A similar case that appeared before the Los Angeles court involved a young Mexican couple. Carmen Hernández, a teenage girl of fifteen, got pregnant several months after she began going out with a young Mexican man who worked as a farm laborer. When the man refused to marry her and then failed to contribute adequately to medical expenses during the pregnancy and to the support of the child, her parents—both of whom were employed as agricultural laborers—had him arrested for statutory rape.[45] The resolutions of such cases are not consistently reported in the court records, but it is clear that in several cases judges ordered the alleged fathers to contribute to the support of the child and to the costs of the young woman's medical care.

Although the economic costs of a nonmarital pregnancy were certainly distressing to working-class families, equally important were the costs to the both the daughter's and the family's reputations. Families worried about the humiliation and limited marriage prospects their daughters would face as unmarried mothers. Such were the concerns of Mrs. Alvarez when she learned of her teenage daughter's pregnancy. Attempting to salvage her daughter's reputation, Alvarez first relied on community pressure to compel the man into marriage. She enlisted several female relatives and neighbors to confront the suspected father where he worked and urge him to marry the girl. When he still refused, Alvarez had him arrested. As she explained in court, "I did because I didn't want my daughter that way, because when a girl is that way, nobody thinks good of her. . . . I told him I wanted him to marry the girl just to give her a name."[46]

In the eyes of some parents, a daughter's out-of-wedlock pregnancy brought shame and dishonor to the whole family, as illustrated in the case of Pauline Taylor. When Mr. and Mrs. Taylor discovered that their fourteen-year-old daughter was four months pregnant, they notified the juvenile authorities of Los Angeles County and filed a rape complaint against the suspected father. The Taylors, according to the probation officer assigned to the case, were poor but respectable people. Mr. Taylor operated a peanut stand, and his wife also worked outside the home to help support their family of four children. The probation officer noted that the Taylors "had no suspicion that their girl was going wrong" and were "overwhelmed with the horror of the situation and seem helpless in regard to it."[47]

The parents sent their daughter to the Truelove Home for unmarried mothers, where she was kept for nearly five months. Her placement in a maternity home served to hide the family's shame—the pregnant daughter—from the public eye. When Pauline gave birth, she wanted to keep the baby, but her parents insisted that she put the child up for adoption. Mr. Taylor was so angry at his daughter and felt so disgraced by the situation that, according to the probation officer, he had not once visited his daughter in the maternity home and refused "to see or recognize the baby or assist in the support and will not allow [Pauline] to come home unless she gives up the child." Anxious to return to her parents, Pauline finally agreed to give up her baby.[48]

As working-class parents turned to the courts to enforce traditional moral codes, their daughters struggled to assert their own social and sexual autonomy. The sexual encounters they described in court did not fit the image of male lust and female victimization promoted in the seduction narratives of purity reformers. Instead of being the helpless victims of evil men, most of the young women were willing participants in a more complicated sexual drama than middle-class reformers or public officials could imagine. In 72 percent of the Alameda cases prosecuted between 1910 and 1920 and 77 percent of the Los Angeles cases in 1920, young women said they had consented to sexual relations with their male partners.[49] The desire for pleasure, adventure, companionship, marriage, and economic support all figured in these young women's decisions about their sexual choices. Most of their male partners were young working-class men, not the older middle-class seducers portrayed by reformers. Seventy-three percent of the defendants in Alameda County were between the ages of eighteen and twenty-nine, the bulk of them between eighteen and twenty-four years.[50] Seventy-four percent of those whose occupation is known were skilled or unskilled laborers.[51] The young men charged with statutory rape in the Los Angeles Juvenile Court were between thirteen and nineteen years of age, with 74 percent between the ages of fifteen and seventeen.[52] They were employed in various working-class occupations such as store clerk, agricultural laborer, and teamster.

The young women in these court cases also challenged prevailing conceptions of female sexual innocence and purity through their dress, language, and behavior. Many had flirted openly with young men on the street, dressed in the latest fashions, and attended dance halls, movie theaters, and amusement parks unchaperoned, often "picking up" young men once they arrived. In so doing, working-class daughters undermined the rigid classification of women as good and bad, angels and prostitutes, a division that was a staple of Victorian culture. They adopted many of the manners associated in the public's mind with prostitution—wearing makeup, smoking cigarettes, going out at night alone, and engaging in sex outside of marriage—yet they clearly disassociated themselves from prostitutes. These young women had not accepted money for sexual favors, and several expressed their clear disapproval of that type of exchange. Yet they acknowledged women's sexual agency and condoned sexual relations in certain circumstances.

Numerous young women had taken an active role in their romantic encounters. On the streets, in movie theaters, and in dance halls, they encouraged and sometimes initiated contact with young men. When asked how she met her sexual partner, one teenage girl explained to court officials: "A flirtation. . . . I turned the corner and looked back and he was standing outside smoking, then I went down a little ways and I looked around again and he was standing on the corner, then he followed me."[53] Another teenager who appeared in court had apparently invited her boyfriend on several occasions to visit her in her bedroom at night without her parents' knowledge. Her family had learned of the relationship when they discovered the following note she had written to the defendant: "Dear [Daniel], I am sleeping in that little room and I felt rather lonesome and cold. I wonder if you couldn't come over to see me tonight about 11:00. . . . From the one that loves you."[54]

Eighteen-year-old Margaret Emerson explained in court how she and her girlfriends met the defendant, George Cheney, and his friends when they went to the "moving picture show" in downtown Oakland one Sunday afternoon. Wearing stylish dresses for the occasion, the girls attracted the attention of the young men, gave out their addresses in East Oakland, and made a date to go to Lincoln Park the following weekend. Margaret explained to the court that "Mama would never let me talk to any fellows unless she saw them." Nevertheless, she went out with George twice before introducing him to her mother. After dating for several months, the couple decided to move in together and made plans to marry once George secured a divorce from his first wife. To get Mrs. Emerson's approval for this arrangement, they told her they had already married and did not mention George's previous venture into marriage.[55]

Like Margaret Emerson, many young women formed intimate relationships with their "steadies," men they had been dating and planned to marry. Yet the expectation of marriage was not always a precondition for engaging in sex. One teenage girl of Mexican descent, Edna Morales, fell in love and became intimately involved with a nineteen-year-old man whom she met at the store where she worked in Los Angeles. When questioned by court officials, Edna plainly stated that she had not engaged in sex because of a promise of marriage, but because of the affection she felt for her partner. The probation officer assigned to the case reported that when she asked the young woman about her sexual relations, "she very boldly said, yes. . . . She did not seem to think there was anything wrong about it but refused to give me the young man's name."[56]

For other young women, sex was not necessarily linked either to marriage or even to love but was simply a form of pleasure, part of an evening's entertainment and adventure. Julia Townsend, who lived with her parents in southern California, made occasional weekend trips to Los Angeles with her two girlfriends to visit dance halls and cafés. On one of these trips, she and her friends arrived in Los Angeles on a Saturday evening, registered at a downtown hotel, and headed for Solomon's Dance Hall. Julia, who was employed as a stenographer, used her own money to pay for the trip and her share of the room. The young women met several young men at the dance hall and invited them to their hotel room. That night the police raided the hotel and arrested the three couples. Julia was charged with "visit[ing] hotels with men to whom she is not married, sleeping and staying in the same room and apartment with these men."[57] Another young woman expressed a liberal sexual standard similar to Julia Townsend's. According to the probation officer who handled her case, "She told me in talking with her that she did not believe there was any wrong in having sexual intercourse with boys, if she would not take money and if she did not become pregnant."[58]

Other young working-class women exchanged sexual favors for an evening's entertainment, a ticket to the amusement park, a meal, or a place to stay for the night. In a society that severely restricted women's access to economic independence and self-support, it is not surprising that many young women chose to barter with sex. Even though employment opportunities for women had expanded during this period, they still earned only approximately 60 percent of the standard men's wages, and women workers typically earned less than the "living wage," which was estimated to be nine or ten dollars a week in 1910.[59] Young women discovered early on that their sexuality was a valued commodity that they could trade for things they wanted or needed. Because of their low wages, working girls often depended on men to "treat" them if they wanted to take part in urban recreations or enjoy a night on the town. In return, the men expected sexual favors, which could range from affectionate companionship to sexual intercourse.[60]

When sixteen-year-old Annie Wilson was asked in court how she became intimately involved with the defendant, she explained that she and her sister had skipped Sunday school to go to the skating rink at Idora Park in Oakland. There they met Andrew Singer, who treated them to refreshments and rides in the park. Later that night Annie returned with the young man to his hotel room and stayed the night. In the meantime her family notified the police, who located her the next morning. When asked by the court why Annie behaved this way, her sister responded, "She didn't like to turn him down, he had given us lunch and paid our way into the rink and she didn't like to turn him down."[61]

Fifteen-year-old Agnes Farrell and her friend Amelia made a similar exchange with sailors they met at the train station in downtown Los Angeles or at the navy dock in San Pedro. They accompanied the sailors to dance halls and to the amusement park at Long Beach and on several occasions spent the night with them in hotels along the beach. Agnes explained to court officials that they did not expect to receive money from the sailors but were merely interested in being taken out and shown a good time.[62]

A number of girls used their sexuality as a strategy for survival after running away from home. Runaways often relied on boyfriends or men they met along the way to pay for meals and hotel rooms. In return for such support, the young women engaged in sexual intercourse with their male companions, following an arrangement that was often unspoken. A teenage runaway with no viable means of economic support often had only her sexuality to trade. One teenage girl left home to escape the heavy domestic duties her family demanded of her. She had no money with which to rent a room, but she met a young man in downtown Los Angeles who found and paid for a hotel room and later helped her to find a job at a nearby cafeteria. In return, she had sexual relations with him.[63] A fifteen-year-old African American girl found herself in a similar situation when she left her aunt's home in a small town in northern California, where she had been living ever since her mother died. She ended up stranded in Oakland with no means of support until she ran into a young black man she knew. He offered to pay for her room and board, and the two lived together for several days until they were arrested by the police.[64]

Other young women exchanged their sexuality, not for entertainment or shelter for the night, but for a promise of marriage. Some hoped marriage would offer a way out of tedious employment or an unhappy or overly strict home. Such was the situation of Louise Howard, who met her boyfriend, Robert Camarillo, at an Oakland dance hall. After they had dated for several weeks, Louise suggested that they get married. She desperately wanted to leave home because of the constant fights she had with her stepfather. Robert promised to marry her once he received the approval of his father. In the meantime, he wanted her to prove her love by having sex with him. Louise agreed to his request, but whenever she brought up the question of marriage, Robert claimed he was still waiting for his father's approval. Eventually Louise's mother learned of the couple's relationship, reported her daughter to juvenile authorities, and had the young man arrested.[65] In another case, a fifteen-year-old Portuguese girl, who worked in a telephone office, agreed to spend the night with a young man she had been dating after he promised to marry her. She was eager to leave her own home because she did not get along with her parents and was particularly distressed by their plan for her to marry a Portuguese man they had selected for her.[66]

Sexuality was a means of rebellion for young women, but it was also clearly an area in which they were exploited. Engaging in sex outside of marriage involved serious risks for them—pregnancy, disease, abandonment, social ostracism. Although they were far from the helpless victims of reformers' accounts, young women nevertheless entered the sexual relationship from a greatly disadvantaged position compared to their male partners. They had far more restricted access to economic independence and faced greater condemnation for their sexual transgressions. Despite the purity reformers' campaign against the double standard, families and society still punished women more harshly than men for illicit sexual activity. Young women also had to contend with a popular male culture that viewed them as sexual bait yet ostracized those who acquiesced as "loose," not fit to be wives and mothers. One young man refused to marry the pregnant teenage girl he had been dating because, as he told court officials in Los Angeles, she was "a girl of easy morals."[67]

One of the greatest risks of sexual experimentation for working-class daughters was out-of-wedlock pregnancy. Mary Reed rebelled against the strict moral code established for young women by drinking with men, going to cafés and dances unchaperoned, and engaging in sexual intercourse. She became pregnant by one young man she had been dating. He refused to marry her and, when arrested, told the court that Mary was promiscuous and had slept with several other men. The court had little sympathy for someone who had violated the social code as Mary had done. Her sexual adventures ended in pregnancy without marriage, a humiliating interrogation by the police and court, and very likely confinement in a reformatory.[68]

Margaret Emerson also found herself unmarried and pregnant after she agreed to move in with her boyfriend, George Cheney. Although George had promised they would marry as soon as he secured a divorce from his first wife, he continually delayed the marriage and finally moved out when Margaret became pregnant a year and a half later. Alone and with few resources, Margaret filed a rape complaint against George and told the court she thought he should marry her and help support the baby.[69]

The grave social and economic costs of out-of-wedlock pregnancy led some young women to resort to illegal abortion, a dangerous and sometimes fatal procedure. One young woman in Los Angeles nearly died from blood poisoning after a botched abortion she received from a local doctor.[70] Another pregnant teenage girl in Alameda County died from an "operation" shortly after an unsuccessful attempt to make her boyfriend marry her by taking him to court.[71]

Young women's increased social autonomy could also make them vulnerable to forcible assault. At times the boundaries and limits of the system of sexual exchange were not entirely clear. In some cases, girls who were reluctant to comply with the expectation of sexual favors were forcibly raped.[72] This was the case with Ruby Haynes, a teenage girl who accepted a date with a young man she met at the movie theater in Oakland. The night they met, Jason Strand took her to the beach, walked her home, and made a date to go to the nickelodeon a few days later. As they were walking home after the second show, Jason took Ruby into a vacant lot and urged her to have sex with him. When she refused, he threw her to the ground and raped her.[73]

Although most of the girls in the court cases studied here had willingly engaged in sex, a number, like Ruby Haynes, had been forcibly assaulted. Twenty-eight percent of the statutory rape cases before the Alameda court were, in fact, forcible assaults.[74] These cases present a different picture of sexual danger than that elaborated by reformers and court officials, who focused on extrafamilial forms of sexual harm, specifically prostitution and white slavery. They believed young women encountered danger when they left home to work in factories and department stores and to play in the new centers of urban recreation. The majority of forcible rape cases, however, suggest that sexual harm was more prevalent in the home itself, where young women and girls faced assaults by male relatives and neighbors, or by male employers if they were domestics.[75]

Forty-three percent of the female victims of sexual assault were attacked by male relatives—fathers, stepfathers, uncles, and brothers. Another 27 percent were assaulted by neighbors or close family friends. Seventeen percent were raped in their place of employment, and all but one of these was employed as a domestic servant.[76] Fifteen-year-old Catherine

Schultz was sexually abused by her father from the time she was seven years old. When her mother died several years later, her father began having sexual relations with her every night. Catherine tried to stop him by locking her bedroom door; when her father threatened to climb through the window, she nailed it shut. Her father became so angry at her growing resistance that he refused to give her any spending money and threatened to put her in a detention home. With the support and encouragement of their twenty-five-year-old housekeeper, Catherine finally reported her father to the police.[77]

In other cases, girls were sexually abused by stepfathers, uncles, brothers, or other male relatives in a position of authority over the girls. One fourteen-year-old girl was repeatedly abused for several years by her stepfather, who always waited until his wife was away from home to assault the daughter. The girl hesitated to tell her mother because she was afraid of her stepfather and also because she feared her mother's reaction: "I didn't tell her anything about it because she has heart failure and I know when I tell her anything she gets sick." When the mother overheard her daughter warning a younger sister about the abuse, she reported her husband to the police.[78]

Domestic servants also faced sexual assault by men residing in the households where they worked. Domestic workers were probably more vulnerable to sexual abuse than female wage-earners in department stores, factories, and offices. They were more isolated and lacked the presence and support of fellow women workers to protect them. Often left alone in the house, they were easy targets for assault by men who lived and boarded there.[79] A fifteen-year-old black girl who boarded with and worked as a domestic servant for a black couple was raped by the man when his wife was away from home one evening. She left the house and notified her father with the following letter: "Dear Papa: I am sorry that I am not going to stay with Mrs. and Mr. [Jones] because he is always so dirty, and you know what that means. I can tell you better when I see you. I am not going to stay here and be disgraced."[80]

A seventeen-year-old Portuguese girl, Isabelle Silva, was assaulted by the male head of the household in the home where she worked as a domestic servant. One day when his wife was away from home, the man followed the young woman into the barn where she was gathering eggs, knocked her to the ground, and raped her. When Isabelle told her parents about the assault, they confronted the man the next day. At first he denied their accusation, then offered to pay them a hundred dollars if they agreed not to report him to the police. The Silvas refused his offer and had him arrested on a charge of statutory rape.[81]

. . .

It is difficult to know just how widespread the sexual abuse of young women within the home was. Most cases were not reported to law enforcement officials, and even fewer were prosecuted in court. Recent historical studies, however, suggest that the problem was far more common than previously believed. Linda Gordon and Paul O'Keefe found evidence of the sexual abuse of children, almost all girls, by male relatives and guardians in 10 percent of the case records from three Boston social work agencies between 1880 and 1960. In a study of gender relations in nineteenth-century New York, Christine Stansell has argued that "sex with girl children was woven into the fabric of life in the tenements and the streets: out-of-the-ordinary, but not extraordinary."[82]

I do not mean to suggest that the public spaces of work and recreation were free of sexual danger. Young women clearly faced assaults by male employers and coworkers in factories and offices and by men they met in recreational venues. But they were particularly vulnerable to sexual abuse in the home because of their greater economic and psychological dependence on male guardians. Domestic servants, and daughters in particular, depended on male heads of households for food and shelter. Some of these victims of familial abuse could and did work, but they rarely earned enough to support themselves independently of their families. As in Catherine Schultz's case, a father could use his daughter's economic dependence to force her compliance to his sexual demands. When Catherine resisted, her father threatened to deprive her of spending money and to throw her out of the house.[83]

Economic dependence aside, most young girls were raised in male-dominated households where they learned subservience to male authority. A number of the victims of familial sexual abuse did not physically resist the sexual advances of their male relatives. When questioned by judges and attorneys about their passivity, the girls said they were afraid or that the man had threatened to harm them if they reported the assaults. Taught at an early age to obey the orders of fathers and other male adults, these girls hesitated to challenge male authority even in cases of sexual abuse.[84]

One clear example is provided by the case of a thirteen-year-old girl who had been sexually abused by her twenty-seven-year-old brother for several years, until an older, married sister found out and reported the offense to the police. Court officials could not understand why the girl had not reported the incident sooner or actively resisted her brother's advances. But as she explained in court, "I couldn't do anything against him, we were the only ones home." She told the judge that she was afraid of her brother, "afraid he'd get me into trouble, afraid of my father too. . . . He might put me away or something."[85]

In a similar case, a fourteen-year-old girl did not actively resist the sexual advances of her uncle, a man fifty-six years of age. She had lived with him and her grandmother from the time she was an infant, after the death of her parents. The following exchange between the girl and an attorney in court demonstrates how difficult it was for young women and girls to challenge sexual abuse by men in authority over them.

Attorney: What you did, you did of your own free will?

A: No, I couldn't help it.

Attorney: You just told the Court that he unbuttoned one side of your panties and you unbuttoned the other side.

A: Yes.

Attorney: That don't look as though you were fighting very hard, did it.

A: No.

Attorney: You were willing?

A: Yes, well yes, I was because I couldn't help it. When he come near me, I just couldn't help it, I had to do it.

Attorney: Why? Were you afraid of him?

A: I was, yes.

Attorney: Did you want to do it?

A: No, I didn't.

The uncle used his position of authority within the home to compel the girl to submit to his sexual demands. The girl's grandmother reported in court that her son locked her out of the house when he planned to have sexual relations with his niece. He told the girl as he took her to the bedroom, "You got to mind me. . . . I am the one that you got to mind."[86]

Given the economic, psychological, and legal factors discouraging them, it is remarkable that some girls did actively resist sexual assault by family members. The older ages of these girls and the support of other women apparently encouraged resistance. Catherine Schultz, for example, submitted to her father's advances until age fifteen, when she gained the courage, with the support of the family housekeeper, to report her father to the police. Another fifteen-year-old girl had endured her stepfather's abuse for two years when she finally declared to her sister that she would "shoot Papa if he tried to grab hold of her again."[87]

Considering the prevalence of domestic sexual abuse, it is at first difficult to understand why public officials and women reformers neglected the issue. Clearly the private nature of such offenses and the reluctance of families to report them made the problem a difficult one to address. Moreover, a general cultural silence about sexual abuse within the family pervaded this period. Although they must have encountered it in the course of their work, police officers, physicians, and court officials ignored the problem, for they were unwilling to seriously challenge male authority within the family. The family was considered a bastion of the social order in America, a place where children supposedly received protection, care, and moral instruction. The very notion of incest made a mockery of this concept of the family. Rather than deal with the problem, it was easier to deny it, to assume that the young women and girls who accused their fathers and other male relatives of sexual abuse were lying. This denial is evident in the case of Catherine Schultz. The male physician who examined Catherine criticized the family housekeeper for encouraging her to file a complaint against her father. He called the housekeeper "a dirty liar" and accused her of putting words in the girl's mouth. "You are putting this girl up to say that and do you realize the trouble you are causing?" he declared.[88] The court apparently shared the physician's view and eventually dismissed the rape charge against Catherine's father.

Women moral reformers had been more willing than most to criticize the institution of the family. In the campaigns for temperance and social purity, for example, they criticized the misuse of male authority within the family and attempted to extend women's domestic influence.[89] They did not, however, seek to undermine the male-dominated family, but rather to reform it. They took their critique only so far both because of powerful opposition by defenders of conservative family values and because of their own dependence on and identification with the family. Middle-class women were dependent on fathers and husbands for economic support. Further, they derived their sense of identity and social purpose from their roles as mothers, as the providers of nurturance, love, and moral guidance to children and husbands. Given these constraints, it was more acceptable for them to address public forms of sexual danger like prostitution and white slavery. But in the end, these campaigns may have diverted attention away from the more imminent sources of sexual harm facing young women and girls.

CHAPTER 3

STATUTORY

RAPE

PROSECUTIONS

IN

CALIFORNIA

*I*n April 1915, Oakland police arrested George Fields, a young man of nineteen years who worked as a jitney bus driver, on a charge of statutory rape. George sat in the county jail for several weeks until his case was heard in the Alameda County Superior Court. Law enforcement officials also apprehended his female partner, thirteen-year-old Louise Blake, and placed her in the county detention home for wayward girls to await the trial. Louise admitted to court officials that she had engaged in sexual relations with the defendant on several occasions. At first George denied any sexual involvement with her but later pleaded guilty to the charge. At the sentencing hearing, the county probation officer recommended probation for the defendant. The young man, he informed the judge, "had previously borne an excellent reputation," while his female partner in the case "was not a pure girl." The officer concluded, "The circumstances of this case are such as would test the moral backbone of persons far better equipped to resist than he had been." Persuaded by this reasoning, the judge granted the young man probation.[1]

The case of George Fields and Louise Blake, along with others heard before the Alameda County Superior Court and the Los Angeles County Juvenile Court, allow us to explore how the criminal justice system responded to the age-of-consent law. (See Appendix for more information on these case records.) Many male court officials were deeply ambivalent about the new legislation and the assumptions on which it was based. Moral reformers had been able to persuade legislators to raise the age of consent but could not ensure that the legal system would enforce the law as they had intended. Like the probation officer and judge in the Fields case, many court officials did not accept the model of female sexual victimization promoted by purity reformers, nor did they share the reformers' commitment to a single standard of morality for both sexes. Rather, they held to a different moral code that tolerated sexual license on the part of men yet expected women to remain chaste. Informed by such attitudes, courts were reluctant to apply the criminal penalties the law called for, particularly in cases in which, like George Fields, the male offenders were young and white and their female partners were thought to be immoral.

With the passage of age-of-consent legislation, the state assumed an active role in monitoring the sexual behavior of working-class women and girls and their male partners. Police officers patrolled train stations, amusement parks, cafés, and dance halls in search of suspected immoral behavior. They also conducted periodic raids of downtown hotels and arrested couples who had violated the law. Adult men arrested for statutory rape typically were detained in the county jail until a preliminary examination could be held in one of the police or justice courts in the county.

At the preliminary hearing, the judge sought to determine if there was sufficient evidence to hold the accused man for trial in superior court, which was the central criminal court for counties in California. Both the prosecution and the defense were permitted to call witnesses for examination and cross-examination. Once the judge decided that prosecution should go forward, which was the outcome in most cases, he set bail to guarantee the defendant's appearance at superior court. If the defendant could not raise bail, he remained confined in the county jail until the trial.[2] At least 36 percent of those charged with statutory rape in the Alameda County Superior Court spent anywhere from one week to six months in jail while awaiting trial.[3]

Although the age-of-consent law was intended to "protect" young women, the prosecution of statutory rape cases proved to be a punitive process for them as well as for the male defendants. Young women and girls were frequently confined in the county detention home for delinquent youth to await court hearings. While in detention, all girls were subjected to compulsory pelvic exams to determine whether they were virgins. If the physician found evidence of sexual experience (a ruptured hymen or relaxed vaginal opening), the girls faced rigorous questioning about their sexual activities by female probation officers, who pressured them to reveal the names of their sexual partners, then turned these names over to the police. During a cross-examination in a police court in Alameda County, the defense attorney asked one girl why she had filed a complaint against the defendant. The girl responded:

A: They made me tell.
Defense: Who made you tell?
A: Miss Rich [probation officer at the detention home]. . . .
Defense: Well, did you tell her you had had sexual intercourse with anyone?
A: Well, she knew it after I was examined. . . .
Defense: How did she happen to have you examined by a doctor?
A: Well, as far as I know, all the girls are who go there.[4]

These inquiries sometimes led to the arrest of several young men for the rape of one girl. In one such case, an unmarried, pregnant teenager, Mary Reed, told the probation officer that the father of her unborn child was a young man she had been dating steadily for the past year. Under questioning by the probation officer, she also confessed to sexual intimacy with several others prior to her current relationship. Rape complaints were filed against all of the young men, even though Mary insisted she only wanted her child's father arrested.[5]

Young women involved in statutory rape cases faced long interrogations about their sex lives at the preliminary hearing. The hearings were meant to determine if sufficient grounds existed to prosecute the defendant, but they usually focused on the moral character of the female witness, too. Male defendants were not required to testify in these hearings, and the vast majority did not. But the young women were routinely questioned by both the prosecution and defense attorneys about their sexual relationships with the accused and usually about past sexual experiences as well. Typical questions included: Where and when did the sex act occur? How did you become undressed? Where did he touch you? What type of underwear were you wearing? What did you say during intercourse? How many times did you have intercourse? The experience was humiliating for many young women and girls, who were compelled to give explicit details of their sexual activities, as in the following exchange between the prosecutor and one female witness:

> *Prosecutor*: And he got on top of you?
> A: Yes sir. . . .
> *Prosecutor*: How were your legs when he had this act of sexual
>   intercourse with you, were they close together or apart?
> A: They were apart.
> *Prosecutor*: And how did they get apart, you put them apart yourself,
>   didn't you?
> A: No sir.
> *Prosecutor*: Sure about that?
> A: Yes sir.
> *Prosecutor*: Who put them apart?
> A: He did. . . .
> *Prosecutor*: What were you doing when he put them apart?
> A: Nothing.
> *Prosecutor*: Where were your hands when he put them apart?
> A: Down at the side.
> *Prosecutor*: What did you say during the time he was putting your
>   limbs, your legs, apart?
> A: Didn't say anything.[6]

In response to these questions, many young women and girls spoke in low voices and gave short, one-word answers whenever possible. One teenage girl expressed the pain and embarrassment that many felt before this type of examination: "Really I don't wish to tell it all," she told the judge. "It humiliates and disgraces me and I don't want to." When the judge threatened to pronounce her in contempt of court and send her to the city jail, she said, "You will have to send me, I can't tell it."[7] One fifteen-year-old African American girl, who had run away from home and moved in with a young man, was asked repeatedly for specific details about her sexual relationship with the defendant. When asked, "What did he do to you when he got into bed with you?" she responded impatiently, "Do you expect me to tell the whole history of my life? . . . I am not going to tell the whole history of my life." After the trial of her male partner in superior court, the district attorney complained that "the little girl was a very unwilling witness while on the stand and did everything possible to shield him, as she said she expected to marry him."[8]

One of the central questions raised in the preliminary hearings was whether the female witness had consented to the sexual act. This issue should have been immaterial in cases of statutory rape, because the law prohibited sexual intercourse with female minors, regardless of their consent. Nonetheless, judges routinely allowed attorneys to question female witnesses about their willingness to engage in sex. When the defense attorney in one case asked a female witness if she had consented to sex with the defendant, the prosecutor objected: "It is absolutely immaterial, Your Honor. The question is whether he had an act of sexual intercourse or not and how he obtained that is not a matter for us here." The judge, in this case and numerous others, demonstrated a marked ambivalence about the issue. He admitted that the question was immaterial but nevertheless permitted the defense attorney to continue his line of questioning: "While I don't believe it is relevant, if you want to ask any direct question as to whether he overpowered her by force or anything of that kind at the time of the act, you may do so."[9]

During another hearing, the judge himself asked the young female witness: "Whatever you did, you did of your own free will?" When she responded affirmatively, the judge demanded: "Well how did you happen to complain against him, then?" The prosecutor became exasperated with the judge's disregard for the law: "Don't you know what the statute is, Judge?" "Yes, I know all about it," he replied, "but I am not so touchy upon this subject [that I can't] try to find out some of the reasons which I have been fishing for since this statute has been changed." The judge continued to badger the witness: "What did you go in the house for? . . . What did you take your clothes off for and go to bed with him? . . . Did you know what you were going to get when you were undressing yourself?"[10]

It is understandable that judges would want to distinguish between forcible and consensual intercourse; a major problem with the age-of-consent law was that it conflated the two by denying women under eighteen years of age the capacity to consent to sex. But judges and attorneys went well beyond establishing consent. They viewed a young woman's willingness to engage in sex as a sign of moral depravity, and they often harassed such young women and girls in court hearings, labeling them "depraved," "wayward," or "loose" and blaming them for the moral transgression.[11]

Like male legislators who had opposed the age-of-consent campaign, some judges and court officials reversed the seduction narrative promoted by moral reformers by portraying teenage girls as temptresses who had lured young men into wrongdoing. In one case, a twenty-three-year-old defendant, employed as a streetcar motorman, had engaged in sex with a teenage girl whom his roommate had met on the street and invited to their apartment. The girl explained in court that she did not want to have sex with the young man and told him so, but she did not actively resist his advances. She had recently left the home where she had been employed as a domestic, was stranded with no money, and needed a place to spend the night. Later the next day, probation officers apprehended and questioned the girl and had the man arrested for statutory rape. Upon hearing the case, Judge Frank B. Ogden of the Alameda County Superior Court claimed that the male defendant was the true "victim" in the case. "A man is a man under those circumstances," he explained. "With a girl over the age of 16 years and of mature appearance it would be pretty hard for a man indeed to so control himself as to eliminate himself from all present danger . . . and under the circumstances it would be a pretty strong man who could escape, a pretty strong man."[12]

In a similar case, a young man of twenty years was arrested for having sexual intercourse with a sixteen-year-old girl who had recently run away from home. She met the defendant at a café, where he worked as a janitor. At his request, the girl agreed to stay at the apartment he shared with several friends until she could find work. During that time the couple formed an intimate relationship. In his report on the case, the probation officer for the court called the young woman "the instigator of the acts" and argued that "there ought to be some protection of youths of his age against girls who get into their beds."[13] The image of female entrapment constructed by court officials, like the seduction narrative of the reformers, served mainly to obscure the actual lived experiences of young working-class women and girls.

Even in cases of forcible assault, judges sometimes scolded the female victims for tempting defendants into immoral behavior. In one instance, sixteen-year-old Ruby Haynes was raped by a young man she had been dating. On their way home from the nickelodeon one evening, the young man pushed Ruby into the yard of a vacant house and demanded that she have sex with him. When she refused, he threw her to the ground and raped her. The judge became impatient with Ruby during the preliminary examination and demanded to know why she had not put up a stronger resistance: "Why didn't you scream, that's what I don't understand. Why don't these girls scream out? Why do you lend yourself to the proposition?"[14] Such encounters, now defined as acquaintance rape, did not fit the court's definition of forcible assault.[15] In the eyes of court officials, Ruby had invited the assault by going out unescorted with a young man she only recently met. She had violated what they considered appropriate codes of conduct for respectable women, thereby becoming "fair game" for men. In commenting on Ruby's case, the judge said, "Wherever she went and whatever she did with that man was voluntary, no force to it at all; she knew what she was going to get when she got it."[16]

Officials responded in a similar fashion to a fourteen-year-old Portuguese girl who was sexually assaulted by the janitor in the cannery where she worked. At the end of a workday this janitor, a twenty-two-year-old man, asked the girl to come into an office. When she did, he pushed her to the floor, held his hand over her mouth to keep her from screaming, and raped her. Once the defendant pleaded guilty, the county probation officer recommended that he be granted probation. "She was an inexperienced girl, it is true, and entitled to protection," the male probation officer stated, "but her willingness to accompany [the defendant] into the office alone, placed him under special temptation." The judge apparently agreed with this reasoning, because he granted the man probation.[17]

At other times, judges might claim that young women and girls had not resisted strongly enough. The court scolded one thirteen-year-old who had been sexually abused by her twenty-seven-year-old brother: "Why did you let him do this, [Pearl], you knew that it was naughty, didn't you? Didn't you know that he hadn't any right to do it to you? . . . Why did you let him?" Pearl tried to explain that the acts were committed against her will: "I couldn't do anything against him. We were the only ones home."[18] In cases like these, the victims of forcible rape were made to feel that *they* had done something wrong and immoral and had somehow invited the attack.

Questions in preliminary hearings furthermore were not confined to the specific sexual encounter or relationship with the accused man. Rather a young woman's entire sexual past was put on display in the courtroom. By the late nineteenth century it had become routine, in rape trials involving adult women, to permit the defense to introduce evidence about the victim's prior sexual experience in an attempt to discredit her before the jury.

···

This practice stood in stark contrast to the handling of male defendants in rape cases. Courts prohibited similar inquiries into a male defendant's sexual history, arguing that such evidence would unfairly prejudice the jury against him. Judges allowed such questions about rape complainants because they held that a woman's sexual past was related to a key issue: whether she had consented to the sexual act. The assumption was that if she had consented to sexual relations in one situation, she was likely to do so in others.[19] As one state appeals court judge pronounced in 1915: "No impartial mind can resist the conclusion that a female who had been in the recent habit of illicit intercourse with others will not be so likely to resist as one who is spotless and pure."[20]

The practice of questioning rape complainants about their sexual pasts was eventually incorporated into standard legal texts on evidence. According to John H. Wigmore, the leading legal scholar on the law of evidence at the time, "When the woman consents to the act, no crime of rape is committed; on such a charge, then, the main issue often is whether the woman did consent. Here the woman's disposition to unchastity would have probative value, and would be admissible on behalf of the accused."[21]

But even after it had become standard legal practice in rape trials to question adult women about past sexual acts, such tactics were still considered improper in cases involving underage females. As Wigmore wrote, "But in a trial for a sex offense where the woman's consent is immaterial and not in issue, it follows that the woman's unchastity would also be immaterial, e.g., a charge of carnal knowledge of a minor (usually miscalled in the statutes 'rape under age' or 'statutory rape')."[22] Despite this rule, it was nonetheless a common practice in Alameda courts to question underage female witnesses about their sexual experience. Some judges did prohibit such questions. One interrupted a defense attorney when he asked the young woman on the stand about her sexual relations with men other than the defendant. "You can't ask her that, [Mr. Brown], she might be a common prostitute, but being under 18 years of age her mouth is closed by law."[23] But other judges were quite willing to bend the rules of evidence. When the prosecution objected to a question about the previous sexual experience of one female witness, Judge Weinmann overruled the objection, explaining, "I will allow a certain number of questions bringing out that side of it, because I think it is no more than fair, while I don't think it is strictly legally admissible."[24] Some judges actually introduced questions themselves about the sexual pasts of female witnesses. Judge George Samuels, for example, asked one teenage girl, "You understood what it was all about, it wasn't your first time? . . . You had been out with these boys more or less quite a number of them right along, that is right isn't it?"[25]

Alameda court officials clearly interpreted the purpose of age-of-consent legislation differently than women reformers did. They saw the law as a tool to be used not so much to protect women from sexual harm as to protect the interests of fathers, future husbands, and the state. According to this view, fathers needed to preserve the chastity of their daughters in order to uphold the family name and reputation and to ensure the daughters' marriageability. One judge chastised a male defendant charged with statutory rape for injuring the father's home and family name by having intercourse with his daughter. According to several judges, the state also had a great interest in the preservation of female chastity. It was necessary, they argued, to ensure the production of a healthy, moral citizenry. Judge Mortimer Smith explained that the "philosophy" behind the law was "that the country depends upon its women to produce good citizens, and a woman who is debauched, that has its effect upon the mind of every child that is born to her and therefore, a sound public policy demands that no man shall have intercourse with a woman under the age of 18 unless he is married to her, and if he does so, that he interferes with the well-being of the community."[26] In a similar vein, Judge Frank Ogden stated that the law aimed "to conserve the woman who is the mother of the children and of the future generations called upon, perchance to rule and govern the state."[27]

Given their understanding of the law and its purpose, it makes sense that court officials were preoccupied with the moral character and sexual experience of young women in statutory rape cases. They deemed sexual intercourse with an "unchaste" girl a less serious offense than the same act with a "chaste" girl. The former was already "ruined," already a liability to her family and a danger to the state, and apparently did not deserve the same legal protection as the latter. One defense attorney stated in court that a man who had relations with a sexually experienced girl, while technically guilty of rape, "has not committed a crime that is as heinous as it would be if he had raped a pure girl."[28] Even the prosecuting attorney expressed this view in the case of a young man of nineteen years charged with the statutory rape of a pregnant fifteen-year-old girl. "This boy is a pretty respectable boy," the prosecutor explained in court. "This girl has been running around with many people, Judge. It is one of those cases where it is too bad that any complaint had been filed at all."[29]

The trial records from Alameda County clearly demonstrate that the sexual double standard still held sway in the courtroom. Male judges, attorneys, and probation officers were impervious to the ideals of male continence and a single standard of morality for men and women, so ardently promoted by purity reformers. Court officials continued to act on traditional views of male and female sexuality. As one judge stated, "The passions concerned are the strongest to control in men, it has been ordained so."[30] The general stance taken in the courtroom was that it was man's nature to be lustful and woman's responsibility to maintain moral standards. Men were expected to "sow their wild oats" during their youth. They could engage in illicit sex and still remain respectable, but when a young woman made a slip of this kind, she was considered permanently "ruined"—a moral threat to society.

Moral reformers in California and elsewhere became increasingly frustrated by the failure of the legal system to enforce the age-of-consent law as they had envisioned, and they pursued various strategies to counter the reluctance of law enforcement officials. In San Francisco and Oakland, members of the Woman's Christian Temperance Union (WCTU) organized to locate violators of the law and pressure courts to prosecute these "cases of outraged girlhood." Rose French of San Francisco was particularly active in this campaign. According to a report issued by the WCTU of Northern California, French helped to initiate numerous prosecutions of male sex offenders.[31] Purity reformers in other parts of the country also worked to ensure the enforcement of age-of-consent legislation. Members of the American Purity Alliance joined forces with the New York Society for the Prevention of Cruelty to Children to find and prosecute men who had sexual intercourse with underage females. Women's clubs in Chicago established a special organization, the Protective Agency for Women and Children, that brought cases of rape and seduction to the attention of the police and the courts. Members of the agency encouraged young women to file complaints and offered them legal assistance in the prosecution of their cases.[32]

Clubwomen also monitored trials of men charged with sex offenses. Women's organizations in Oakland, for example, arranged to have their members in daily attendance at the 1906 trial of a man who was accused of assaulting a young woman.[33] Their object was to provide emotional support for the women who had to testify in court and to assert their moral influence in a courtroom dominated by men. The Protective Agency for Women and Children carried out this work on a regular basis in Chicago courts. According to the *Union Signal*, the official publication of the National WCTU, members of the agency "have repeatedly gone to the police court, and stood by the girl through all the trying ordeal. Their presence changes the moral tone of the police court, and imparts courage to the timid girl whose very innocence confuses her in the presence of strange, sneering men."[34]

Although important, this type of moral support in the courtroom was limited in what it could accomplish. Organized clubwomen came to believe that they needed to have real power within the political and legal systems to influence the prosecution of sex offenses. Political enfranchisement would enable them to shape legislation and to elect judges and prosecutors who were sympathetic with their goals. Concern about sex crimes helped to fuel the burgeoning suffrage movement of the late nineteenth and early twentieth centuries, and it was a key issue for California suffragists. After they won the vote in 1911, one of their first legislative goals was to raise the age of consent from sixteen to eighteen.[35]

Once that goal was achieved, clubwomen and reformers used their newly acquired political voice to recall a San Francisco police court judge because of his lenient treatment of male sex offenders. The recall effort began in 1913, when Judge Charles Weller lowered the bail of a defendant charged with the rape of a young woman. The accused man made bail; shortly thereafter he left the city and was never located by law enforcement officials. Angered by the judge's action, clubwomen investigated his record and found that Weller consistently set low bail for rape suspects and dismissed cases in face of what they considered incriminating evidence. They formed the Weller Recall League and circulated petitions to have the recall placed on the ballot for the next election. The struggle to oust Weller became a cause célèbre for clubwomen throughout the state.[36] The California Federation of Women's Clubs threw its support behind the campaign and printed the following statement from the Recall League in its journal, the *Woman's Bulletin*: "We are working steadily and faithfully that this condition of injustice and immorality we have inherited from the fathers in our city, who have allowed this system of vice to grow, may be uprooted by the mothers of our city and be supplanted by courts of justice which do not belie their names and where a girl's virtue may be considered the foundation of good citizenship."[37] Recall proponents gathered enough support to defeat Weller and to elect another judge, Wiley Crist, who pledged to use his office to protect womanhood.

After the success of the recall campaign, women reformers in California broadened their quest for authority in the courtroom by demanding the right to sit on juries. The California Civic League (earlier the California Equal Suffrage Association) organized its members to lobby for a state law that would extend jury service to include women. The absence of women on juries, they argued, prevented fair rulings, particularly in the prosecution of sexual offenses. As one female activist explained, "Women witnesses, often young, often wronged, often ignorant, need the protection of their own sex in the hour of trial as well as of temptation."[38] Their efforts finally paid off in 1917 with the passage of the Woman Jury Bill, which made California one of the first states to legalize women jurors. The actual implementation of this bill, however, comprised an ongoing struggle between women reformers and a reluctant criminal justice system.[39]

The reformers' concerns about sexual offenses evoked greater sympathy from male justices on the juvenile court. The juvenile court was a product of the late-nineteenth- and early twentieth-century movement to reform the criminal justice system. Established in California in 1903, the juvenile court removed youths from the adult criminal justice system and handled them in special courts designed to address their particular problems. The first judges on the Los Angeles Juvenile Court had played an important role in the foundation of this system, and they shared many of the goals and ideals of women reformers. Curtis D. Wilbur, who served on the court from 1903 to 1913, helped to draft the Juvenile Court Law of California. He and Judge Sidney Reeve, who served on the court from 1915 to 1921, worked closely with women activists in Los Angeles to enact and enforce penal reform measures.[40]

Under Judges Wilbur and Reeve, the prosecution of statutory rape proceeded very differently than in the adult criminal court of Alameda County. In court hearings Wilbur and Reeve spoke out against the double standard of morality and chastised young male moral offenders for their wrongdoing. Judge Reeve sounded remarkably similar to women moral reformers when he scolded one young man for having sexual relations with a teenage girl: "There is not a meaner beast on earth than a fellow who will start a girl or try to induce a girl who has been a good girl before on a career of that kind. He is the meanest kind of cuss, just a low down cuss, just a little beast; and that is what you have been."[41] When another teenage boy charged with statutory rape appeared before him, Judge Reeve lectured about the dangers that illicit activity posed for future generations: "The life that you lead from the time you start in past the period of adolescence up to the time you die, is reflected in future generations twofold. I want to tell you that. And just through parties such as were pulled off here, through associations such as are pulled off here, conditions develop where we have the defective and we have the blind—they are with us all the time and you can put them all right down to just carelessness."[42]

During these juvenile court hearings judges tried to impress upon young men the importance of the single standard of morality, to instruct them that men as well as women had a responsibility to remain chaste. When one sixteen-year-old boy tried to excuse his behavior by claiming his female partner was "of easy morals," Judge Reeve scolded him: "Now, there are no two standards in this world; there is only one. It doesn't make any difference if this girl had sexual intercourse with 20 men, it wouldn't lessen your offense under the law. But the part I hate to see is that when these boys get in trouble, they say, 'Well, I was not as much to blame as the girl.'" Reeve went on to remark, "You might be in the eyes of some boys a hero, but you are not. . . . Supposing some fellow went along and did what you did to this girl, to your sister."[43] To emphasize the seriousness of the offense, judges often made male youths read aloud the law on statutory rape, particularly the section stating that a man found guilty of this crime faced up to fifty years in prison. (In California, the penalty for both forcible rape and intercourse with girls under sixteen was a maximum of fifty years; the punishment for intercourse with girls between sixteen and eighteen was either confinement in the county jail for not more than one year or in the state prison for not more than fifty years.)[44]

In their pursuit of male sex offenders, the juvenile courts met with resistance from police departments and from the adult criminal justice system. Judge Reeve became particularly disturbed in one instance when the police and the district attorney failed to follow up a complaint that had been filed against a nineteen-year-old sailor. According to the report filed by a probation officer for the juvenile court, the sailor had engaged in sexual relations with one teenage girl in Los Angeles and was responsible for the pregnancy of another young woman he had dated earlier. Judge Reeve criticized the leniency shown to male offenders by the police: "Now the great difficulty is that it seems the double standard is very prominently fixed in the eyes of the Police Department and they want the girl filed on and put away and they want to let the boys be turned loose. I don't believe in it and never have believed in it. I don't believe there is any boy that has ever been tied up and forced to commit an act of this kind."[45] In an effort to correct police bias and to send a message to other young men, Reeve sentenced the sailor to one year in a reform school.

TABLE 4. *Disposition of Statutory Rape Cases in Alameda County, California, 1910–1920*

Disposition	Total Cases		Consent Cases		Force Cases	
	N	%	N	%	N	%
Dismissed by court	17	15	14	18	3	10
Convicted by jury	18	16	4	5	13	43
Acquitted by jury	14	13	8	11	4	13
Transferred to juvenile court	6	5	6	8	0	0
Guilty plea	54	48	44	58	10	33
Guilty plea to lesser charge	3	3	0	0	0	0
Total	112		76		30	

Note: The number of cases in the Consent and Force columns do not add up to the total number of cases because in six cases the court records did not indicate whether or not force had been used.

Most young men prosecuted for statutory rape in the Los Angeles Juvenile Court, however, did not face institutional confinement, because juvenile offenders were not subject to the same criminal penalties as their adult counterparts. Judges for the juvenile court were expected to devise a sentence appropriate to each individual case, based on the youth's character, attitude, and family background, as well as the particular offense he committed. Juvenile officials tried to avoid the incarceration of young criminal offenders whenever possible. The favored form of correctional treatment was probation, which aimed to rehabilitate delinquent youth in their own homes under the supervision of a probation officer.[46] The court's handling of statutory rape cases generally followed a predictable pattern. After administering a severe scolding in the court hearing, judges typically released the young men from detention and placed them on probation. Of the twenty-three defendants charged with statutory rape before the Los Angeles court in 1920, more than four-fifths (82 percent) were placed on probation and less than one-tenth (9 percent) were sent to reform institutions. The remaining cases were either dismissed or sent to adult criminal court.

Those convicted in adult criminal court were more likely to be incarcer-

TABLE 5. *Sentencing in Statutory Rape Cases, Alameda County, California, 1910–1920*

Sentence	Total Cases		Consent Cases		Force Cases	
	N	%	N	%	N	%
Probation	37	49	33	66	4	17
County jail	10	13	8	16	1	4
State prison	25	33	8	16	16	69
Juvenile institution	3	4	1	2	2	9
Total	75		50		23	

Note: The number of cases in the Consent and Force columns do not add up to the total number of cases because in two cases the court records did not indicate whether or not force had been used.

ated than were juvenile offenders, but they, too, had a decent chance of receiving probation. Adult probation, introduced in California in 1903, offered an alternative to imprisonment in felony cases. It became common for defendants to plead guilty in the hopes of receiving a lighter sentence, preferably probation.[47] Forty-eight percent of the defendants charged with statutory rape in the Alameda County Superior Court between 1910 and 1920 pleaded guilty. Another 13 percent were acquitted by a jury, 16 percent were convicted, and 15 percent of the cases were dismissed before going to trial (see Table 4).[48] The high number of guilty pleas indicates the growing use of plea bargains in which the defendant made a deal with the prosecution, promising to plead guilty in return for a lesser charge or a reduced sentence. Many defendants entered a guilty plea immediately; others first pleaded not guilty and later changed their plea to guilty, a sign of probable bargaining between the defense and prosecution.[49] Defendant's hopes of receiving probation were often fulfilled. Approximately half (49 percent) of those found guilty of statutory rape in the Alameda County Superior Court were granted probation (see Table 5).[50]

Various factors—including the defendant's age, the nature of the sexual encounter (whether or not force was used), the moral character of the female witness, and the defendant's race and ethnicity—determined whether convicted men would receive probation or incarceration. In particular, judges were far less likely to send younger men to prison or jail. Sixty-four percent of convicted defendants age thirty or younger were placed on probation, while just over a third (36 percent) were incarcerated in prison, jail, or reform school.[51] In contrast, approximately one-fifth (22 percent) of the convicted defendants over age thirty received probation, while nearly four-fifths (78 percent) were incarcerated.[52] Courts tended to be lenient with young offenders because, as one official explained, "With a youth up to the early twenties a slip of this kind can be condoned."[53] The age of a twenty-one-year-old defendant clearly influenced Judge William Donahue's decision to grant him probation. As Donahue explained, "In your case you are young. I can understand why a man of the age of twenty-one only, and the girl was about seventeen, how that could occur, and there might be extenuating circumstances. If you were an older man I would not place you upon probation. I would send you to prison. But seeing you are a young man I am going to give you probation."[54]

Superior court judges were also less likely to order incarceration in cases in which the female partner had consented to intercourse. Sixty-six percent of those convicted of statutory rape in consent cases were granted probation, and 32 percent were sent to prison or jail.[55] But only 17 percent of those found guilty in cases involving forcible rape were placed on probation, while 73 percent were incarcerated in prison or jail (see Table 5).[56]

Even in cases of forcible assault, judges typically showed more concern for the loss of female chastity than for the physical and emotional harm done to young women and girls. Male perpetrators received harsh sentences not so much because they had raped a young girl, sometimes with violence, but because they had destroyed her moral purity. After sentencing one man to prison for raping an eight-year-old girl, the judge lamented that she was now "marred and marked . . . with the stigma that will attach to her in the future."[57] In another case, a fifteen-year-old girl was raped by her male employer in the home where she worked as a domestic. The judge sentenced the man to prison, but he expressed little interest in the harm done to the girl, instead stressing the importance of female chastity for the creation of a racially and morally pure social order. "[O]ur children, our girls," he stated to the defendant, "should be kept clean from contamination so they can become mothers of a better race. It devolves upon the court to sentence you, and after you have gained your liberty I hope that you may come out a better man."[58]

When determining sentences, court officials also took into account what they judged to be the moral character of the female witness. Young women were deemed immoral on a variety of grounds: if they had consented to sex; if they had previous sexual experience; if they engaged in what was considered inappropriate behavior for respectable women, such as walking the streets at night, going out alone with men, drinking liquor in cafés, or living away from home. Judges frequently granted lenient sentences to defendants in cases involving young women of suspect character. Judge J. D. Murphey based his decision to award probation to one defendant on the supposed immorality of the fourteen-year-old female witness. The defendant had met the teenager and her girlfriend at a dance and invited them to stay in his hotel room for the night. After studying the case, Judge Murphey ordered the man released from custody and placed on probation: "The record appears to me to sustain the proposition very fairly that these girls themselves were not good at all. They were wayward girls and disposed to do anything probably, and while, understand, it is not any excuse from a legal point of view, [Anderson], it may in a way assist the Court upon the recommendation of all your friends to see its way clear to grant you this requested probation."[59]

The dubious character of the fifteen-year-old female witness in another case led Judge James G. Quinn to grant probation to a fifty-seven-year-old man. Quinn stated in court that "this is the first case of a serious nature such as this, with a man of this age, where probation has even been considered." The older man deserved leniency, he explained, because the teenage girl "has the appearance of being a much older woman," and "her habits and morality are not alone questioned, but are absolutely proved to be bad."[60]

Other factors that influenced sentencing decisions in the Alameda County Superior Court were the ethnicity and race of the defendant. It is impossible to provide firm statistical evidence of the relation between sentence and ethnic background because court records do not consistently indicate the ethnicity or birthplace of male defendants. The court transcripts do, however, suggest that judges took this factor into account. Louis Albertoli, a twenty-four-year-old Italian immigrant, faced deportation and a five-year prison sentence for having sex with a fourteen-year-old girl who lived in his neighborhood. In handing down his decision to incarcerate the young man, Judge Ogden explained that American society could not afford to tolerate the supposedly degraded customs of certain immigrant groups:

I do not feel that we ought to have people come to this country unless they are able and willing to abide by our laws. I realize that in some foreign countries the same code of morals is not present that is present in this country. . . . It is a fact that in some of the countries today a man can forcibly take his woman that he looks to and wants to have for his own and these consider it a marriage, but of course, we do not call those countries civilized, but as I said before if we permit these customs to prevail upon this soil instead of having the higher code of ethics, we would descend to the code of ethics and morals of the other communities.[61]

A stronger case can be made for the role of race in shaping sentencing decisions. Both statistical data and court transcripts indicate that African American men were more likely to be incarcerated for engaging in sex with female minors than were white defendants. All five of the African Americans prosecuted for statutory rape in Alameda County during these years received the court's harshest punishment—incarceration in the state prison. In one of these cases, a young black man, Raymond Thompson, was arrested when he was found living with Lucy Somers, a black teenager of fifteen years. Lucy had left her aunt's home and decided to move in with Raymond. The couple had known each other for several months and hoped to marry soon, despite the aunt's objections. Like most defendants in similar cases, Raymond pleaded guilty in the hope of receiving lenient treatment. At the sentencing hearing, his attorney urged the judge to grant Raymond probation. He explained that the couple wanted to marry and that Raymond was currently employed in a good job as a barber and was capable of supporting a wife. But in contrast to other cases of this nature, the prosecutor pressed hard for a prison sentence. He pointed out that Raymond had been married before and was therefore unreliable as a husband.

The prosecutor also made an issue of Raymond's race in presenting his case for incarceration. A stiff sentence, he argued, would serve to warn the black community to reform their supposedly lax and immoral habits. "It is about time that we should educate these colored people and tell them that they have to obey the laws," the prosecutor explained to the judge. The defense was quick to point out that white defendants typically received probation even in violent cases: "For the last two years, I can show fifteen cases where the circumstances and facts have been of the most aggravated character in rape cases where white people have had probation, but the trouble is that Mr. Smith [prosecutor] is biased against the probation proposition." The defense attorney also made use of racial stereotypes in presenting his case to the judge. He argued that the court should not expect blacks to maintain the same moral standards as whites. In the end, the prosecutor's arguments proved more persuasive, and the judge sentenced Raymond to ten years in San Quentin.[62]

The court clearly had different standards for black or foreign-born and for native-born white defendants. Judge Ogden, who sent Louis Albertoli to prison, granted probation to a twenty-three-year-old white man in a similar case because he believed the man was the true "victim." It would require a very strong man, he had explained, to escape from the trap set by the sixteen-year-old female witness.[63] When a white man had sex with an underage female, he was seen as the victim of her loose and immoral ways. When an immigrant or African American man did the same, he was labeled a product of an uncivilized and depraved racial group.

As all these cases show, the actual enforcement of age-of-consent legislation in California had consequences that moral reformers had not intended and could not control. Most male police and court officials in the criminal justice system showed little concern for, if not outright hostility to, the reformers' goals of ending the double standard and male sexual privilege. In their hands, enforcement of the law became a punitive process for the young women and girls it was meant to protect, as they faced possible confinement in detention centers and reformatories and had to endure grueling interrogations by male judges and attorneys who frequently labeled them promiscuous and immoral. Furthermore, officials used the law to reinforce racial bias within the legal system by targeting African American and immigrant men for the harshest forms of punishment.

Frances Willard in 1895.
As president of the Woman's Christian Temperance Union (WCTU)
from 1879 to 1898, Willard was a major national leader in the age-of-consent
campaign in the late nineteenth century.
(Reprinted from Gordon, *Beautiful Life of Frances Willard*, 1898)

Many Americans in the late nineteenth and early twentieth centuries believed that "white slavery" rings were operating in cities throughout the country, kidnapping young women and girls and forcing them into lives of prostitution. This illustration, which appeared in a white slave tract in 1910, depicts a young woman trapped inside a brothel with an evil procurer lurking behind her. (Reprinted from Bell, *Fighting the Traffic in Young Girls*, 1910)

Reformers and public officials considered public dance halls particularly dangerous places for young women because of the drinking and close dancing that went on and the strange men they encountered there. In this illustration, a suspicious-looking man lures an innocent young woman into a dance hall. (Reprinted from Bell, *Fighting the Traffic in Young Girls*, 1910)

In the late nineteenth and early twentieth centuries,
young women found new employment opportunities
that took them outside of the home.
They often labored alongside men in workplaces free of
family supervision and control, such as in this fruit-packing factory
in Los Angeles County (ca. 1915) and the telephone company office
shown in the next photograph.
(Courtesy of the California Historical Society/Title Insurance
and Trust Photo Collection, Department of Special Collections,
University of Southern California Library)

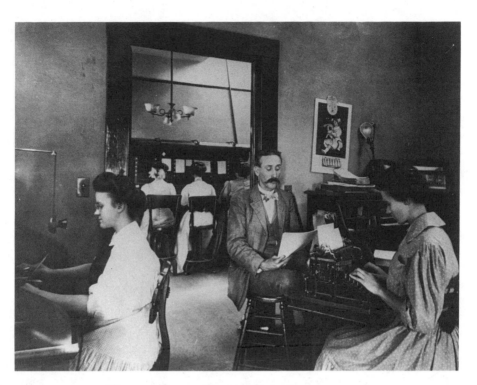

Women office workers at a telephone company
in Los Angeles County, circa 1910.
(Courtesy of the Security Pacific National Bank
Photograph Collection,
Los Angeles Public Library)

Set at the edge of the ocean,
the amusement park at Long Beach, California,
known as the Pike (shown here in 1920),
was one of the most popular entertainment spots
for young people in Los Angeles County
in the early twentieth century.
(Courtesy of the Security Pacific National Bank
Photograph Collection,
Los Angeles Public Library)

Young working men and women flocked to the promenade
at the Long Beach amusement park, shown here in 1909,
to enjoy the cafés, ice-cream parlors, penny arcades, shooting galleries,
and the Majestic and Silver Spray dancing pavilions.
(Courtesy of the Huntington Library, San Marino, California)

Young women model their stylish
bathing costumes in the surf at Long Beach in 1910.
(Courtesy of the California Historical Society/Title Insurance
and Trust Photo Collection,
Department of Special Collections,
University of Southern California Library)

Young immigrant women and men,
like these Mexican youths at Venice Beach (ca. 1925),
joined the crowds on the beaches of southern California
to enjoy their leisure hours away from work.
(Courtesy of the Security Pacific National Bank
Photograph Collection,
Los Angeles Public Library)

Alice Stebbins Wells,
who joined the Los Angeles Police Department in 1910,
was the first female police officer in the country.
She is shown here with her police badge
soon after her appointment.
(Courtesy of the Charles Pierce Collection,
Department of Special Collections,
University of California, Los Angeles, Library)

Janie Porter Barrett, president of the Virginia Federation of Colored Women's Clubs, was founder and director of one of the first Progressive reformatories for African American youths, the Virginia Industrial School for Colored Girls, which opened in 1915. (Courtesy of the Hampton University Archives)

In 1911, under pressure from Progressive reformers, Los Angeles County opened a new juvenile detention center, known as Juvenile Hall, to keep young offenders out of city jails. Juvenile Hall was also the place where female referees presided over the cases of delinquent girls. (Reprinted from Los Angeles County Board of Supervisors, *Annual Report*, 1914)

Miriam Van Waters, shown here in 1925,
promoted Progressive policies for adolescent girls in the
various positions she held in the juvenile justice system of
Los Angeles County. She was superintendent of Juvenile Hall
from 1917 to 1920, founder of the El Retiro School for Girls in 1919,
and referee of the juvenile court from 1920 to 1929.
(Courtesy of the Miriam Van Waters Papers,
Schlesinger Library, Radcliffe College)

CHAPTER 4

THE 'DELINQUENT GIRL' AND PROGRESSIVE REFORM

$\mathcal{E}$arly in the twentieth century, even as purity activists continued to battle the courts and the legislatures over the age of consent, a new generation of white women reformers began to view female immorality in a different light and, consequently, sought different methods of regulating it. College-educated women involved in the Progressive movement disagreed with the Victorian assumption of girlhood sexual passivity and victimization. Instead, they acknowledged female sexual agency and thought of young women who engaged in illicit encounters as "delinquents" in need of guidance and control. These reformers did not blame evil men for young women's moral downfall, but rather, influenced by recent trends in the social sciences, they looked to societal and family environments to explain sexual delinquency among young working-class women.

With this reformulation of the problem came efforts to find new methods of sexual regulation. Progressive reformers advocated a much broader program of state intervention that focused more directly on controlling working-class females and their social environments instead of their male partners. They called for the establishment of special police forces, juvenile courts, detention centers, and reformatories to monitor and correct sexual misconduct among young women and girls. Past experience with male police officers and court officials led reformers to demand that women be given a role in the enforcement process. They insisted that women professionals should manage the new institutions set up to oversee the treatment and care of delinquent girls; they lobbied successfully for the appointment of women police officers, juvenile court judges, probation officers, and staff at the correctional institutions. Policing working-class female sexuality thus expanded female authority within the criminal justice system and created new professional opportunities for educated, middle-class women.

This new interpretation of the problem of female immorality emerged at a time when public anxiety about the sexuality of young, unmarried women had greatly intensified and had spread well beyond the circle of moral reformers who launched the age-of-consent campaign. During the first two decades of the twentieth century, public officials, business leaders, physicians, and social scientists, in addition to women reformers, expressed mounting concern about the apparent rise in sexual promiscuity among young working-class women in American cities and cautioned that such behavior posed serious moral, social, and health threats to the rest of society. A heated antiprostitution campaign that took shape in the Progressive Era heightened public fears about the sexuality of young, unmarried women. Vice crusaders warned that many young women workers and migrants to the city were being lured into prostitution. In response to such concerns, most major cities in the country formed vice commissions to investigate and find solutions to the problem of prostitution.[1]

The eugenics movement linked illicit sex on the part of young women to racial decline and degeneration. Its advocates considered the "immoral" young woman a major threat to their goal of purifying the genetic composition of the American population. They regarded her behavior as a result of faulty heredity and asserted that she endangered society through the propagation of defective and degraded children. Eugenicists adopted increasingly racist tones in the face of an influx of immigrants from southern and eastern Europe, Mexico, and Asia, who, they declared, threatened to pollute the nation's gene pool.[2] Sexually active young women supposedly presented another danger by spreading venereal disease. In the early twentieth century, physicians and public health experts launched a national campaign to combat venereal disease through social hygiene education and the repression of prostitution and illicit sex. Influenced by prevailing social attitudes rather than medical reality, they identified the "immoral" woman as the primary source of infection.[3] Americans soon came to perceive the sexuality of young, unmarried women as a major social problem that threatened society with vice, family breakdown, disease, and racial degeneration.

During this time of social turmoil over illicit sex, competing cultural perceptions of female sexuality circulated in American society and the popular media. The older images of female victimization and female depravity that fueled the debates over the age of consent in the late nineteenth century persisted well into the twentieth century. Many vice crusaders remained convinced that young prostitutes had been victimized by evil "white slavers." They warned that an international ring of pimps and procurers operated in American cities to entrap young women and girls and force them into prostitution.[4]

The agitation over white slavery was expressed vividly in numerous books, films, and articles. Polemical tracts on the subject flooded the American public between 1909 and 1914 under such titles as *The Great War on White Slavery, Fighting the Traffic in Young Girls, The Girl That Disappears, House of Bondage,* and *Modern Herodians or Slaughterers of Innocents.* Films like *The Traffic in Souls* and *The Inside of the White Slave Traffic* were shown in theaters throughout the country, attracting large audiences. All these books and films told variants of the same tale of an innocent, native-born white girl who left the safety of her home in the country for the adventures and opportunities of the city. Once there, she typically fell victim to sinister procurers who used various forms of trickery—a drugged drink, the promise of marriage, and violence if necessary—to lure her into a life of prostitution.[5] Public anxiety over this problem led to numerous municipal investigations in the 1910s and a U.S. Senate investigation in 1909–10. Various antivice groups pressed for legislation that would punish procurers and "white slave" traders. Eventually, forty-four states passed laws prohibiting "compulsory prostitution," and in 1910 the federal government passed the "White Slavery" or Mann Act, which prohibited the transportation of women across state lines for immoral purposes.[6]

The image of innate female depravity also persisted into the Progressive Era, particularly among proponents of the eugenics movement, who attempted to give scientific validity to the view that female moral offenders were inherently depraved and dangerous to men. Eugenicists held that sexual immorality, like other forms of deviant behavior, was the result of an inherited mental defect, or "feeble-mindedness" as it was called at the time. The feeble-minded girl supposedly posed a grave social menace because she contributed to the spread of immorality, disease, and the propagation of "defective" and "unfit" offspring. A leading eugenicist, Walter E. Fernald, stated at a meeting of the National Conference of Charities and Corrections in 1904: "It is well known that feeble-minded women and girls are very liable to become sources of unspeakable debauchery and licentiousness which pollutes the whole life of the young boys and youth of the community. They frequently disseminate in a wholesale way the most loathsome and deadly diseases, permanently poisoning the minds and bodies of thoughtless youths at the very threshold of manhood."[7] Henry Goddard of the Vineland Training School, another key proponent of eugenics, wrote in 1911 that mentally defective girls "must always be a trouble, must always be a disappointment, incapable of bearing the responsibilities that have been put upon them, and, what is worse, they will be, as many of them already are, mothers of more feeble-minded and deficient persons."[8]

Eugenicists and their supporters advocated rigorous measures to control female moral offenders. Offering little hope of reforming such women and girls because of the supposed hereditary nature of their condition, they argued that the best course of action was permanent incarceration in a growing number of custodial institutions for the feeble-minded. Some eugenicists also advocated sterilization to remove even the slightest possibility of such a person's reproducing her own kind. In response to eugenic concerns, forty-three states had established institutions for the feeble-minded by 1923, and by 1931, thirty states had passed laws allowing for the sterilization of "unfit" and feeble-minded persons.[9]

It was within this context of conflicting perceptions of illicit female sexuality that Progressive women reformers developed their new framework for explaining the problem and worked to shape public policies in accordance with their view. Rejecting the conventional images of female victimization and depravity, they constructed a model of delinquency that both acknowledged the sexual agency of teenage girls and emphasized their lack of experience and need for guidance. The Progressives' explanation of female immorality blamed neither male vice nor innate mental defect, but rather the difficulties of adolescence and the social conditions in which working-class girls lived.[10]

Progressive women differed in several important respects from the female moral reformers who had launched the age-of-consent campaign in the late nineteenth century. Most had attended college, and a number went on to graduate school to obtain higher degrees in law, medicine, social work, and the social sciences. They tended not to follow the traditional path for women of marriage and motherhood but devoted their lives to public service and social reform. Instead of religion-based organizations like the Woman's Christian Temperance Union, they were drawn to more secular reform efforts such as social settlements, the Women's Trade Union League, the Juvenile Protective Association, and the National Consumer's League. A number of these reformers became self-supporting professionals who forged new career paths for women in the areas of social work, public health, and nursing.[11]

This new generation of women reformers comprised an important part of the Progressive movement that swept through American cities in the period from 1890 to the end of World War I. This movement was composed primarily of middle-class men and women who attempted to address the array of social problems that accompanied rapid urban growth and industrialization, including poverty, crime, disease, political corruption, labor unrest, and the abuse of corporate power. Ideologically, Progressives stood between American socialists, who called for a radical restructuring of the economic system, and conservative business leaders and politicians, who adamantly opposed government interference in economic affairs and saw nothing wrong with existing power structures. Progressives aimed to reform the worst abuses of the capitalist system without, in the end, undermining that system. To accomplish this goal, they sought a wide range of economic, political, and social reforms, such as antitrust legislation, civil service reform, factory inspection laws, pure food and drug laws, and social insurance for victims of industrial accidents.[12] Female reformers were especially active in efforts that aimed to protect women, children, and the home from the harmful effects of rapid urban growth and industrial capitalism. They targeted issues of child labor, juvenile delinquency, prostitution, unsanitary housing, and low wages and poor working conditions for women laborers.

Several characteristics distinguish Progressivism from earlier middle-class philanthropic efforts. First, Progressive reformers developed innovative methods of social analysis. They used the techniques of empirical research and sociological investigation to study the ills that afflicted American society. Second, they did not see poverty and unemployment as the result of individual moral failings, as did nineteenth-century charity workers and philanthropists, but rather as the result of environmental forces over which the poor had little control. Finally, these reformers developed new solutions to the social problems they addressed. In a departure from strict laissez-faire principles, they called on the state to intervene in social and economic relations in order to protect the common good and provide opportunity for everyone. Progressives applied the principles of science and efficiency in developing their reform programs. They created bureaucracies and commissions to manage social problems and relied on trained experts to develop and administer policies.

This reform context underlay Progressive women's new approach to the problem of female immorality. Instead of telling melodramatic stories of seduction as nineteenth-century moral reformers had, they conducted systematic studies of young working-class women in urban neighborhoods. Three works in particular illustrate their reinterpretation of adolescent female sexuality. In *The Delinquent Child and the Home*, published in 1912, Sophonisba Breckinridge and Edith Abbott assessed the causes of juvenile delinquency among Chicago youths based on court and reformatory records from the first ten years of the Cook County Juvenile Court and interviews with court officials and the families of delinquents.[13] They wrote their study while employed as researchers for the Chicago School of Civics and Philanthropy. Both women had doctoral degrees in the social sciences from the University of Chicago and were part of the reform community living at Hull House.

The following year, the National Federation of Settlements conducted an investigation of the "problem of the adolescent girl of the tenement-house family and the city factory or department store" and published the results in a book entitled *Young Working Girls*. Edited by the federation's secretaries, Robert A. Woods and Albert J. Kennedy, the study was based on information provided by two thousand social workers from across the country. They reported on the family backgrounds, employment, recreational activities, and moral behavior and attitudes of the working-class girls in their neighborhoods. Ruth True, a social investigator for the Bureau of Social Research of the New York School of Philanthropy, produced a similar study that examined the nature and causes of moral delinquency among working-class girls living on New York's West Side, an Irish and German neighborhood along the Hudson River. True and her two assistants conducted lengthy interviews with sixty-five girls and published the results in 1914 in *The Neglected Girl*.[14]

In forming their analyses, women investigators were influenced by several intellectual developments of the period. One was the new theory of adolescence developed by eminent psychologist and child study expert G. Stanley Hall. Hall was the first to develop a systematic conceptualization of adolescence as a distinct stage in life. He wrote numerous papers on the subject in the 1890s and in 1904 published a monumental two-volume study called *Adolescence: Its Psychology and Its Relations to Physiology, Anthropology, Sociology, Sex, Crime, Religion, and Education*, which had a great effect on educators, social workers, and social scientists. Hall described adolescence as a turbulent period of physical, emotional, and sexual development during which youths needed to be shielded from adult duties and expectations. This theory encouraged the prolongation of a period of dependence and segregation of youths from the world and the pressures of adulthood.[15]

In his writings about adolescent sexuality, Hall was influenced by the work of Sigmund Freud and other European sexologists. He considered sexual urges and desires a normal part of adolescent development for both girls and boys. This marked a clear departure from Victorian notions of female passionlessness and childhood sexual innocence. The adolescent girl, according to Hall, was acutely aware of her sexuality and exhibited a keen interest in the opposite sex. "The *other sex* as such now dawns upon her horizon," he wrote. "A year or two ago boys were just playmates, often too rough, teasing, and perhaps generally horrid; and in the affairs of older gentlemen and young men she had no part or lot. . . . But now individual young people of the male sex begin to stand out from the mass, and she gradually begins to practice the great selective function of women in comparing and judging, approving and disapproving."[16] Although Hall considered sexual urges normal for adolescents, he did not encourage the open expression of these feelings. Rather, he held that adolescent sexual energy needed to be sublimated and directed into other channels, such as religion, athletics, education, or music, until adulthood and marriage. Hall considered this redirection particularly critical for girls, because he believed that sexuality occupied and defined their lives to a far greater extent than it did for boys.[17]

Hall recommended close supervision and guidance of young girls during adolescence, particularly by their mothers. He explicitly instructed mothers and educators in the proper care of adolescent girls, calling for plain diets, plenty of sleep, little mental strain, regular exercise, and careful instruction in sex hygiene. Hall particularly urged mothers to teach their daughters about sex with an emphasis on motherhood rather than on the sex relation itself. "In this way," he explained, "the girl will be anchored betimes to what is really the essential thing, viz., reproduction and the carrying beneath her heart and then bearing children which are the hope of the world. . . . Love when it came would thus never be entirely divorced from thoughts of motherhood."[18]

Reformers did not accept many of the conservative conclusions Hall drew from his understanding of female adolescence and sexuality. For example, he spoke out strongly against higher education for women for fear that the mental strain would interfere with their reproductive capacities. But Progressive reformers did assimilate Hall's portrayal of female adolescence as a time of emotional upheaval and sexual awakening that required careful supervision and guidance. The study of working girls conducted by the National Federation of Settlements clearly reflected the influence of Hall's thinking when it described female adolescence as a "period of feverish physical, mental, and emotional activity." The authors explained that during this time:

> A practically overwhelming consciousness of sex, combined with a growing desire for companionship, leads the girl into short-lived and cliquey alliances with those of her own sex, and into various forms of adventure with members of the opposite sex. She develops an absorbing interest in the individualizing, aesthetic, and associational aspects of dress. She longs to be popular with men, craves a "beau" or "steady," and begins to think of marriage. The longing for companionship adds strength to the natural desire for a "good time," and intensifies her delight in parties, "shows," and dances.[19]

Hall's theory of adolescence defined a middle-class experience. Most working-class families possessed neither the economic resources nor the cultural values that would have supported such an extended period of dependence and close supervision of youth. Thus, when reformers examined the adolescent experience of working-class daughters, they found much to alarm them. The conditions of these young women's lives seemed to promote sexual delinquency. Ruth True warned that the working-class daughter did not have athletics, education, and wholesome recreation to divert her newly awakened sexual urges. With the dawn of adolescence, she was swept "inevitably out of the simplicity of little girlhood into the thousand temptations of her environment, if not, perhaps, into one of the commonest of neighborhood tragedies."[20]

Another influence on Progressive theories was the environmental explanation of deviancy. The dominant school of criminology in the late nineteenth century had traced criminal behavior to inherited physical and mental traits. By the early twentieth century, some social scientists began to challenge hereditarian explanations and to stress the role of family life, education, and economic conditions in the development of criminal and delinquent behavior.[21] In keeping with this trend, Progressive women reformers looked to social and environmental factors to explain female sexual delinquency. They identified poverty, premature entrance into the work force, modern commercial amusements, and inadequate home life as the major causes of illicit behavior among young women and girls.

In *The Delinquent Child and the Home*, a classic Progressive explanation of juvenile delinquency, Sophonisba Breckinridge and Edith Abbott argued forcefully that one had to look to the harsh economic and social conditions in which working-class youth lived in order to explain their deviant behavior. "When we see all the wide background of deprivation in their lives," they wrote, "the longing for a little money to spend, for the delights of the nickel theater, for the joy of owning a pigeon, or for the glowing adventure of a ride on the train, it is not hard to understand how the simple fact of being poor is many times a sufficient explanation of delinquency." Urbanization and industrialization, they argued, had caused great economic hardship and disrupted family life among workers and immigrants. Crowded, unsanitary housing, congested neighborhoods, and the meager earnings of their parents deprived working-class children of a safe, wholesome upbringing.[22]

Progressive reformers also pointed to the numerous moral dangers and temptations that surrounded working-class daughters as they entered the paid labor force. Their places of employment in factories, stores, and offices did not provide the kind of supervision that was deemed necessary for adolescent girls. They worked alongside men in poorly regulated work environments, a situation that encouraged girls to "become careless in their conduct, slack in manners and conversation, immodest in dress, and familiar to a degree that lays them open to danger."[23] Social investigators also feared that the low wages typical of most women's jobs caused some working girls to turn to prostitution and led others to offer sexual favors to their male partners in return for new clothes or a ticket to the movies or amusement park.

The moral dangers associated with wage work were nowhere more glaringly apparent to reformers than in department stores, an increasingly popular place of employment for young women. Members of the National Federation of Settlements feared that the salesgirl, surrounded by expensive clothes, jewelry, and other finery, would develop a longing for an extravagant lifestyle and hence "become dissatisfied with simple, wholesome living." Unable to purchase the store's fine items on her meager salary, she was likely to sacrifice her moral virtue to obtain them. Furthermore, the store setting exposed her to solicitation and flattery from male bosses, coworkers, and strangers passing through the store. As Woods and Kennedy explained, "Her work locates her in such a way that she may with fatal ease become involved with traveling men, procuresses, and other designing people."[24] So great was the public anxiety about the "department store girl" that reformers and vice investigators conducted special analyses of the problem in several cities, including New York and Chicago.[25]

Another perceived source of moral danger for working girls was the commercialized amusements that they were so eager to attend in the evenings after work. Social investigators acknowledged that a "deep-seated desire for spontaneous action" was a normal part of adolescence.[26] The problem was that working-class girls lacked wholesome forms of recreation and instead sought diversion in the dance halls, amusement parks, and movie theaters so prevalent on the urban landscape. Such entertainments, reformers charged, exploited youths' need for play and encouraged illicit behavior. They considered the public dance hall, in particular, "a source of evil." With "its air of license, its dark corners and balconies, its tough dancing, and its heavy drinking," the dance hall supposedly weakened moral inhibitions and led many girls astray.[27]

In assessing the problem of female delinquency, Progressives drew special attention to the difficulties faced by young immigrant women. Abbott and Breckinridge found that many female youths charged with delinquency in Chicago were immigrants or the children of immigrants, but they rejected the nativist view that the foreign-born were innately more prone to criminality. Instead, they attributed the delinquent behavior to economic hardship and the trauma of adjusting to life in modern American cities and factories, an adjustment that was particularly hard for immigrant families of rural backgrounds.[28] To a more limited degree, Progressive reformers also noted the dangers facing young African American women in American cities. They pointed to poverty, poor housing, lack of adequate educational and employment opportunities, and racial discrimination as the major causes of delinquent behavior among black female youths.[29]

• • •

Through their studies and investigations, Progressive reformers directed public attention to the economic and social conditions that contributed to female delinquency. They indicted the modern city and urban industrialism for failing to meet the needs of young immigrant and working-class women and called on local and state governments to address the problem. Their environmental analysis, however, also targeted working-class home life as a major cause of female delinquency. Abbott and Breckinridge asserted that deviancy was inevitable when children were raised in "degraded" homes, "homes in which they have been accustomed from their earliest infancy to drunkenness, immorality, obscene and vulgar language, filthy and degraded conditions of living."[30] Unlike many nineteenth-century philanthropists and charity workers, Progressive reformers did not think that working-class people were inherently depraved. Rather, they held that urbanization and industrialization had disrupted their family lives and made it difficult for them to provide a safe, moral upbringing for adolescent girls.

Progressives nevertheless placed the working-class home at the center of their analysis of the causes of female delinquency. And a major thrust of their reform program involved the reconstruction of working-class family life according to middle-class standards. This understanding was expressed clearly in the study produced by the National Federation of Settlements: "It is easily evident that practically all the sources of moral contamination to which girls are exposed find an approach through some failure or inadequacy in home and family life; and that the home, therefore, marks the chief point at which constructive social work must center."[31]

The family ideal envisioned by reformers consisted of the nuclear family of father, mother, and two to three children who resided together in a private home. Fathers were the breadwinners for the family, while mothers stayed at home caring for the children and keeping house. According to Woods and Kennedy, "The good mother must be a thrifty and capable housewife, in possession of stable moral standards, and with time and energy to give to the needs of her children." In this ideal family, the parents would not depend on adolescent children to assume wage-earning responsibilities at too early an age, because, during the turbulent period of adolescence, they belonged at home or in school, where they would receive careful guidance by mothers and teachers.[32]

Working-class home life, according to reformers, fell short of this ideal and thereby contributed to daughters' delinquency in numerous ways. The "overcrowded" working-class household was repeatedly blamed for causing a decline in moral standards. Many working-class parents had more children than the middle-class norm; furthermore, they often shared their homes with extended family members—aunts, uncles, cousins, and grandparents—and frequently took in boarders to supplement the family income. Reformers referred to such living arrangements as "confused family groupings." They asserted that overcrowding in the home "breaks down the feeling of privacy, and hence brings on loss of self-respect, of modesty, of order, of neatness."[33] According to Breckinridge and Abbott, almost any departure from the nuclear family norm apparently threatened proper adolescent development:

> If the family is large, if the home is crowded, if the mother is distracted by the presence of many children and can give little attention to any one of them; if the burden of custody and discipline during her absence falls upon the eldest or upon the eldest at home; if there are relatives or lodgers lending complexity to an already confused situation; if there is an unsympathetic step-parent and a mixed family of children, there is little hope that the nervous system of the child, started unfavorably on its career, will have its proper chance to mature into self-control, or the character to develop into dignified manhood or womanhood.[34]

Reformers held that working-class parents further endangered the moral development of their adolescent daughters by pushing them prematurely into the work force so that they could contribute to the family income. Working for wages not only exposed adolescent girls to moral dangers in the workplace but also gave them a level of power and autonomy within the family that reformers considered inappropriate and even dangerous for ones so young and unstable. Daughters, they feared, would use their new status to demand privileges such as staying out late or going to dance halls unchaperoned. As Woods and Kennedy warned, the wage-earning daughter "begins to enter into hitherto forbidden amusements, and justifies herself by the claim, 'I am earning my own living and can do as I please.'"[35]

In their scrutiny of working-class home life, reformers paid particular attention to the role of mothers. According to the middle-class conception of adolescence, the mother bore more responsibility than anyone else for guiding her daughter safely through the stormy period of adolescence. But reformers concluded that many working-class mothers, although perhaps concerned about their daughters, were largely incompetent in dealing with them. With large families and heavy domestic duties, they were often too tired and overworked to devote sufficient time to their daughters. Furthermore, working-class mothers, particularly the foreign-born, failed to understand the current environment in which their daughters lived. According to the National Federation of Settlements study, "Their standards are often wholly inept and they find themselves incapable of supplying that advice which would meet the daughter's more modern experience and common sense."[36]

One of the gravest moral dangers for girls, to the reformers' way of thinking, was the working mother. Because she was away from home for a good part of the day, she could not provide the careful guidance and supervision that adolescent girls supposedly needed, and social reformers perceived a direct connection between this neglect and the delinquent child. Abbott and Breckinridge asserted that "almost inevitably the fact that the mother goes out to work means that the home is cheerless and untidy and that the children have every opportunity to stay away from school and live that life of the streets which is at once so alluring and so demoralizing."[37] The link between working mothers and juvenile delinquency was increasingly emphasized in the writings of reformers and social workers in the late 1910s and 1920s.

Women reformers were not unaware of or insensitive to the difficult conditions that propelled some mothers into the work force. They understood that the low wages, unemployment, and disabilities that beset many husbands forced working-class mothers to find jobs outside of the home and that the situation was particularly dire for single mothers who had lost their husbands through death or desertion. But in addressing the problems of needy mothers and their children, reformers ultimately supported a conservative solution. They continued to insist on the incompatibility of motherhood and paid labor. They advocated mothers' pensions, which would maintain women's primary roles as mother and housekeeper, over policies that would strengthen their positions as wage-earners, such as state-supported child care and job training.[38]

. . .

Progressives had shifted the focus from the male seducer to the home and social environments as the critical elements in a girl's moral downfall. Their reformulation of the problem of female immorality led them to call for different methods of sexual regulation than those advocated by nineteenth-century moral reformers. In place of the legal restraint and punishment of male seducers, Progressives advocated policies that aimed to control young women and their social surroundings.

Historians have generally argued that one of the hallmarks of Progressive reform was an emphasis on environmental strategies to eliminate vice, crime, and delinquency. According to this interpretation, Progressives rejected an earlier emphasis on institutionalization and legal coercion and sought instead to prevent deviant behavior by improving the home, workplace, and city environment.[39] It is true that Progressive women reformers did advocate a wide array of preventive measures to deal with the problem of sex delinquency: higher wages and limited hours of work for women wage-earners; employment bureaus to direct them to safe jobs; public parks, social clubs, and regulated dance halls to provide wholesome recreation; mothers' pensions, compulsory schooling, and child labor legislation to reform family life; and supervised boarding homes for young women living apart from families. These preventive strategies have received considerable attention from historians of Progressivism and female reform movements.[40]

What has received far less attention is the extent to which women reformers also relied on legal coercion to deal with female delinquency. The distinction between "environmental" and "coercive" strategies, between preventive and institutional solutions, is not as clear as some historians have suggested. The same women reformers who proposed preventive measures also supported the expansion of the criminal justice system—the creation of special police bureaus, juvenile courts, detention centers, and reformatories to monitor and correct the sexual misconduct of working-class female youth. The Progressive Era, in fact, witnessed the dramatic growth of a state institutional and legal network for the surveillance and control of young female moral offenders. Scholars' confusion over this development in part stems from the way in which reformers understood and described their policies on behalf of female youth as "protective work." They did aim to shield teenage girls from sexual exploitation, unfit homes, and dangerous forms of work and recreation, but the protective work they advocated had a coercive side. It entailed using the state for the purposes of surveillance, legal prosecution, detention, and institutionalization of young women and girls who engaged in suspect behavior.

In calling for state regulation of female sexuality, women reformers specifically envisioned a maternal state. Their experience with the criminal justice system had shown them that male police and legal officials often treated female offenders unfairly and ignored their particular needs and problems. Reformers thus insisted that trained women professionals should handle young female sex offenders in order to provide them with the maternal care and guidance they supposedly lacked in their own homes. Progressives maintained that they could make "the State as near as possible a real mother to the girls" if they could get women appointed as police officers, juvenile court judges, probation officers, and superintendents of correctional facilities for female youth. In this way, they simultaneously tackled the problem of female delinquency, extended female authority within the criminal justice system, and created new professional opportunities for educated, middle-class women.[41]

The reform of the juvenile justice system proceeded at varying speeds in cities throughout the country. Women reformers and social workers in Chicago, New York, and Los Angeles were among the first to implement innovative legal policies to deal with female delinquency. In doing so, they drew upon a nineteenth-century tradition of penal reform in the United States. Women prison reformers in the Northeast and Midwest first initiated the demand for women's control over female offenders in the 1840s. Outraged by the neglect and poor treatment of female inmates in men's prisons, they called for the establishment of separate institutions for women under the control of female staff and administrators. They believed that women prisoners faced abuse and degradation when handled by male officials and that women, because of their maternal qualities, were better suited to protect and reform female offenders.[42] In a similar vein, Progressive women criticized the existing male-controlled criminal justice system both for dealing too harshly with young female offenders and for neglecting their special needs.

Though following in the footsteps of nineteenth-century prison reformers, Progressive women differed from them in several important respects. The Progressives aspired to a much broader role for women within the criminal justice system. They hoped to extend female authority to all aspects of the system, including prevention programs, police surveillance, and judicial processing as well as institutional care. Furthermore, reformers believed that maternal sympathy, although important, was not enough for the effective control and rehabilitation of female delinquents. As part of the new generation of college-educated reformers and professionals, they emphasized the importance of "scientific" methods of diagnosis and treatment.[43] This emphasis was a critical part of the new approach to juvenile corrections developed during the Progressive Era. Scientific diagnosis entailed physical and mental examinations and extensive social investigations of delinquent youths, the results of which supposedly enabled court officials to assess the individual needs of the offender and to determine the appropriate form of correctional treatment.[44] The women professionals who filled the new positions in the juvenile justice system attempted to combine maternal values with those of "scientific" social work in their work with young female offenders.

One of the first goals of Progressive reformers was the hiring of women police officers. Beginning in the early years of the twentieth century, they began to lobby municipal governments to hire female officers to monitor and work with delinquent girls. In May 1910, Los Angeles social reformer Alice Stebbins Wells, with the support of prominent clubwomen in the city, petitioned the mayor of the city to appoint her as a police officer to do "preventive-protective" work with wayward women and girls. Wells argued that she could better address the problems of young female moral offenders if she had an official position within the police department instead of working simply as a volunteer for a charity organization. "A volunteer cannot keep order nearly as well as someone with authority," she explained. Under the instructions of Progressive mayor George Alexander, the Los Angeles police department hired Wells on September 13, 1910. With her appointment, Los Angeles became the first city in the country to hire policewomen on a permanent, full-time basis. A second policewoman was hired in 1912, and by 1914, five female officers were patrolling the streets of Los Angeles.[45]

Wells's appointment immediately attracted national attention and provoked both enthusiastic and hostile responses. Some journalists portrayed her as a masculine, gruff woman with glasses, wearing her hair in a tight bun and grasping a revolver. Despite such caricatures and the staunch opposition of some police departments, her success in Los Angeles generated demands for women police in many other cities. She was inundated with speaking requests from women's clubs, civic organizations, churches, parent-teacher associations, and universities. During the next few years Wells spoke in over 100 cities in all regions of the country. By 1915 at least 25 other cities had hired full-time, paid policewomen, and by 1920 at least 146 cities employed women officers. Women officers gained professional legitimacy with the formation of the International Association of Police Women in 1915 and with the establishment of university training programs for them in numerous cities by 1920.[46]

Though female officers theoretically exercised full police powers, their actual duties differed from those of male officers. Their primary function, according to Wells, was "protective work for women, children, and the home."[47] "The woman officer does not and should not do the kind of work our police officers are actually doing," explained Chicago settlement worker Edith Abbott. "She is not a 'policeman' engaged primarily in detecting crime; she is a social worker engaged in the most difficult kinds of public welfare work."[48]

One of the central tasks of women officers was to monitor young women in public places and to apprehend those who seemed in moral danger. Aletha Gilbert, one of the first policewomen hired in Los Angeles, described the work of women officers in this way: "We shall have three women patrolling the streets from 3:30 to 11:30 and when young girls are found standing on street corners ogling men and boys or hanging about theater entrances, they will be taken home. And we will then try to find out why their parents did not know what they were doing."[49] Policewomen performed another important function through the questioning and investigation of young women held in custody. According to Los Angeles Police Chief Charles Sebastian, "Such work is delegated solely to these women assistants, who by their womanly sympathy and intuition are enabled to gain the confidence of their younger sisters."[50]

Setting their sights beyond the police department, reformers also aimed to shape policies and extend female authority within the juvenile court system. Contemporaries considered the foundation of juvenile courts one of the most significant of Progressive penal reforms. These courts, the first of which was established in Cook County (Chicago) in 1899, removed children and youths from the adult criminal justice system and handled them in special proceedings that emphasized rehabilitation instead of punishment. The primary aim of juvenile courts, in contrast to criminal courts, was not to determine guilt or innocence but to assess the conditions in a youth's life that had led to delinquency. Judges and probation officers focused more on the youth's character, habits, family background, and up-bringing than on the particular offense he or she had committed.[51]

Once the juvenile courts were in operation, women reformers called for the hiring of female probation officers to handle girls' cases, and in response, the courts appointed a number of college-educated women, often with social work experience, to work with the delinquent girls. Because they were responsible for investigating the nature and causes of delinquent behavior and for monitoring the girls who were placed on probation by the court, probation officers played a critical role in the regulation and correction of femal sexual delinquency.[52]

Not content with probationary work, however, women reformers broadened their demands for female authority within the juvenile justice system to include calls for women judges. Members of the National Association of Women Lawyers, an organization based in New York City, argued strenuously for this cause in a series of articles and editorials published in the *Women Lawyers' Journal* between 1912 and 1915. The writers held that male judges either handled the cases of female juvenile offenders superficially to avoid the embarrassment of a thorough examination, or they destroyed the girls' "feminine modesty" by interrogating them about intimate matters before an audience that included men. The attitude of most men toward a girl's immorality, asserted one writer, "is far too light and flippant a one." They failed to understand that a girl's "misstep is more vital to the race than destruction of millions of dollars' worth of property, or even destruction of life. It is an attack upon motherhood, it is the poisoning of the sources of life, it requires more immediate, intimate and expert attention than bodily ailments which require the woman physician. Place a man at the task and you dam the mainspring of a better race at its source."[53]

Bowing to this kind of pressure, several juvenile courts did hire women to handle girls' cases. In 1913 juvenile court judge Merritt Pickney of Chicago appointed the lawyer and settlement worker Mary M. Bartelme to hear cases involving young women and girls. Acting in the position of assistant to the judge, she held private hearings with the girls and their parents and made recommendations about the cases to the judge. Bartelme served in this capacity until 1923, when she was elected circuit court judge for Cook County, which gave her full judicial authority over girls' cases. In 1927 she became the presiding judge of the juvenile court, a position she held until she retired in 1933.[54]

The Los Angeles Juvenile Court, however, was the first in the country to grant women full judicial authority over girls' cases. In 1915 women reformers and their supporters successfully lobbied California legislators to create the position of a female "referee" who was responsible for handling such cases in juvenile court. The reformers had succeeded in convincing juvenile court judge Sidney Reeve that "a woman dealing with women would naturally have a better understanding of any given case and a better conception of the method of reformation or correction than a man." In November 1915, Orfa Jean Shontz, a lawyer and former juvenile probation officer, was appointed the first female referee of the Los Angeles Juvenile Court. When Shontz resigned in 1920, Miriam Van Waters, a social worker and graduate of Clark University, assumed the position of referee and played a major role in juvenile justice reform until she left the city in 1929.[55]

When they heard girls' cases, these women professionals sought to avoid any resemblance to a typical criminal court hearing. In Los Angeles, referees held private, informal hearings with the girls in Juvenile Hall, away from the Hall of Justice where criminal trials were heard. The referee wore street clothes instead of a robe and sat at a table with the girl and her parents instead of presiding over them from a judge's bench. According to one account, in the courtroom of Orfa Jean Shontz, "There are good pictures on the walls, curtains, not bars, at the windows; and a big vase of roses, fresh from the garden is in front of the girl." Most important, male court officials were excluded from these hearings; the clerk and bailiff, as well as the judge, were women: "When a girl is brought into this little courtroom she sees only three faces and they are the faces of three of her own sex, whose hope is to aid and not to punish."[56]

Women reformers attempted to foster a maternal approach in juvenile detention centers as well as in the courts. Progressives strongly objected to young female offenders being held in jails and police stations, where they supposedly faced further corruption by more hardened adult criminals. As an alternative, reformers called for "detention homes" that would be staffed by trained female superintendents. Maude Miner, a probation officer for female offenders in New York City, played an instrumental role in promoting the detention home idea. Miner, who graduated from Smith College and received a master's degree from Columbia University, worked as a probation officer for the magistrates' court in New York City from 1906 to 1909. While serving in this position, and with the help of other reformers in the city, she founded a private detention home in 1908, called Waverly House, for young female offenders awaiting trial. The founders formed the New York Probation and Protective Association and assumed responsibility for managing Waverly House and for administering a program of "reformative and protective work" to aid delinquent women and girls.[57] Thanks to the success of Waverly House, the association convinced city officials in 1910 to establish a municipal detention center for female offenders and to hire a female superintendent.

Miner and social reformers in other areas of the country popularized the detention home idea in numerous published articles and talks they gave before public officials and civic groups. Through their efforts, detention centers modeled along Progressive lines were quickly founded in numerous cities. By the end of 1910, at least fifteen states had passed laws requiring the establishment of detention homes for juvenile offenders to keep them out of jails.[58]

The juvenile detention center served not only as a temporary "home" but also as a center for the scientific diagnosis of delinquent youths. Physicians and psychologists conducted physical and mental examinations of all detainees in order to identify medical conditions and mental problems that might have contributed to delinquent behavior. In addition, all female inmates faced compulsory pelvic exams to determine if they were virgins and compulsory testing and treatment for venereal disease. Treatment typically entailed confinement in a detention hospital until they were considered cured. At the same time, probation officers also conducted detailed social investigations that would enable judges to assess the causes of delinquency and the best method for correcting it. The officers questioned delinquent girls, parents, relatives, employers, teachers, and neighbors for information about the girls' behavior, lifestyles, and associates. Their findings, along with the results from the physical and mental exams, were compiled in a report for the judge to study before hearing the case.[59]

In addition to new policies governing court procedures, women reformers and social workers devised new methods of correctional treatment for delinquent girls. Juvenile justice reformers of the Progressive Era rejected the prevalent nineteenth-century belief that delinquents were of a single type and were best treated through a single program of institutionalization. They promoted alternatives to incarceration with delinquency prevention measures and, most important, with the use of probation, which sought to rehabilitate delinquent youths in their own homes, under the supervision of a probation officer, rather than sending them to correctional institutions.[60]

In spite of the growing enthusiasm for juvenile probation, though, reformers and court officials continued to promote institutional commitment for female sex delinquents. Delinquent girls, they argued, more often required institutionalization than delinquent boys, for several reasons. Settlement workers Edith Abbott and Sophonisba Breckinridge explained in *The Delinquent Child and the Home* that the girl's offense was of a far more serious nature. The delinquent girl, they wrote, "is in a peril which threatens the ruin of her whole life, and the situation demands immediate action. . . . The delinquent boy, on the other hand, is frequently only a troublesome nuisance who needs discipline but who, as the probation officer so often says, is 'not really a bad boy' and 'with a little watching he is sure to come out all right.' " Furthermore, social workers believed that a girl's delinquency more often resulted from a degraded or inadequate family life and that her rehabilitation demanded prompt removal from that environment. According to Abbott and Breckinridge, "the only hope is to remove her entirely from influences that threaten destruction and to place her in an institution until the critical years are past."[61]

Juvenile court statistics from this period indicate that girls were, in fact, more likely to be institutionalized and less likely to receive probation than boys. A study covering the first ten years of the juvenile court in Chicago found that 59 percent of the boys who appeared there were returned to their homes under the care of a probation officer, and only 21 percent were sent to institutions. With girls the proportions were reversed. More than half (51 percent) were committed to institutions, while only 37 percent were placed on probation. Similar low rates of probation and high rates of institutional commitment for girls in juvenile court during this period have been reported for other cities, including Memphis, Los Angeles, and Milwaukee.[62]

The growing number of young women and girls arrested for sexual delinquency, coupled with the courts' reluctance to place them on probation, prompted the establishment of many new state reformatories for girls during the Progressive Era. Before that time, most existing institutions for girls were private religious homes, such as the Florence Crittenton and Salvation Army homes administered by Protestant missionaries. A Catholic order of nuns, the Sisters of the Good Shepherd, had also founded correctional schools for girls in numerous U.S. cities and towns in the nineteenth century. These institutions relied on a combination of religious instruction and domestic training to reform wayward girls.[63] In the early years of the twentieth century, Progressive women reformers began to agitate for the establishment of state-run public reformatories that would utilize modern methods of rehabilitation. As a result, the early twentieth century witnessed a dramatic increase in the number of state reformatories for girls throughout the country. In the period between 1850 and 1910, an average of fewer than five new public correctional institutions for girls were established per decade. Between 1910 and 1920, however, twenty-three new reformatories were founded. Furthermore, older institutions were expanded in size, staff, and clientele during this decade.[64]

The women behind the reformatory movement took their cue from recent trends in penal reform that emphasized rehabilitation instead of punishment and individualized treatment instead of regimented control. Reformer and social worker Martha Falconer was at the forefront of this effort. Falconer served as superintendent of Sleighton Farm, a reformatory for girls in Pennsylvania, from 1906 to 1918 and in this position introduced many of the Progressive measures that other girls' reformatories later adopted. Miriam Van Waters called Falconer "the beloved builder of the new idea of correctional education for wayward youth." Before her appointment at Sleighton Farm, Falconer had been a settlement worker at the Chicago Commons and one of the first probation officers for the Cook County Juvenile Court. She also worked for seven years with Hastings Hart at the Illinois Children's Home and Aid Society in Chicago, where she handled child placement and juvenile probation matters. At the end of 1905 Falconer left Chicago to become superintendent of the Girls' Department of the House of Refuge in Philadelphia. In 1910 that institution was moved to a farm near the town of Glen Mills, Pennsylvania, where it became known as Sleighton Farm.[65]

At Sleighton Farm, Falconer sought to create a home environment for the girls by organizing the reformatory according to the cottage system (as opposed to the congregate system), whereby inmates were divided into individual surrogate "families," each headed by a matron. The families, Falconer noted, would serve as a "socializing element" for the girls. Sleighton Farm did away with guards, uniforms, and harsh forms of punishment such as flogging, solitary confinement, and limited diets. The girls at Sleighton Farm were permitted to wear their own clothes and were disciplined in a gentler, noncorporal fashion, mainly by deprivation of privileges. Perhaps Falconer's most widely acclaimed reform was the introduction of student government. Inmates elected officers and held regular student body meetings in which they planned activities, aired complaints, and exercised a limited role in the institution's affairs.[66]

Falconer recruited a number of college-educated women to staff the institution and to administer a program of academic training, cultural development, and recreational activities. This diverse program distinguished Sleighton Farm from more traditional correctional institutions where female inmates spent most of their time doing heavy domestic work in congregate kitchens and laundries. At Sleighton Farm, all girls spent half of each day in the classroom, where they received instruction from trained teachers. The reform school also regarded recreation as an important part of the rehabilitative process and hired a recreation leader to plan and supervise a program of exercise and play. Occasionally girls were permitted to leave the institution, accompanied by a staff member, to visit the park or attend concerts and lectures in town.[67]

Although Falconer had moved away from the single-minded focus on domestic labor that characterized traditional institutions, domestic training and housework still formed a critical part of the rehabilitation program at Sleighton Farm. A central goal of the reformatory was to train girls to become good housewives and mothers, to channel their misguided sexual energy into preparation for marriage and motherhood. This was accomplished with daily doses of domestic work for inmates, leading to their placement as domestic servants when the girls were paroled from the institution. After their half-day of schooling, inmates spent the rest of the day performing domestic chores in the institution. "The new girl enters the washing department," explained Falconer. "When she has learned to wash she is promoted to the ironing room; then to plain sewing, dress making, etc., until by the time she is ready to leave the house she has been thoroughly trained in all kinds of general housework."[68]

Girls who completed their sentences at Sleighton Farm were not simply released into the community to return to their homes and old neighborhoods. As Falconer explained, "If the girl were simply dismissed from the house when her term expired, in all probability she would drift back among her old associates, into the bad environment that caused her former offense." To prevent such an occurrence, parolees were typically placed with a private family as a "mother's helper" to perform domestic work and child care. In a study of girls on parole in Massachusetts, Edith Burleigh and Frances Harris strongly recommended this form of placement for several reasons. Service with a family, they argued, "helps to confirm into habits the rules of hygiene inculcated at the Industrial School," which her "poor or ignorant home" could not teach her. Also, "an intelligent employer will be more keen and alert in providing protective care for the girl than an ignorant mother, no matter how much she loves her child." And finally, "living in a family often helps to crystallize for the girl her vague hopes and longings for a home and children of her own."[69] Through its policies of institutional commitment and parole, then, the reformatory aimed to mold delinquent girls into the middle-class ideal of respectable womanhood by changing their attitudes about sex and fostering in them a desire for home, marriage, and family.

The Progressive methods Falconer introduced at Sleighton Farm were adopted at a growing number of girls' reformatories headed by energetic, reform-minded superintendents. Foremost among these superintendents and their institutions were Fannie French Morse at the Sauk Center Reform School in Minnesota, Mary "Molly" Dewson at the Massachusetts Industrial School for Girls, Carrie Weaver Smith at the Texas State School for Girls, Janie Porter Barrett at the Virginia Industrial School for Colored Girls, and Miriam Van Waters at the El Retiro School for Girls in Los Angeles County. A survey of thirty-eight girls' reformatories, conducted by Van Waters in 1921 and financed by Chicago reformer Ethel Sturges Dummer, clearly showed the Progressive influence in correctional homes for delinquent girls. Following the Sleighton Farm model, many institutions had abolished corporal punishment and the wearing of uniforms. They had adopted the cottage plan of organization, instituted student governments, and developed programs that combined academics, recreation, and vocational and domestic training, administered by staffs of educated women.[70]

The Progressive reformatory has been viewed by its contemporaries and by some historians as more humane and sympathetic than traditional custodial institutions.[71] But although the reformatory movement certainly improved conditions for female inmates, it is also important to remember that it expanded state surveillance and control of working-class female youths. As a result of the reformatory movement, many more young women and girls were institutionalized for moral offenses than had been previously. Furthermore, they frequently faced long commitment terms of several years. Teenage girls remanded by the Los Angeles Juvenile Court, for example, remained in the state reformatory an average of 2.6 years; those committed at age fourteen stayed an average of 3.7 years. Women court officials and superintendents believed that an extended period of institutionalization was necessary for successful rehabilitation, and they considered it best to have girls committed throughout the critical years of adolescence.

African American clubwomen and reformers also engaged in "preventive-protective work" for the young women in their communities during the Progressive Era. Though still relying mainly on voluntary efforts within the black community, they too began to ask the state to address the problem of female delinquency. Like white women reformers, they supported the formation of juvenile courts and reformatories for delinquent youths, but at the same time they were very concerned about the problem of racial discrimination within the legal system. They called for the hiring of African Americans to oversee the care of black boys and girls in juvenile institutions, for experience had shown them that white officials either ignored or mistreated troubled black youths. Numerous state and local women's clubs, supported by the National Association of Colored Women (NACW), organized and raised funds for the hiring of black juvenile probation officers and for the establishment of reformatories staffed by black superintendents and teachers.[72]

A leading figure in the reformatory movement among African American women was Janie Porter Barrett. Barrett founded the Locust Street Social Settlement in Hampton, Virginia, the first settlement in Virginia and one of the first in the country for African Americans. In 1908 she was elected president of the Virginia State Federation of Colored Women's Clubs. Under her leadership, the federation launched a campaign to establish a reformatory for delinquent black girls that would be staffed by black women. Barrett spoke before women's clubs, civic organizations, and the state legislature to gain attention and raise money for the project. She explained that African American girls charged with delinquency were being sent to jails and prisons because there were no proper juvenile facilities for them. After three years of fund raising, the federation purchased a farm north of Richmond in 1914 and the following year opened the Virginia Industrial School for Colored Girls at the location. Barrett became the resident director of the institution and remained in this position for the next twenty-five years. She incorporated Progressive correctional methods by instituting the cottage system, prohibiting corporal punishment, and providing educational and vocational instruction to the girls. In 1920 Barrett was able to persuade the state legislature to fully fund the institution.[73] Following in Barrett's footsteps, members of the Alabama State Federation of Colored Women's Clubs organized and raised funds for a girls' reformatory, which was opened in Mt. Meigs, Alabama, in 1921. By the mid-1920s, seven new reformatories for black female youths had been established that were wholly or partially supported through public funds.[74]

Despite establishing some reformatories, however, African American women ultimately had far less access to professional positions within the juvenile justice system than did white women and thus had little ability to influence public policies concerning female delinquency. They exercised no judicial or police authority and met with only limited success in their campaign for black juvenile probation officers. A few black officers were hired in Chicago, Denver, Pittsburgh, and Atlanta, but most local governments refused to consider African Americans for this position. In Los Angeles, for example, African American citizens had organized in 1914 and 1921 to demand the instatement of black juvenile probation officers, but the probation department would not alter its hiring practices.[75]

A study published in 1909 by Atlanta University commented on the serious barriers that African Americans faced when they tried to influence the state's handling of delinquency and crime in their communities. For the most part, they were denied any voice in the legal system, particularly in the South, where most blacks lived. According to the study, "In the South, and especially the lower South, the colored people are almost helpless; they have few or no representatives on the police force; no influence in the police courts; no control over the jail and methods of punishment. Personal influence may do something, but for the most part, they have to sit by and see children punished unintelligently and men and women unjustly."[76]

Given their exclusion from the criminal justice system, African American women continued to rely heavily on private, self-help efforts within their own communities to address the problem of female delinquency; these efforts, begun in the late nineteenth century, expanded greatly in the early years of the twentieth. The reformers worked primarily through an extensive network of women's clubs and organizations and relied on donations from African American organizations and individuals and occasionally from interested white philanthropists. Clubwomen engaged in a range of activities to prevent young women from going astray. They established traveler's aid societies, social clubs, and boarding homes in cities throughout the country to provide moral protection and guidance for young black women who lived and worked away from their families.

Jane Edna Hunter, a nurse and social welfare leader in the black community of Cleveland, was particularly active in the latter area. In 1913 she established the Phillis Wheatley Home for the protection of young black women workers. The home provided lodging, vocational instruction, and a recreational center, employment department, and cafeteria for its residents. The Cleveland home became the model for a network of residences, clubs, and employment services throughout the country sponsored by the NACW.[77] In addition to setting up boarding homes for the moral protection of female youths, black clubwomen also carried out reformatory work with young women and girls "who are already fallen into vice." Local women's clubs established and administered private reformatories and maternity homes for wayward girls in numerous cities, including Pittsburgh, New York City, Topeka, St. Louis, Los Angeles, Kansas City, and Indianapolis.[78]

. . .

Whereas African American women were excluded from the legal system, white, middle-class women came to administer an extensive legal and institutional network for the correction and control of female delinquency through the positions they held in reformatories, detention centers, juvenile courts, and police stations. But even though they acquired considerable influence, these women could not always administer programs and institutions in accordance with their goals of protection and rehabilitation. As they worked within the larger criminal justice system, they sometimes became implicated in repressive and discriminatory policies directed against young female offenders.

This tendency was most clearly demonstrated during World War I, when the problem of the female sex delinquent assumed national proportions. According to military and government pronouncements, promiscuous girls posed a serious danger to soldiers through the spread of venereal disease. To combat the threat, federal officials embarked on a massive and ambitious campaign to eliminate immorality and disease from the armed forces, and as part of that campaign they enlisted the services of women professionals who had been active in juvenile corrections. These women initially viewed their appointments as a great opportunity to disseminate Progressive policies for the prevention and control of female delinquency. They soon discovered, however, that working for the federal government meant enforcing a punitive program of compulsory examinations and the quarantine of morally suspect women and girls. In April 1917, soon after the United States began to mobilize for war, Secretary of War Newton Baker created the Commission on Training Camp Activities (CTCA), which was charged with making military training camps wholesome environments, cleansed of sexual vice and venereal disease. The CTCA, under the direction of lawyer and reformer Raymond Fosdick, launched a comprehensive program of educational and coercive measures.

Within the camps themselves, the commission organized recreational and athletic activities to develop soldiers' self-control and redirect their sexual impulses. Troops also received regular instruction in social hygiene to warn them of the moral and health threats posed by illicit sexual activity.[79]

More than just a program of education and uplift of the soldier, the CTCA plan also involved an aggressive campaign against prostitution to prevent the spread of venereal disease. Military and medical authorities viewed prostitution as a major source of venereal infection and believed its repression was essential to the health, moral virtue, and efficiency of the armed forces. This view lay behind the passage of section 13 of the Selective Service Act, which prohibited prostitution within a five-mile radius of all training camps. The CTCA created a Law Enforcement Division to monitor these "moral zones" and to eliminate prostitution and liquor from cities and towns near the training camps. With the support of local officials, the division maintained a vigorous offensive against vice; by the end of the war, it claimed to have closed down 110 red-light districts.[80]

Eventually, however, CTCA officials came to realize that prostitution was not the sole source of immorality and disease. Fosdick received reports from investigators and social workers throughout the country that "khaki-mad girls" who were not professional prostitutes were flocking to training-camp cities in search of love, excitement, and adventure. Warren Olney, chairman of the California division of the CTCA, wrote to Fosdick in August 1917: "One of the very difficult problems to meet in connection with military camps and posts at the present time is that of young girls, innocent and otherwise, visiting the camps and hanging about. The inevitable result is all kinds of trouble and demoralization." An article in *The Survey* confirmed the findings of Olney and others. "The social hygiene problem created by this war," wrote the author, "is not a problem of commercialized prostitution. It is a problem of the individual soldier and the individual girl—the man cut away from his ordinary amusements and social life, the girl responding to the unusual and romantic glamour of the uniform."[81]

To address the "girl problem," as it came to be called, Fosdick created the Committee on Protective Work for Girls (CPWG) in September 1917 and sought the support of women professionals and social workers in the field of female delinquency. He appointed Maude Miner of the New York Probation and Protective Association to head the CPWG and named Chicago reformer Ethel Sturges Dummer and Martha Falconer of the Sleighton Farm reformatory, among others, to serve as advisory members of the committee.[82]

As director of the CPWG, Miner proposed a broad program of "protective work" aimed at preventing sex delinquency among young women and girls. She urged the hiring of "protective officers" to patrol the streets, dance halls, and amusement parks in training-camp towns. These officers performed duties very similar to those of policewomen. As Miner explained, "They do scouting work on the city streets and in the parks, and speak to young girls who are going off into the dark places with soldiers. They go to the dance halls and the moving picture theatres and to the amusement parks to see if ordinances are enforced and to find girls in need of protective care. They discover the young runaways who have come to camp cities and often send them back to their homes."[83]

Protective officers also did "personal work with girls"; they visited them at home, talked with their mothers, and got them involved in girls' clubs and other wholesome activities. Women officers also had police powers to arrest and detain female moral offenders when necessary. Within the first several months of the founding of the CPWG, Miner hired seventy-five female protective officers and six district supervisors to work near national army and navy training stations and in cities where large numbers of soldiers and sailors were stationed.[84] The country's first policewoman, Alice Stebbins Wells, who at the time was president of the International Association of Policewomen, held a summer course at the University of Southern California to offer training in "preventive and protective police work" for women officers and social service workers to address the wartime emergency.[85]

It soon became evident that there was a marked conflict between the goals of government officials and those of women social workers. Fosdick and other CTCA officials were primarily concerned with eliminating disease and vice from the military bases, while the social workers emphasized the prevention and rehabilitation of female delinquency. This conflict was obvious in the educational program of the social hygiene campaign. Miner originally proposed that the CTCA adopt the educational series developed by the National Young Women's Christian Association (YWCA). The YWCA had appointed more than fifty female physicians to meet with young women near camp communities "to promote sex instruction and to emphasize the responsibility of women and girls for right social standards."[86] The physicians also met with mothers of teenage girls to discuss their concerns about female adolescence and sexual development. In March 1918, CTCA officials did adopt the YWCA program, but they altered its purpose and direction. Fosdick appointed Katherine Bement Davis to direct the education campaign through the CTCA's newly created Social Hygiene Division. Under Davis, educational efforts concentrated primarily on keeping soldiers free of vice and disease by warning women and girls about the serious moral and health risks associated with illicit sex. In addition to presenting a lecture series, the Social Hygiene Division carried out its work through the distribution of pamphlets, placards, exhibits, and a film called *End of the Road*. All these materials were intended to frighten young women and girls into chaste behavior by demonstrating the horrible illnesses, physical deformities, and terrible social consequences that could result from venereal disease. During the war and demobilization period, a staff of 145 women physicians traveled across the country and delivered over six thousand lectures, reaching an audience of nearly one million women and girls.[87]

Maude Miner became increasingly disturbed by the narrow focus of the CTCA campaign and complained to Fosdick that the social hygiene program "does not permit of the broader scope which this Committee had in view in the educational work."[88] Their disagreement intensified when Miner submitted a budget for a broad program of "protective and reformative" work that included funding for protective officers, probationary work, and institutional care for young women and girls. After reviewing the proposed budget, federal officials appropriated funds only for institutions to house women infected with venereal diseases and rejected all other funding requests.[89]

The conflict came to a head in early 1918, when the Law Enforcement Division of the CTCA adopted a policy of compulsory physical examination, detention, and quarantine of women suspected of harboring a venereal disease infection. With strong encouragement from the Law Enforcement Division, local governments enacted laws that allowed for the detention of any woman "reasonably suspected" of carrying venereal disease; she could be arrested and detained without bail until examined and found free of disease. By March 1918, thirty-two states had enacted such measures. The U.S. attorney general not only endorsed these local regulations but also ordered that trials of female offenders could be delayed until they were examined and treated for venereal disease.[90]

The policy of compulsory examination and detention prompted protests from a small number of female reformers and eventually led Miner to resign from the CPWG in April 1918. "I could not be satisfied," she explained, "to see the girls' interests entirely subordinated to the interests of the soldier and the only reason for caring for the girls in the detention or reformatories reduced to just that."[91] It was not that Miner and other opponents of the new policy objected to the detention and examination of female moral offenders. As already seen, they had helped to implement such policies before the war in New York, Los Angeles, and other cities. What they frowned upon was the use of reform institutions merely to track down female venereal disease carriers and isolate them from the rest of society. Miner thought these institutions should seek to rehabilitate female offenders and provide them with education and job training. Reformers also objected to the clear sex bias in the CTCA policy. "Why should women be imprisoned for a disease when the man, as responsible, goes scott free?" Ethel Sturges Dummer demanded to know.[92] Despite the protests, CTCA officials made no effort to detain and quarantine infected men during the war.

Aside from a small vocal opposition, most female social workers did not publicly protest the repressive measures adopted by the CTCA. In fact, numerous women such as Martha Falconer, Jane Deeter Rippen, Katharine Bement Davis, Jessie Binford, and many local female police and court officials continued to work with the CTCA and helped to implement its aggressive campaign against female sex offenders. Fosdick appointed Jane Deeter Rippen to replace Miner as director. He renamed the committee the Section on Women and Girls and placed it under the Law Enforcement Division of the CTCA. As a result of this reorganization, the section was charged with helping the Law Enforcement Division to enforce vice laws against women and to apprehend those thought to be carriers of venereal disease. The duties of "protective officers," now known as field agents, changed accordingly. Field agents helped to track down venereal disease carriers and arranged for their examination and incarceration.[93]

At this time, the CTCA also recruited Martha Falconer to direct the Section on Reformatories and Houses of Detention, which was to oversee the construction of additional facilities for the incarceration of delinquent women and girls. In February 1918, President Woodrow Wilson set aside $250,000 from the National Security and Defense Fund for this purpose. In July 1918, Congress also took action by enacting the Chamberlain-Kahn Bill, which created a "civilian quarantine and isolation fund" to assist states with building institutions for the incarceration and treatment of suspected venereal disease carriers.[94] Falconer attempted to implement the Progressive policies of delinquency control that she and other social workers had developed over the previous decade. She called for the establishment of detention homes to provide scientific analysis and treatment of female offenders and proposed the construction of reformatories based on the Sleighton Farm model, with a program of schooling and vocational training, a staff of educated women, and a system of self-government.[95]

Despite Falconer's intentions, the detention centers and reformatories constructed and used during the war were used mainly to identify and isolate venereal disease carriers. These institutions often resembled prisons, complete with barbed wire and guards, instead of the homelike institutions envisioned by Progressive reformers. The Los Feliz Hospital in Los Angeles, for example, was surrounded by a high barbed-wired fence to keep its female inmates from escaping. Even one major supporter of the wartime venereal disease policy in California admitted that the fence gave "the sense of oppression which one feels on entering a prison."[96] Instead of receiving schooling and job training, the women confined in Los Feliz spent their days performing heavy domestic labor.

Regardless of these harsh measures, Falconer did not question the policy of compulsory examination and quarantine. She, like many social work professionals, came to accept the government's interpretation of the problem. Female offenders must be made to realize, Falconer stated, that the government will "come down harder and harder upon them as they prove a menace to our efficiency."[97] With Falconer's assistance, the federal government helped to finance the construction and expansion of numerous other institutions throughout the country for the incarceration of female moral offenders. Between April 1918 and July 1920, federal funds totaling $427,089 were used for the construction of twenty-three new detention centers and four new reformatories and for the expansion of sixteen existing correctional institutions for women. Throughout the remainder of the war and the demobilization period, field agents and law enforcement officials apprehended an estimated 30,000 women and girls suspected of illicit activity, prostitution, or venereal disease. Many of these were found to be first-time offenders and were therefore released on probation, but at least 18,000 were committed to institutions between 1918 and 1920.[98]

Through their involvement with the CTCA, women reformers and social workers played a central role in implementing this massive wartime program of incarceration and compulsory examination. Drawing on their experience and expertise, they sought to disseminate modern methods of delinquency prevention and control to other regions of the country.

These methods were originally intended both to protect and to rehabilitate women and girls and to prevent the spread of vice and disease among the armed forces. The CTCA campaign, however, increasingly focused on the eradication of venereal disease through the incarceration of morally suspect females. Unable to alter this direction, some reformers resigned, but most accepted the government's reasoning and lent their services to the repressive campaign.

With the end of the war, the social hysteria about venereal disease subsided, along with the mass arrests and detention of young women and girls. What remained, however, were the legal mechanisms of sexual control—female police and probation officers, the courts, detention centers, and reformatories—which continued to monitor and regulate working-class female sexuality.

CHAPTER 5

MATERNAL JUSTICE IN THE JUVENILE COURT

*I*n 1920 eighteen-year-old Thelma Gilbert appeared before the Los Angeles County Juvenile Court on a charge of sexual misconduct. She had been arrested by the police for having intercourse with a young Hungarian man she had been dating. A female probation officer investigated the case and learned that Thelma and her partner first met at a hotel in Long Beach where they both worked. They had been dating for a while and had talked about getting married. The probation officer later discovered that the man already had a wife and child in Hungary and was seeking to end that marriage. The court had him arrested, and he was sentenced to a ninety-day jail sentence on a charge of disorderly conduct. Thelma was held in the juvenile detention center known as Juvenile Hall, where she was examined by a woman physician and closely questioned by the probation officer about her sexual activities. At the court hearing the referee, Miriam Van Waters, lectured Thelma about the dangers of sex outside of marriage. "If you care for anyone enough to marry him," she said, "you better find out if he is married already and you better not have intercourse with him until you are married, understand that?" The court detained Thelma in Juvenile Hall for two months and then sent her away from Los Angeles to live with relatives in Kansas.[1]

Middle-class white women in southern California had succeeded in gaining significant influence within the juvenile justice system through the appointment of women probation officers, judges, police officers, and reform-school superintendents. Their professional victory, however, had ambiguous consequences for the working-class teenage girls, like Thelma Gilbert, who were subject to court control. On the one hand, these women professionals rejected the harsh attitudes toward and discriminatory treatment of female moral offenders that had been common in the existing criminal justice system. They sought to understand and ameliorate the social circumstances that led young women into trouble. On the other hand, women officials exercised extensive authority over the lives of working-class girls and their families in their effort to correct the problem of sex delinquency. In the name of "protection," they disciplined young women and girls for sexual misconduct and their parents for supposedly inept methods of child rearing. (See Appendix for information on the case records used in this chapter.)

The creation of official positions for women within the juvenile justice system attracted an impressive group of women professionals to Los Angeles, where they worked together to implement Progressive policies for the care and rehabilitation of delinquent girls. They helped to create and administer one of the most innovative and humane systems of female juvenile justice in the country at the time; an examination of this system demonstrates well both the accomplishments and limitations of Progressive juvenile justice at its best.

Foremost among the pioneering women professionals in Los Angeles were the first female judges or referees of the juvenile court, Orfa Jean Shontz and Miriam Van Waters. Born and raised in Iowa, Shontz moved to California in 1911 and studied law at the University of Southern California. She was admitted to the bar in 1913, one year before her graduation.

In 1911, while in law school, Shontz became one of the first female probation officers for the Los Angeles County Juvenile Court, and in 1915 she
was appointed the first female referee of the court. She resigned from this
position in 1920 to become city clerk of Los Angeles, but she maintained
close ties with her former colleagues in the juvenile justice system and
continued to support their work.[2]

Shontz's close friend and ally in juvenile justice reform was the young
social worker Miriam Van Waters. Van Waters was born in 1887 in Greens-
burg, Pennsylvania, and grew up in Portland, Oregon, where she lived
with her parents and three younger siblings. She attended the University
of Oregon, where she graduated with honors in philosophy in 1908 and two
years later earned a master's degree in psychology. Encouraged by her
professors, Van Waters applied for and won a fellowship for graduate
study at Clark University in Worcester, Massachusetts. She graduated in
1913 with a doctoral degree in anthropology. After her graduation from
Clark, Van Waters became active in juvenile justice reform. She worked
first as an agent for the Boston Children's Aid Society, where she was in
charge of girls appearing before the juvenile court. In 1914 she returned to
Portland to serve as superintendant of Frazer Hall, the county juvenile
detention center, and in this position introduced numerous reform measures. When she moved to Los Angeles in 1917, she quickly became a
leading figure in the juvenile justice system, promoting Progressive policies for female juvenile offenders in a variety of positions she held: as
superintendent of Juvenile Hall from 1917 to 1920, as founder of the El
Retiro reform school for girls in 1919, and as referee of the juvenile court
from 1920 to 1929.[3]

Van Waters soon gained national recognition for her work in juvenile
corrections in Los Angeles and for her extensive body of writing, which
included many articles and two major books, *Youth in Conflict* (1925) and
Parents on Probation (1927). In 1927 Felix Frankfurter invited her to take
part in the Harvard Law School Crime Survey, and two years later, President Herbert Hoover asked her to serve on the National Commission on
Law Observance and Enforcement (the Wickersham Commission) as a
consultant on juvenile corrections. That same year, Van Waters was elected president of the major professional organization of social workers in
the country, the National Conference of Social Work.[4]

Van Waters and Shontz firmly opposed the harsh attitudes and methods of punishment that were commonly leveled against young female offenders in the existing criminal justice system. They rejected the use of

guards, confining walls, uniforms, and corporal punishment in the juvenile institutions that they managed.[5] In place of this punitive approach, they promoted a model of juvenile corrections that conceived of the juvenile court and its related institutions as substitute parents. As Van Waters wrote in one article, "In theory this court is parental, a court of guardianship—not a criminal or quasi-criminal court, but a court where the paramount issue is the welfare of the child."[6] Female juvenile offenders, she argued, should not be treated as criminals but as troubled youths in need of maternal guidance and supervision.

In keeping with this view, women professionals rejected the view, held by many male police officers and legal officials, that young women who engaged in sex were permanently "ruined" and became a source of moral contamination for the rest of society. Miriam Van Waters was particularly adamant in contesting this belief. In a speech delivered at the California Conference of Social Agencies in 1920, Van Waters dismissed the notion that "an anatomical condition which once having been reached in a young girl forever separates her from the good woman." As she wrote to her friend and supporter Ethel Sturges Dummer, "One need only go to an El Retiro Student Meeting to discover what rot all that is!"[7]

Instead of dispensing moral condemnation, these women argued, those who worked with delinquent girls should focus on the social conditions that led them to sexual delinquency. Van Waters urged, "By all means let us let go of the concept of the moral judgment and seek as patiently as social physicians must, the causes that underlie behavior."[8] She and her colleagues in Los Angeles believed that young female offenders could be reformed through the wise counseling and guidance of trained women social workers.

Shontz and Van Waters promoted their ideas about juvenile justice throughout the Los Angeles community. They spoke regularly before women's clubs, churches, and parent-teacher organizations on such subjects as "Preventive Work and the Juvenile Detention Home," "The Woman Judge," and "The New Opportunity of the Juvenile Court." In 1918 Van Waters delivered more than forty lectures and talks to, among others, the Catholic Bureau of Charities, the Colored Federation of Women's Clubs, the Friday Morning Club, the State Normal School, the Hollywood Christian Church, the Pasadena Methodist Church, and the Boyle Heights Parent-Teacher Association.[9]

As they developed their contacts with community organizations, Van Waters and Shontz also established close ties with other young professional women working within the juvenile justice system. They recruited like-minded, college-educated women to fill staff positions in the court, Juvenile Hall, and El Retiro and provided a source of support and companionship for them at the home they shared with two other colleagues. The Colony, as they called their home, became a place where women professionals gathered to thrash out their ideas and strategies for reform.[10]

Backed by this support network, Van Waters and Shontz defended and expanded Progressive policies within the juvenile justice system in Los Angeles in the 1910s and 1920s. During this time, however, they also encountered considerable opposition to their reform agenda from conservative public officials and law enforcement authorities. A continual source of trouble was the district attorney's office. In 1921 D.A. Thomas Woolwine backed a bill before the state legislature that would have made juvenile offenders subject to adult criminal court proceedings. With the help of local clubwomen and concerned citizens, Van Waters and Shontz managed to defeat this bill, but they faced Woolwine's continued opposition the following year when he supported a conservative judge to head the juvenile court, a man whom Van Waters described as "utterly inexperienced and committed to the policy of ignoring the legislation providing for the juvenile court." The Progressive group once again blocked the district attorney's plan by getting their own candidate for judge appointed to the juvenile department.[11]

Women reformers and professionals faced yet another struggle in 1921, this time with county supervisors over the hiring of a new superintendent of Juvenile Hall. As a political favor to an influential supporter, the supervisors agreed to appoint to the position a certain man who had little training in juvenile corrections. When women officials learned of the plan, they worked quickly and effectively to block it. In a letter to her father, Miriam Van Waters denounced the supervisors' action and vowed to fight it. She wrote, "How any sane person could think a man could run an institution for children, one half of whom are girls, and one fourth of whom are suffering and in need of hospital care for venereal infection is more than I can see. . . . Of course I have not the slightest idea of letting them do this, but unless I were here a man would surely go in."[12] She called on prominent local and national women reformers (including Martha Falconer) to write letters to the board of supervisors detailing the problems with male superintendents. In response to the pressure, the board agreed to appoint Margaret Bullen, a young woman whom Van Waters had personally trained and selected for the position.[13]

A particular target of conservative officials was the Progressive program of rehabilitation in place at the El Retiro reformatory. Van Waters had designed the plan for El Retiro when it opened in 1919, and although she held no official position at the institution, she continued to influence its administration and hiring decisions during the time she was referee of the Los Angeles County Juvenile Court. Influenced by Martha Falconer's work at Sleighton Farm in Pennsylvania, Van Waters prohibited the use of corporal punishment, guards, bars in the windows, and uniforms for the young inmates. She introduced a system of self-government and staffed the institution with educated women who administered a well-rounded program of schooling, recreation, and vocational training.[14] Ethel Sturges Dummer, a major philanthropist and reformer in Chicago, was so impressed with the institution when she visited in 1920 that she commissioned Van Waters to conduct a national survey of girls' reformatories in order to disseminate El Retiro's methods throughout the country. Van Waters discussed the results of this study in an article, "Where Girls Go Right," that appeared in the national reform journal *The Survey* in 1922.[15]

Despite this national recognition, Van Waters and her colleagues faced opposition from local county officials who objected to the lenient disciplinary methods and to what they considered the "free and easy manners" of the El Retiro girls. At one point the chief of the county probation department threatened to build a fence around El Retiro to tighten security and discipline there.[16] In 1923, when Van Waters had a staff member fired for hitting inmates, the county supervisors warned her against further interference with the management of the school. Van Waters, however, continued to oversee policies and staff appointments at El Retiro. As she explained to a friend, "But I have made this statement to officials that I simply assume the right to see that the girls are properly treated and that the school maintains its tradition. If they deny that right they must prove that I do not possess it. They must challenge it!"[17]

In 1920 Van Waters introduced a policy that was particularly controversial when she permitted El Retiro girls to enroll in the local high school in San Fernando. Her reasoning was that reform school girls should be integrated into the community as far as possible in order to remove any sense of shame and isolation they might feel. Her action met with stiff opposition by a group of businessmen from the chamber of commerce, who argued before the board of education that inmates from El Retiro posed a serious moral threat to the other students and should not be permitted in the school. Van Waters countered the businessmen's resistance by meeting separately with mothers of the high school students and by speaking with parent-teacher organizations and members of the board of education. Persuaded by her arguments and the community support she had attracted, the board voted a week later to permit El Retiro girls to attend the school.[18]

Even as they battled the opponents of Progressive correctional methods, women officials were exercising a far-reaching authority over young female offenders within the system. Although they rejected harsh forms of correctional treatment, women court workers never doubted that young women and girls should in fact be apprehended and disciplined for sexual misconduct. They used their legal authority to monitor and correct sexual delinquency among working-class teenage girls and to instruct the girls' parents in proper methods of child rearing.

The system they administered targeted primarily working-class and poor teenage girls. Most (80 percent) of these girls' fathers or male guardians were employed in a range of skilled, semiskilled, or unskilled occupations as carpenters, teamsters, tailors, railroad workers, factory hands, fruit packers, and agricultural laborers. The rest (19 percent) either owned small shops or worked in low-level white-collar jobs as clerks or salesmen. Only one father, a physician, worked in a professional occupation.[19] A fairly large share of the mothers or female guardians also worked outside the home. In 1920, when only one-ninth of all married women were wage-earners, almost one-third (31 percent) of the mothers of delinquent girls were employed in the paid labor force.[20] These working mothers were concentrated in low-paying occupations as domestics, laundry workers, and janitors. Only two of the working mothers were professionals, both nurses, and only four were skilled workers, all employed as seamstresses.

The girls themselves came from a range of racial and ethnic backgrounds. Fifty-four percent of the girls arrested in 1920 were native-born whites, 5 percent were native-born blacks, and 41 percent were either immigrants or the children of immigrants. Half of the immigrant families were of Mexican origin, and the rest came from a number of different countries including England, Canada, Italy, Germany, and Russia.[21]

Most of the girls and their families—native-born as well as immigrant— were newcomers to California. Of the native-born girls whose birthplace is known, only 25 percent were born in California. The rest came from all regions of the country. The largest number (34 percent) were from the Midwest; 21 percent were from the West, 13 percent from the Northeast, and 7 percent from the South.[22]

Many of these teenage girls came from homes marked by poverty, hardship, and family instability. Their parents faced unsteady employment, low wages, and poor health as they struggled to raise their children, and some relied on public and private charities in an attempt to make ends meet. Others had been forced to place their children temporarily with relatives, foster families, or in orphanages while they coped with economic difficulties. By the time they appeared in court, most of the girls had experienced severe family disruptions that contributed significantly to the economic insecurity of their lives. Sixty-six percent came from homes in which one or both natural parents no longer resided. Twenty-five percent of the girls had parents who were divorced or separated, and 41 percent had faced the death of one or both parents.[23] Although some divorced or widowed parents did remarry, more than half (52 percent) of the girls still lived in single-parent households, most of these headed by mothers or female guardians. Single mothers, in particular, struggled against great hardships to raise their children. Many were compelled to enter the paid labor force, where they typically were relegated to the lowest-paying jobs as domestics, janitors, and unskilled factory laborers. Furthermore, they received little help in the way of child care or financial assistance from public and private agencies and thus had to juggle work and family responsibilities on their own.[24]

Such straightened circumstances led many teenage girls to work outside of the home to help support their families. These girls typically left school at age sixteen—or even earlier—to take jobs as waitresses, sales clerks, factory hands, office workers, and domestics. In addition, many of the girls shouldered heavy responsibilities in their own homes, where they were expected to do domestic chores and care for their younger siblings after work to assist their parents.

These young women ended up in juvenile court through a variety of channels. Twenty-seven percent were sent there by law enforcement officials, often by policewomen. Another 25 percent were reported by school officials (principals, teachers, and attendance officers), social welfare agencies, and private individuals. Nearly half (47 percent) of the cases were initiated by parents, guardians, or relatives of the girls.[25]

Under the California juvenile court act, youths under the age of twenty-one could be arrested and detained for a wide range of activities, including incorrigibility, disobeying parents, skipping school, running away from home, associating with disreputable companions, or simply being "in danger of growing up to lead an idle, dissolute or immoral life."[26] The vast

majority of girls (81 percent) were apprehended for moral or sexual offenses. Most (63 percent) were charged with "sex delinquency," which
meant engaging in heterosexual intercourse outside of marriage. Others
(18 percent) were charged with moral offenses that officials feared would
lead to sex delinquency, such as attending dance halls and cafés unchaperoned, drinking alcohol, flirting with sailors, staying out late at night, or
dressing in a provocative manner.[27] In one such case, a school principal
reported a female student to juvenile authorities because she "persisted in
wearing tight skirts, high-heeled shoes, and silk stockings and dressing
her hair in a manner disapproved of by the teacher."[28] The vice-principal of
another school reported twelve-year-old Guadalupe Rodríquez to court
authorities because she had been "idle and in conversation with boys on
Main St. and various places and finally I thought for the good of the other
girls something must be done."[29] The court apprehended a seventeen-
year-old girl for loitering at beachside cafés until late hours, drinking alcohol and smoking cigarettes with young men.[30]

The more common, and more serious, charge levied against female
youths was that of having sex outside of marriage. Many of these teenagers were intimately involved with one partner, often a steady boyfriend;
other young women had sexual relations with several men; very few (less
than 1 percent) were involved in prostitution. Many girls who initially
were apprehended for non–sex-related offenses, such as stealing, running
away, or disobeying their parents, found themselves labeled "sex delinquents" if court officials discovered that they had engaged in intercourse
at any time in the past.

The charge of sex delinquency does little to explain the complex social
circumstances, needs, and longings that figured into the sexual relationships of working-class female youths. For many of these girls, sex was a
form of self-assertion and rebellion against rigid social conventions, parental restrictions, and lives scored by poverty, neglect, and instability. A
number of them had been sent to court for engaging in sexual relations
with their boyfriends. These girls were exploring sexual intimacy in the
context of steady relationships, sometimes—but not always—with men
they intended to marry; but their behavior often conflicted with parental
and societal expectations of proper female conduct. Such was the case of
nineteen-year-old Cora Stevens, who left home over the strong objections
of her father and moved in with her boyfriend, a young man employed as a
machinist. Before this, Cora had lived with her widowed father and her
one-year-old daughter from a previous marriage. She and her boyfriend

were planning to marry but had to wait until her divorce was final. They decided to live together until that happened, but they were arrested by juvenile authorities within a few weeks.[31]

Sixteen-year-old Augusta Garland was also arrested for engaging in sex with her boyfriend. Garland's sexual behavior was an assertion of social autonomy in the face of parental restrictions and confining moral codes. When her parents prohibited her from going out at night with her boyfriend, she moved out of the house, found a room in a downtown hotel, and worked to support herself. Once on her own, Augusta spent her evenings as she pleased and on several occasions invited her boyfriend to spend the night with her. The couple had been dating for three months and had plans to marry until they were apprehended in the hotel one evening by a woman police officer. The officer sent Augusta to Juvenile Hall, with a police report stating: "She confesses to having sexual intercourse with him at this time and many times before."[32]

Although some young women like Cora and Augusta formed sexual relationships with men they intended to marry, others did not necessarily link sex with marriage. Edna Morales, a teenage girl of Mexican descent, became intimate with a nineteen-year-old man she had been dating. The couple met and fell in love while working together in a store in Los Angeles. When questioned by court officials, Edna explained that they had no particular plans to marry but had engaged in sex because they cared so much for one another.[33]

For other girls, sex was part of a search for excitement and pleasure in the context of lives that were circumscribed by economic hardship and family instability. They sought relief from the difficulties of their everyday lives by enjoying the night life and commercialized leisures of the big city—venues in which it was easy to meet and form romantic relationships with young men. Los Angeles offered many opportunities for pleasure and romance at its beaches, coastal amusement parks in Venice and Long Beach, dance halls, cafés, and movie theaters.[34]

Eighteen-year-old Rose Lafite was eager to take part in this urban youth culture. As the oldest child in a poor, female-headed home, Rose bore considerable family responsibilities. During the day she performed household chores and cared for her three younger siblings while her mother worked as a domestic. In the evenings Rose worked at a local café to earn money for the support of her family. After a long and tiring day, the teenager insisted on spending her free time as she wished. Several nights a week after work she went dancing with her "girl chums" in the Silver

Spray Dance Hall at the Long Beach amusement park. Rose also insisted on her right to sexual freedom and autonomy; she often dated young men she met at the dance hall and formed sexual relationships with some of them. Police officers found Rose and her male partner together in a hotel room one evening and arrested them.[35]

An African American teenager, Mattie Wright, also looked for excitement in the urban amusements and night life of the city. Mattie lived with her divorced mother and younger brother. The year before she was arrested, Mattie was forced to leave school in order to help support her family. She worked as a domestic, virtually the only type of employment open to African American women, who were excluded from the higher-status jobs as office workers, store clerks, and factory operatives.[36] Mattie sought relief from the tedium and strenuous labor of her job by frequenting dance halls and cafés with friends at night after work. She soon started going out with young men and on several occasions stayed out all night with them, until her mother notified the juvenile authorities.[37]

A number of teenage girls became involved in sexual relationships as a strategy for survival. This was particularly true for runaways, who constituted one-fifth (20 percent) of those charged with delinquency.[38] As they struggled to live on their own, runaway girls often depended on boyfriends or men they met to pay their living expenses and, in exchange, had sex with them. These girls left home for a variety of reasons. Sixteen-year-old Stella Browne wanted to escape the restrictions her family had placed on her. She lived with her aunt and uncle because her own parents could not care for her. Stella's mother was an invalid, and her father had abandoned the family when Stella was a small child. Stella paid her aunt and uncle room and board from the wages she earned as an operator for the telephone company; in return, she expected to enjoy a certain amount of independence. She wanted to go out at night with her friends, but her aunt prohibited this and punished Stella when she disobeyed. Tired of her aunt's strict control, Stella left home to try to make it on her own. She found a job as a waitress in a small town near Los Angeles but was struggling to make ends meet. Then she started dating a young man and soon moved in with him, and he helped to pay for her room and board.[39]

Other young women left home to escape physical and sexual abuse at the hands of their guardians or relatives. Fourteen percent of the girls in the court cases studied here had been victims of physical or sexual assault in their homes.[40] This figure clearly underestimates the true number of incidents, in part because families were hesitant to reveal such problems to court authorities. One eighteen-year-old Jewish girl, Bess Fanburg, endured a particularly abusive upbringing. Her father began having sex with her when she was sixteen, soon after her mother's death. Later Bess began to resist her father's advances, but she paid a high price for her rebellion: "As I got older," she explained to court officials, "I would not have anything to do with him and then he got cruel to me and would be cross at me all the time and beat me and not buy me any clothes or let me go out any place at all." When Bess started dating a young man, her father became very angry and forbade her to see him. The couple continued to meet on the sly, became engaged, and eventually Bess left her father's house.[41]

Another girl of fourteen, Elizabeth Danton, left her parents' home to escape the constant fighting, physical abuse, and overwork she faced there. Her father was a heavy drinker who regularly fought with his wife and sometimes beat her and the children. When her mother became ill, conditions grew worse for Elizabeth, who was made responsible for all the housework and the care of her invalid mother and younger sister. According to the probation officer's report, Elizabeth ran away because "she got tired of this work and no one seemed to think she needed any relief or change." After she left home, however, Elizabeth was stranded without adequate means of support. She managed to find various jobs as a waitress and chorus girl and also relied on men she met to help pay for meals and hotel rooms; in exchange, she had sexual relations with them. She was eventually picked up by the police and sent to Juvenile Hall.[42]

The search for social and sexual autonomy led teenage girls into serious trouble. Due to their age, gender, and class, working-class teenage girls faced grave social, economic, and physical risks when they engaged in sex outside of marriage. Despite their defiance of strict moral codes, these young women still lived in a sexist culture that labeled them as ruined, immoral, and unfit for marriage because of their sexual experience. A number of teenage girls were distressed to learn that the men who had been so eager to date them and to have intimate relations had no intention of marrying them or even treating them as serious girlfriends. In one case, the male partner of a teenage girl claimed that the only reason he made a date with her at all was because he heard she was "easy" and he expected to have sex with her.[43] Another young man refused to marry the pregnant teenage girl he had been dating because he claimed that she was "a girl of easy morals."[44]

Sexual experimentation could also be physically dangerous for teenage girls. Thirty-five percent of the girls in the Los Angeles court cases were infected with venereal disease, which could lead to serious illnesses, sterility, and pelvic disorders. Another problem faced by approximately one-tenth (9 percent) of the girls was out-of-wedlock pregnancy.[45] For working-class girls, such a pregnancy often led to financial hardship, social ostracism, and family rejection. When sixteen-year-old Anna Jones discovered that she was pregnant, she was abandoned by her male partner and kicked out of her home. Anna had been orphaned as an infant and had spent the first fourteen years of her life in a Catholic orphanage before she was adopted by her aunt, Mrs. Patterson. But once the aunt learned of Anna's pregnancy, she refused to take her back home. According to the probation officer, Patterson stated "that she wished the girl put somewhere, wherever the court judged best, and that the baby should be adopted out and she refused to assume any further responsibility in the matter."[46]

The pregnancy of another teenage girl proved a traumatic experience for her and her family. When Pauline Taylor first discovered she was pregnant, she drank turpentine in a failed attempt to induce an abortion. Her parents were greatly distressed when they learned of her condition and had her placed in a home for unwed mothers. Mr. Taylor, in particular, was so angry that he refused to have any contact with his daughter. According to the probation officer, the father "had not visited the girl since she was taken away from home. Until very recently he did not even inquire after her welfare." Once she gave birth, Pauline wanted to keep the child, but her parents insisted that she give it up for adoption before they would allow her to return home.[47]

Another danger that some teenage girls encountered in their search for social freedom was sexual assault. Several young women and girls had been raped by boyfriends or by strangers whom they met in dance halls, parks, and on the street. One sixteen-year-old girl was assaulted by a young man she had been dating. Before going out together one evening, he asked her to accompany him to his home so that he could introduce her to his mother. Once they were inside the house, he locked the door and raped her.[48] Another young woman was assaulted by five young men she met at a dance hall one evening. The men offered to give her and two of her girlfriends a ride home from the dance. After dropping off the two friends, the men gang-raped the young woman who was left in the car.[49]

Although the search for social and sexual freedom led to serious hardship and pain for many young women, numerous others safely negotiated their sexual relationships until the time of their arrest by juvenile court officials. Some were experienced at using birth control methods to avoid out-of-wedlock pregnancy. Furthermore, not all young women encountered exploitation and rejection in their sexual interactions with men. Some had developed solid relationships with men who cared for them and did not consider them unfit for marriage because of their sexual activity. This was the experience of Stella Browne, who had left home to escape her aunt's punishment and moved in with a young man she met while living on her own. The couple cared for one another, shared living expenses, and had made plans to marry. Stella's arrest and detention by juvenile authorities interfered with these plans.[50]

Regardless of how well some teenage girls managed their relationships, women officials nonetheless perceived it as their duty to apprehend the girls for sexual misbehavior and then to reform them. These women dealt with young female offenders in a distinctly different manner than that of most male law enforcement officials. Assuming the role of maternal guardians, they rejected conventional attitudes within the criminal justice system that their charges were inherently bad and menaces to society. Instead, they held that young female offenders could be rehabilitated if given the right training, and that their problems were largely the result of poor social and home environments. In the case of fourteen-year-old Elizabeth Danton, women officials clearly articulated their differences with their male colleagues. The male police officers who arrested Elizabeth wanted to have her locked up, claiming that she was "a girl of the street" and "common property for anyone and everyone who came along." Women juvenile authorities adamantly denied those accusations. They countered that "the child's trouble was largely due to home conditions" and insisted that "she is a very promising child and can, with proper training, grow into a good, clean young woman."[51]

In their handling of delinquency cases, women probation officers and referees tried to address the difficulties that teenage girls faced as a result of their sexual activities. Whenever possible, they arrested the male partners and tried to hold them accountable for out-of-wedlock pregnancies and sexual assaults. Women officials had the male partner of pregnant teenager Anna Jones arrested and prosecuted for statutory rape. He was eventually granted probation, but was ordered to contribute to the support of the child.[52] While investigating the case of Thelma Gilbert, the probation officer discovered that Thelma had been sexually abused by her older brother. The court made a concerted, though ultimately unsuccessful, effort to locate and arrest this man for his crime.[53]

In their role as maternal guardians, women court officials showed great concern and sympathy for the teenagers who came under their care, but at the same time they expected to exercise considerable authority over the young women's lives. Acutely aware of the gender biases that influenced male police and legal functionaries, women officials were far less sensitive to the class and ethnic biases that shaped their own responses to delinquent girls. They assumed that the working-class girls who passed through the court system needed supervision and rehabilitation and that middle-class women professionals were the best ones to provide it. Women officials tried to reform the sexual behavior and attitudes of working-class teenage girls by instructing them in middle-class standards of female respectability and by dispensing the maternal guidance and discipline supposedly lacking in the girls' own homes. Referees and probation officers scolded their charges for wearing too much makeup and dressing in a provocative manner. One referee warned an eighteen-year-old, "Any girl who will go before the public with her hair and eyelashes beaded and paint on her face is going to attract attention . . . [and] is surely inviting trouble."[54]

Other girls were chastised for visiting amusement resorts that the court deemed inappropriate and dangerous for adolescents. Women officials had identified several areas in Los Angeles as trouble spots; these included the so-called "rough" dance halls, such as Solomon's and Rutherford's, and the beachside amusement parks at Venice and Long Beach. Referee Miriam Van Waters cautioned one teenager, "The dance halls, [Patricia], are no place for young girls. You will get in very serious difficulty if you frequent them."[55] She lectured another girl for spending her evenings at the Long Beach amusement park, known at the time as the Pike. The Pike, insisted Van Waters, "is nothing but a place of assignation. . . . The beach is no place for a girl."[56]

Women officials stressed the idea that sex before marriage was wrong and would lead to hardship and trouble. When Edna Morales was apprehended for having intimate relations with her boyfriend, court officials were disturbed to learn that she did not see anything wrong with her behavior. Her probation officer reported, "I talked with her and asked her about it and she very boldly said yes. . . . She did not seem to think there was anything wrong about it but refused to give me the young man's name." Edna was confined in Juvenile Hall and received a stern lecture from referee Orfa Jean Shontz about the dangers of illicit sex. Under pressure, Edna eventually revealed her lover's name and acknowledged her wrongdoing. "There is not any danger of my ever doing anything anymore again," she promised the referee. Once she agreed to stop seeing her boyfriend, the court permitted Edna to return to her family.[57]

Particularly disturbing to court officials was the casual attitude toward sex displayed by some young women. For a number of girls like Rose Lafite, sex was not linked to marriage or even to love, but was just part of an evening's entertainment. Rose was arrested with her male partner in a hotel room after they had spent the evening together at a dance hall. Police officers reported that they had seen the couple enter a drugstore to buy condoms before going to the hotel. The referee sharply reprimanded Rose for her behavior: "You know little girl you have gotten your foot in a nice mess and you don't seem to realize it at all. Your actions and answers are defiant. You think you have a perfect right to do these things and no one should say a word about it. I want to tell you this is a serious matter and you don't realize it in any way." Rose was detained in Juvenile Hall and eventually her case was transferred to the juvenile court in Orange County, where she lived with her mother. Before releasing the teenager to Orange County officials, the referee threatened to send her to the state reformatory if she was picked up by the Los Angeles police again.[58]

In their efforts to reform delinquent girls, women officials often carried out policies that stigmatized the girls and subjected them to punitive and intrusive methods of control. To a large extent, they were constrained by the system in which they operated. Women professionals had chosen to deal with the problem of adolescent female sexuality through the criminal justice system. They had worked hard to reform that system; they sought to make the juvenile court into a concerned and caring surrogate parent. But the court was still part of the criminal justice system and as such relied on coercive methods—arrest, surveillance, detention, and institutionalization—to accomplish its ends. As officials within that system, the women became implicated in its repressive and discriminatory policies.

In their various positions as policewomen, probation officers, and referees, women officials assisted state efforts to monitor and correct female sexual delinquency. When a girl was arrested, probation officers questioned her relatives, neighbors, employers, and school officials to gather details about her sexual misconduct and, in the process, alerted them that she was a delinquent in trouble with the law. Once apprehended, the teenage girls were usually detained in Juvenile Hall, where they were interrogated about their sexual lives. During these interrogations, court officials did not focus solely on the specific act leading to the arrest but wanted to know a girl's entire sexual history, beginning with the first act of intercourse. They pressured the young women to reveal the names of their male partners, the time and place of each encounter, and the number of times they had had sexual relations. Those who failed to give satisfactory answers faced court discipline. In the following exchange, referee Van Waters questioned one seventeen-year-old girl who had initially refused to reveal the details of her sex life:

> *Referee*: Now, [Eliza], when you were at the beach how many men or boys did you have intercourse with? . . .
> *A*: I have not had anything to do with anyone but [Franklin]. . . .
> *Referee*: How long had you known him when this happened?
> *A*: 24 hours.
> *Referee*: You want us to believe that is the only one you had intercourse with while you were away?
> *A*: Yes it is so.
> *Referee*: [Eliza], you can easily see we don't place reliance on what you have said. . . . You tell us the truth now or we will send you back where you came from. You have got to come across now with a clean sheet.[59]

Although they had objected to similar lines of questioning by male judges and probation officers, women court officials themselves felt no hesitancy in probing for the intimate details of girls' sexual relations. They felt that, as female professionals, they were best equipped to address the special problems of delinquent girls. And in order to carry out this task, they needed full access to the girls' social and sexual histories. Miriam Van Waters defended such procedures in one of the numerous articles she wrote about the juvenile justice system. The juvenile court, she explained, "can demand the whole truth because it has the power to save, to protect, and to remedy."[60]

As part of the court process, female youths also had their bodies probed and examined for signs of sex delinquency. Women court officials helped to make pelvic examinations and testing and treatment for venereal disease routine procedures for all delinquent girls, defending such procedures on the grounds that they were necessary health measures and provided important evidence for determining the causes of delinquency and the proper methods of rehabilitation.[61] But in practice, these measures also served to stigmatize and punish young women and girls who had engaged in unsanctioned sexual behavior.

Women physicians in Juvenile Hall conducted compulsory pelvic examinations of all young women charged with delinquency to determine if they were virgins. Even girls originally arrested for non–sex-related offenses such as truancy or stealing were forced to undergo the exams. Physicians would examine the condition of the hymen and the size of the vaginal opening and report these findings to the girl's probation officer and the court referee. A medical report by one physician in 1910 read as follows: "Have examined [Ida Woods] and find her not a virgin, the hymen is destroyed and she admits practicing self-abuse. She admits having been with a boy of twenty."[62] By 1920 most medical reports on young women who had sexual experience simply stated that there was "clinical evidence of delinquency." These girls were labeled "sex delinquents" and confined to a special ward in Juvenile Hall to separate them from the presumably innocent girls.

Another routine procedure was compulsory examination and treatment for venereal disease. In response to the national social hygiene campaign to combat venereal disease, Los Angeles court officials arranged to test all youths detained in Juvenile Hall for syphilis and gonorrhea. A woman physician administered the tests to girls using the latest diagnostic methods—the Wasserman blood test for syphilis and microscopic smears for gonorrhea. In 1915 Juvenile Hall also opened a detention hospital and instituted compulsory treatment for all infected girls. Staffed by a full-time female physician and a nurse, the hospital was equipped to handle up to twenty girls. During and immediately following World War I, when the social anxiety about venereal disease greatly intensified, the hospital held as many as fifty girls at a time.[63]

This concern with disease was not unfounded, considering that more than one-third (35 percent) of the girls who came before the court in 1920 tested positive for venereal disease.[64] Court policies, however, were sexually biased and unnecessarily harsh. Juvenile Hall physicians tested boys but did not require their quarantine and confinement, as they did for girls. In fact, the hospital had no facilities for housing boys and thus permitted them to receive treatments on an outpatient basis. In contrast, girls found to be infected were detained in the hospital for the course of their treatments, which generally lasted from one to three months and sometimes as long as a year. During that time, the girls were not allowed to mingle with the rest of the youths in Juvenile Hall and, unlike the other inmates, were compelled to wear gray nightgowns at all times instead of their street clothes.[65]

Once their cases had been investigated and analyzed, delinquent girls faced correctional treatment and rehabilitation. Women court officials relied primarily on three methods: (1) closely supervised probation in the home of parents or other relatives; (2) placement in a private home to perform domestic work; or (3) institutionalization in a private or public correctional facility. Probation was a central feature of juvenile justice reform in the Progressive Era. Reformers and court officials increasingly viewed it as a more humane and effective form of rehabilitation than institutionalization.[66] As noted in the last chapter, however, the juvenile courts were more willing to grant probation to boys than to girls. In the Los Angeles Juvenile Court, only 26 percent of the teenage girls charged with delinquency were placed on probation after the initial court hearing, compared with 44 percent of the boys.[67]

Women referees typically required specific changes in behavior and lifestyle before they would agree to probation. They instructed teenage girls to end relationships with their boyfriends, to stay out of dance halls, or to quit certain jobs that were considered inappropriate. Once the girls were permitted to return to their parents, they remained under the supervision of probation officers, usually for a period of several years and often until they turned twenty-one. During this time, the officers visited homes, workplaces, and schools to ensure that the girls and their families were abiding by court instructions. Those who violated court orders could be sent back to Juvenile Hall to face more rigorous methods of punishment.

Nearly half (47 percent) of the girls charged with delinquency were removed from their homes and placed in institutions or private homes to work as domestics at some point between the initial petition and the final dismissal of the case.[68] The court's reliance on domestic service to rehabilitate the girls seems odd in light of the goals of Progressive women regarding women's work and self-support. Through their efforts on the court and at El Retiro, reformers like Miriam Van Waters and Orfa Jean Shontz sought to provide young women with education and job training that would enable them to pursue a wide range of occupations in business, clerical work, sales, and manufacturing. Van Waters, in fact, considered domestic service one of the least desirable forms of employment for young women because of the "long hours, monotonous routine, restricted opportunities for harmless social life, few companions their own age, and insufficient protection from domestic conflicts in homes where they labor."[69]

Nevertheless, the court administered by Shontz and Van Waters placed 30 percent of all the young women who were removed from their parents' care in private homes to do domestic work. This decision was in large part a function of limited public funds. It was cheaper for the county to place girls as domestics than to provide them with job training. But it is also clear that women officials thought that placement in a middle-class home would provide teenage girls with the maternal supervision and household training supposedly lacking in their own homes. Regardless of the intentions of court officials, however, most teenage girls detested live-in domestic service. They considered it a degrading form of work and objected to the greater restrictions and demands on their time that it entailed. One girl probably expressed the feelings of many when she told her probation officer that she would rather go to hell than work as a domestic servant.[70]

Still other girls faced a more stringent form of rehabilitation. The court determined that one-third (33 percent) of those charged with delinquency required institutional commitment to one of several private and public custodial facilities.[71] Women reformers in California had worked hard to establish public reformatories for girls that incorporated Progressive ideas about correctional treatment. These included staffing by trained women professionals, the abolition of corporal punishment, a system of student government, and a diverse program of schooling, job training, and recreational activities for the female inmates. The reformers achieved considerable success when California legislators opened the first state reformatory for girls in Ventura in 1915 and the county of Los Angeles established the El Retiro School for Girls in 1919.[72]

These victories notwithstanding, most teenage girls sent to institutions by the Los Angeles County Juvenile Court did not experience Progressive correctional methods. In the first place, Progressive institutions often failed to live up to the ideals of their founders. This was particularly true for the state reformatory at Ventura, where the court placed 9 percent of its institutional cases in 1920.[73] Within three years of its opening, the reformatory faced charges by the State Board of Charities and Corrections for using inhumane punishments to discipline the girls, including restricted diets of bread and water, solitary confinement, deprivation of medical care, and hosings with cold water.[74]

The El Retiro reform school came much closer to achieving the Progressive ideal, largely due to the efforts of Miriam Van Waters. Van Waters kept a close eye on the management of the institution and made sure that the girls were treated decently and that they had access to proper schooling, recreation, and job training. She forbade the use of corporal punishment and fired staff members who resorted to such measures. Further, she encouraged the teachers and staff at El Retiro to form personal relationships with the girls, for she believed that human warmth and interaction were important in the rehabilitation process. Van Waters herself developed close ties with many of the El Retiro inmates. During her years in Los Angeles, she visited the institution weekly, had dinner with the girls, and attended student body meetings and the plays and concerts they organized. She took an avid interest in the girls' lives and counseled them about marriage, education, and family problems. Some girls referred to her as "Mother" or "Aunt Miriam," and many continued to stay in touch with her through letters and visits long after they left El Retiro.[75]

Despite Van Waters's achievements at the reform school, the court sent only 25 percent of its institutional cases to El Retiro in 1920, demonstrating the second reason that few girls experienced Progressive rehabilitation: the juvenile court continued to rely heavily on more traditional private correctional facilities run by religious groups. In 1920 the court placed nearly half (44 percent) of its institutional cases in such facilities, including the House of the Good Shepherd, which was administered by Catholic nuns, and the Florence Crittenton Home and the Truelove Home for unmarried mothers, which were under the direction of Protestant missionaries.[76]

The House of the Good Shepherd alone received 30 percent of the court's institutional cases, making it the most frequently used institution of all. Built in 1904, the House could hold up to 120 inmates and accepted girls of all races and creeds. Rather than the Progressive methods practiced at El Retiro, the sisters of the Good Shepherd relied on heavy doses of prayer and labor to reform delinquent girls. When a girl entered the institution, her family name was dropped and never mentioned again "till she has retrieved her right to it, as she goes forth purified and strengthened for a new life." Instead, each female inmate bore the name of a saint during her confinement. The sisters kept the girls busy throughout the day, either praying or working in one of four areas—laundry, sewing, cooking, and cleaning. According to a report by the State Board of Charities and Corrections, inmates sixteen years and older worked forty-eight hours a week and received little or no schooling. Those under sixteen labored thirty-three hours a week and attended classes for only twelve hours a week.[77]

Whatever the nature of the correctional facility, it is clear that young women perceived institutionalization as a severe and unjust form of punishment. Even many of those sent to El Retiro strenuously objected to being taken away from their families. A rare collection of writings by El

Retiro inmates in the 1920s allows us to explore what they thought and felt about their experiences with the juvenile justice system. These girls apparently were asked to express their views of the juvenile court as part of an assignment. Many used the opportunity to protest the court's policy of institutionalization. They argued that it was unnecessarily harsh, particularly in light of the kinds of offenses they had committed. One teenager expressed the views of numerous others when she wrote, "I think the cause of unhappiness today and of a lot of the girls today is the Juvenile Court. In a lot of cases it isn't justice. If a girl gets in Juvenile Hall for the first time and for some petty offense she is sent out here [El Retiro] or to Good Shepherd. And when she has a home and parents I think it is a crime. The object of being in the Hall and of having court and all that should be enough punishment for the first offense. And a girl that can make good, if she is given a chance realizes that."[78]

Another girl criticized the court's tendency to penalize poor youths and their parents for failing to live up to middle-class standards of home life: "If a child is taken under the court the first thing that is done is to investigate the child's home, if that home doesn't suit the investigator's critical eye the child is generally taken from his home. His or her parents aren't wealthy, they can't possibly find a nicer looking home and it isn't always a wise thing to take a child away from its mother. There is always a better time for everyone, and these parents may be trying their best to get a nice house, but they have to wait for more money."[79]

A number of other girls emphasized the hardships that their families had suffered as a result of their removal from home. The situation was particularly difficult for female-headed families, who depended heavily on the wages and domestic help of teenage daughters. As one girl explained, "I think that boys and girls should not be taken away from their mothers and fathers so frequently as they are being taken. Especially boys and girls that have no fathers. Their poor mothers left to grieve. I think that nine out of ten would do right if they were given more chances for their mothers' sake. . . . Why must we be taken away. My own mother has suffered hell and no doubt many others have. On account of courts, always courts."[80] Another El Retiro girl voiced a similar criticism of the court's policy of institutionalization. She wrote: "When there is only the mother and daughter alone and the mother has had a hard struggle all thru life I firmly believe the child and mother should not be separated, also when there is a large family and only one older child they should be allowed to stay home." She went on to argue that "there are plenty other ways devised to show the girl is in the wrong other than taking them away from home."[81] Despite such protests, these young women had little ability to alter the court's placement decisions. Court officials continued to view institutionalization as an important and necessary means of rehabilitation for delinquent girls.

The juvenile court functioned as a place of moral instruction and discipline of working-class parents as well as their daughters. Parents were required to attend court hearings with their daughters, and there they frequently found themselves subject to the scrutiny of court officials. Influenced by current social-work literature on juvenile delinquency, most probation officers and referees considered a troubled family life a leading cause of sex delinquency among female youths. As they investigated working-class homes, these women officials did frequently encounter serious problems, which they tried to address. Many of the teenage girls lived in poor, unstable homes; they were deprived of adequate schooling, often overworked, and sometimes treated harshly. Their parents were struggling against poverty, sickness, and family dislocation and could not always provide their children with a secure, well-supervised home life.

Even though they confronted indisputably real problems, court officers often carried out policies that exacerbated the hardships facing teenage girls and their families. These officials tended to judge working-class homes according to a middle-class ideal of family life. In this ideal setting, fathers were the full-time breadwinners while mothers remained at home to care for the children and the household. Daughters remained in school until they had completed high school, and when they did enter the labor force, their parents ensured that they found safe, well-supervised jobs. Many working-class parents had neither the economic resources nor the cultural values to maintain this model of family life. Those who refused or were unable to live up to such standards faced court censure and risked having their daughters removed from their care.

Such was the case of Mr. Tanner, a shipyard worker who lived in Los Angeles with his sixteen-year-old daughter, Mae. Tanner was called into court after Mae had been arrested for having sexual relations with a sailor. According to women officials, Tanner fell short of court family standards and contributed to his daughter's delinquency in several ways. He was divorced from his wife and lived alone with Mae in an apartment building. His worst offense, in the eyes of the court, was that he had consented to let his daughter work in one of the concession stands at the Pike, the amusement park in Long Beach. It was there that Mae had met young men and arranged dates with them. As the referee in the case, Miriam Van Waters chastised Tanner for allowing his daughter to take such a job. But Tanner had a different idea of his parental role and responsibility. "She said she had got a job," he told the referee. "I don't believe in her being idle. I was willing to meet the bills and thought an idle person got into mischief." The referee responded: "Most of the jobs on the Pike are for girls to get boys' money. It is nothing but a place of assignation and everyone knows it. She used this job for the purposes of meeting young men who afterward took her to the hotel and had intercourse with her." The court ultimately removed Mae from her father's care and placed her as a domestic with a family who lived outside of Los Angeles. When Mae's relatives objected to this decision, the probation officer warned them not to interfere with the court's policies. They were told that Mae "has been placed with a very nice family here in the city where she can earn her own living and at the same time have the proper supervision that a girl in the city needs and if you are wise you will not say anything to make her dissatisfied or in any way unhappy in these new surroundings."[82]

Mr. Franz, a German father, was also taken to task for his child-rearing practices when his sixteen-year-old daughter Marguerite appeared in juvenile court. Women officials criticized Franz for taking his daughter out of school when she was only fourteen and sending her into the work force. They were further disturbed to learn that Franz frequently yelled at his two teenage daughters and sometimes hit them when they disobeyed his orders. The probation officer noted in her report that Franz "has not undertaken his duty as to the training of his child, the girls are in perfect horror of him all the time, and [Marguerite] says this, she thinks he wants her to go to work so that she will give him the money." Franz clearly had a different understanding of the roles and responsibilities of his adolescent children. He believed that wage-earning was an obligation that youths owed their parents for supporting them through childhood. He told the court that his daughter was too old for school and did not learn anything useful there, anyway. Court officials judged that Marguerite's home was unfit for an adolescent girl. They first tried to place her as a domestic in a private home and then, when she refused to stay there, sent her to the state reformatory in Ventura.[83]

Mothers were the objects of particularly close scrutiny by the court, because they were thought to have the primary responsibility for the upbringing of their daughters. As court referee, Van Waters reproached one mother for allowing her daughter to skip school during the day and stay out at night. Mrs. Warren, a single mother with three children, explained that she was sick and needed her daughter's help at home. She further informed court officials that whenever her daughter went out at night she was always accompanied by neighbors. When the referee next complained about the girl's style of dressing, Warren responded defensively, "Now look here, that is what makes me so mad. Because she has to wear things that are given her, she has got to be criticized. We do the best we can on what we have got." Van Waters then reprimanded the mother, "I am talking about this girl's appearance as a young girl. She is over dressed, her hair and general appearance is anything but modest and girlish. You as a mother should be very glad to have her told so."[84] The court eventually removed this girl from her mother's care and sent her to live with her grandmother, who promised to see that she attended school regularly and dressed in a modest fashion.

The court held another mother responsible for her daughter's sexual misconduct and late-night carousing. Fifteen-year-old Julia Anderson had been frequenting the cafés and amusement park at Venice beach with her boyfriend and on several occasions had stayed out all night. When a probation officer investigated the girl's home, she learned that Julia was the oldest of nine children in her family. Her father had died the previous year, leaving her mother to raise the children on her own. To make ends meet, Mrs. Anderson received assistance from county charities and also relied heavily on Julia's help with child care and household tasks. The probation officer attributed the girl's trouble to her mother's inept parenting. Anderson, she wrote, "seems to have no interest in her children excepting to get all the work out of them that is possible. [Julia] was called upon day after day to work at tasks which were bound to be very uncongenial, for instance, washing diapers, and naturally rebelled at the constant labor." At this officer's recommendation, Julia was removed from her mother's care and placed in the El Retiro reform school. "To permit her to return," wrote the officer, "would be to invite a repetition of the acts which brought her here in the first place." The court's decision clearly worsened the plight of this female-headed family, for Anderson was deprived of the crucial assistance of her eldest daughter. Julia was also very unhappy with the decision, and she ran away from El Retiro several weeks after being sent there.[85]

One of the court's greatest concerns was the working mother. Referees and probation officers believed that having a mother who worked outside the home contributed to a daughter's delinquency. Working mothers, they thought, could not provide adequate supervision and guidance and thus exposed their daughters to moral dangers and temptations. Referee Van Waters considered one mother's employment a major cause of her daughter's delinquency and instructed her to quit this job. Mrs. Goldman, a Russian Jew, was separated from her husband and worked nights as a waitress at a local café. Her seventeen-year-old daughter Beatrice had been arrested in a hotel room in downtown Los Angeles with two other teenage girls and four young men. Although Beatrice denied any wrongdoing, her physical exam at Juvenile Hall indicated that she had engaged in sexual relations, if not on this particular night, then on previous occasions.

At the court hearing, Goldman as well as her daughter came under the referee's critical eye. Van Waters reprimanded Goldman, taxing her in particular for working away from home: "Then while you are away at work you don't know what your girls are doing?" Goldman admitted her guilt, saying, "I think myself, it is more my fault than her fault." She promised, "I am going to do no more night work." Van Waters ordered that Beatrice remain in Juvenile Hall: "The girl will have to stay here until further order and you will have to change your work and make different arrangements so you will be home evenings."

At a subsequent court hearing, Goldman reported that she had adjusted her home situation to meet the court's requirements. She no longer worked outside the home but instead earned an income by taking in boarders. Perhaps in an additional effort to please the court, she explained that she had decided to live with her husband again. Van Waters permitted Beatrice to return to her parents but issued a final warning: "I want it understood if this girl goes home, there is not going to be any foolishness about it at all. She has fooled you and everybody and fooled her father and she has got in this trouble, now she is going to behave herself or we will know why and if it is your fault we will get after you."[86]

Though they concentrated primarily on the reformation of delinquent girls and their parents, women officials also used their legal authority to discipline male moral offenders, with the aim of undermining the double standard of morality that had long operated in the criminal justice system. Typically, women probation officers and referees urged parents to file legal complaints against the men who had engaged in sex with their daughters and called on judges and police officers to arrest and prosecute the offenders. Men in such cases could be charged either with statutory rape or with contributing to the delinquency of a minor.

The referee and probation officer in Bessie Simons's case made a concerted effort to identify and arrest her sexual partner. Once the teenage girl identified seventeen-year-old Daniel Cameron, referee Van Waters ordered the young man to appear in juvenile court, where she chastised him for his immoral behavior. Van Waters then encouraged Bessie's father to file a statutory rape complaint against the young man:

> *Referee*: Well, Mr. [Simons], what do you think of this young fellow sitting there beside you taking advantage of your daughter this way and hurting her reputation?
> *Mr. [Simons]*: I think it is the meanest, terrible thing he could do. Of course I can't understand it.
> *Referee*: It is your privilege to defend your daughter. It would be a good thing for him if you would take him out and horsewhip him. We will put him in charge of the sheriff.

At the referee's urging, Simons did file a complaint against Daniel, who was arrested on a charge of statutory rape.[87]

In yet another case, women court officials vigorously pursued the arrest of four teenage boys who had sexual intercourse with a pregnant teenage girl, Pauline Taylor. The boys were made to appear at Pauline's court hearing, where they received a severe scolding from Van Waters: "Now you four boys are not going to get out of this as easily as you think. This girl will be marked the rest of her life and every one of you boys have had a hand in marking her. Every one of you are going to be arrested and you are going to answer to the superior court for treating this child as you have and that other girl."[88] Van Waters urged Pauline's parents to file statutory rape complaints against the young men, explaining that "if they put this girl in this condition, they will do it to others." Their arrest, she pointed out, would be a warning to other boys "to straighten up and behave themselves."[89] The Taylors, like numerous other parents, subsequently filed complaints that led to the arrest of the young men.

Other parents were not as cooperative, however. Some were reluctant to press charges because of the notoriety it would bring to their daughters and families. When Van Waters urged the aunt and guardian of a pregnant teenage girl to file a complaint against the young man involved, the woman refused, explaining: "We don't want any publicity at all. If we can keep the girl—I feel that among our own people, anyway, and our friends around, she has still got a good name, they still don't know anything about the trouble [Evelyn] has been in—we want to keep it to ourselves."[90]

In their pursuit of these male moral offenders, women officials encountered more serious resistance from the police department itself. Male police officers proved reluctant to arrest men who had been sexually involved with female minors. In numerous cases, they detained the young women but released the men found with them in hotel rooms or other trysting spots. When two policemen discovered Eliza Hayden and a young sailor "in the act of sexual intercourse," they took the couple to the police station, booked the young woman as a vagrant, and returned the sailor to his battleship.[91] The unequal treatment of male and female offenders became a bone of contention between the police and the Progressive officials who staffed the juvenile court. In Eliza Hayden's case, referee Van Waters upbraided the two officers for releasing the young sailor. "You merely turned him over to the battleship?" she asked with exasperation at the court hearing. Then she instructed one of her assistants to follow through with the arrest of the sailor.[92]

In a similar case involving a nineteen-year-old sailor, juvenile court judge Sidney Reeve also criticized the lenient treatment accorded male moral offenders by the police. "Now the great difficulty," he declared in court, "is that it seems the double standard is very prominently fixed in the eyes of the Police Department and they want the girl filed on and put away and they want to let the boys be turned loose. I don't believe in it and never have believed in it."[93] Reeve and other male juvenile court judges generally cooperated with women officials in their efforts to hold male sex offenders accountable for their actions. In court hearings, these judges chastised the young men and lectured them on the importance of the single standard of morality. Judge Reeve warned one sixteen-year-old boy charged with statutory rape: "Now there are no two standards in this world; there is only one. It doesn't make any difference if this girl had sexual intercourse with 20 men, it wouldn't lessen your offense under the law.... You might be in the eyes of some boys a hero, but you are not."[94] To impress upon the accused youths the seriousness of their offenses, judges made them read aloud the state law on statutory rape, which stated that men accused of this crime faced up to fifty years in prison.

Despite these efforts, a strong gender bias persisted within the juvenile justice system. This is evident both in the different types of charges leveled against male and female youths and in the different degrees of punishment they received. As noted earlier, the vast majority (81 percent) of charges filed against girls were for moral offenses. In contrast, less than 5 percent of male youths who were arrested faced such charges. Most boys (67 percent) were arrested for criminal offenses, primarily theft and assault.[95] Young women also faced stiffer punishments for their offenses than did their male counterparts. The court was far more likely to separate girls from their families and place them in institutions or foster homes. Nearly half (47 percent) of the girls but only one-quarter (25 percent) of the boys were removed from their homes by the court. Furthermore, girls were more likely to be institutionalized than boys. Whereas one-third (33 percent) of the girls faced long-term institutional confinement, only one-fifth (21 percent) of the boys did.[96] The inequality of punishment appears even greater when one examines the sentences for moral offenders. Male juvenile court judges may have given stern lectures and threatened harsh punishments, but they generally handed down lenient sentences to young male sex offenders. Only 9 percent of the juvenile boys charged with statutory rape in 1920 were removed from their homes and sent to institutions or foster homes. Four-fifths (82 percent) were granted probation and released to their families. The remaining cases (8 percent) were either dismissed or transferred to the adult criminal court.[97]

Two cases provide specific examples of the unequal treatment meted out to male and female juveniles charged with moral offenses in juvenile court. When Bessie Simons and her partner, Daniel Cameron, were apprehended for engaging in sex, the female referee had Bessie detained for two months in Juvenile Hall and then placed her in the House of the Good Shepherd for a longer period of confinement. Daniel, on the other hand, received a stern scolding from Judge Reeve but was permitted to return to his home after the court hearing.[98] Pauline Taylor also received a harsher punishment for her sexual activity than did her male partners. The court did order the young men to contribute to the cost of caring for Pauline during her pregnancy, but none of them were held in detention or institutionalized as she was.[99]

Although juvenile court officials made some effort to hold male partners responsible for their part in sexual encounters, they ultimately punished the young women who were involved more often and more rigorously. Even though women professionals had gained some influence within the juvenile justice system, they still confronted serious restrictions on their ability to shape the operation of justice. They were confined to handling girls' cases and thus could not control how judges and law enforcement officials dealt with male offenders. But women, too, bear some responsibility for the continuation of the gender bias. Despite the legal system's lenient treatment of male offenders, they continued to subject young women and girls to arrest and to stringent methods of control for sexual misbehavior.

CHAPTER 6

'THIS
TERRIBLE
FREEDOM'

Generational Conflicts in Working-class Families

On November 10, 1910, a probation officer with the Los Angeles County Juvenile Court received the following letter concerning a teenage girl:

As an interested mother I wish to call your attention to a fourteen-year-old girl which had been running around three and four nights a week with street car conductors on the Stephenson Ave. car line until eleven, twelve, one at night. Her mother has been dead one year and her father seems to have no control over her and came to me to ask my advice and to report it to head quarters.

She is a girl that has a very bad temper and is very headstrong and uses such profane language, making it very hard to reason or control her. Her father wishes that she be taken to the detention home until they know what is to be done with her. . . . We have reasons to know that she is an immoral girl as she has said so in her talk.

Please call at the earliest convenience as the father is anxious to act at once. The father does not want the child to know that this letter has been written and at his request I write these few lines.[1]

As the father requested, a woman probation officer visited the home soon after receiving this letter and took the daughter to the juvenile detention center, where she was held until her court appearance. After hearing the case, the court referee placed the teenager in an institution for wayward girls.

In this case, as in many others involving female delinquency that were heard by the Los Angeles court in the early twentieth century, it was the parents who were responsible for reporting their daughters to juvenile authorities. In fact, family members—mostly parents—initiated almost half (47 percent) of the girls' cases that came before the court in 1920.[2] (See Appendix for more information on these case records.)

Middle-class reformers and professionals created and administered the juvenile justice system to promote their own agenda: to control and reform the socially unacceptable habits of working-class youths and their parents. But once this system was in place, working-class parents attempted to use it for their own purposes, namely to restrain children whose behavior conflicted with family needs and expectations. In addition to initiating proceedings against their daughters, parents also tried, although not always successfully, to influence the court's decisions in accordance with their interests. Rather than seeing the court system as a top-down model of class control, then, we should conceive of it as a triangulated network of struggles and negotiations among working-class parents, their teenage daughters, and court officials.[3] The first part of this chapter explores the conflicts that originally brought parents and daughters into court. The second part examines the complex negotiations that took place between parents and court officials over the care and treatment of delinquent daughters.

· · ·

Working-class parents from a wide range of racial and ethnic backgrounds turned to the courts for help in dealing with rebellious daughters. The majority (72 percent) were from white working-class families, including both native-born Americans and immigrants from Canada and various European countries. Twenty-one percent of the parental referrals in 1920 came from Latin American immigrants, most of these from Mexico. African Americans comprised another 6 percent of the parents who sought court intervention.[4]

These parents all hoped that the court would help strengthen their flagging authority over the social and sexual activities of their teenage daughters. Many families were experiencing serious generational conflicts as daughters asserted increasing autonomy over their lives. The massive economic and social changes taking place in early twentieth-century American cities expanded opportunities for young working-class women and offered them unprecedented freedom from family restrictions.[5] As they became wage-earners and began to spend their leisure hours in dance halls and movie theaters, young women and girls also began to challenge traditional family expectations and to resist their parents' attempts to control their labor, free time, social interactions, and sexuality. Some refused to turn their wages over to their parents; others neglected to perform the domestic tasks expected of them, preferring instead to go out in the evenings. Still others insisted on dating and marrying young men of their own choice, over their parents' objections. Many daughters challenged family moral codes by engaging in sex outside of marriage.

Generational conflicts proved particularly intense among immigrant families, in which the growing social autonomy of young women in American cities conflicted most sharply with traditional family roles and expectations. Many of the non-native families who turned to the courts—a group that included Mexican, Italian, German, Russian-Jewish, Irish, and Canadian immigrants—came from peasant or artisanal societies in which families expected to exercise considerable control over their daughters' labor power, social lives, and courtship activities. Such societies were based on a family structure that was both patriarchal and cooperative. The fathers controlled economic resources and determined the responsibilities of all members of the family unit—wife, children, and servants. Everyone who lived in the same household pooled their labor and any wages they might earn for the economic maintenance of the whole family.[6] In the towns and rural communities of Europe and Mexico, daughters usually worked under the supervision of family members in farm households or family workshops and small businesses. There was a growing female factory proletariat among some groups, such as Eastern European Jews, but even in those cases industrial homework was still far more common than factory labor.[7]

Once settled in the United States, immigrant families still relied heavily on daughters' contributions to the family economy, but now the young women worked outside of family settings, in stores, factories, canneries, and laundries. Although many groups initially disapproved of women working outside of the home, economic need compelled them to send their daughters into the paid labor force; at the same time, though, these families continued to depend on adolescent girls to assist with cooking, cleaning, and the care of younger siblings, particularly if their mothers were sick, deceased, or also worked outside the home.

Some daughters, however, used their newly gained economic power as wage-earners to challenge familial control over their labor and free time, which became a major area of conflict in some immigrant families and led many parents to seek court intervention. Such was the case of Heinrich Franz, a native of Germany, who reported his sixteen-year-old daughter Marguerite to the juvenile court authorities. As he complained to the referee, "She don't mind when I tell her she is to stay at home. She makes her toilet and breakfast and she wants to go out of the house, and out she goes, and then she comes in about 9:00 and goes back, and does nothing at the house. She said, 'I don't want to work.'"[8] When he first settled in Los Angeles, Franz was unable to support his wife and children on his earnings alone. To supplement the household income, his wife worked as a waitress and his daughter left school at age fifteen to enter the labor force. Franz expected his daughter to return home immediately after work to assist her mother with household chores, but Marguerite soon began to resist this strict control by skipping work occasionally and neglecting her domestic duties to attend movies with friends. Franz first tried to discipline his daughter with reprimands and beatings; then, when this failed, he turned her over to the juvenile court.

Most immigrant daughters did not refuse to work, but they did insist on a certain amount of social autonomy once they began earning an income for the family. Some used a portion of their wages to buy clothes and makeup or to attend movies and other entertainments. Like their brothers, they were eager to participate in the new urban amusements in the evenings after work, to the alarm of their parents, who expected the girls to return home and spend their leisure time in the safety of the family and neighborhood. One Italian family was greatly disturbed when the sixteen-year-old daughter began to attend dance halls on a regular basis. Mr. Alberti complained to juvenile authorities that his daughter Patricia stayed out late at night at disreputable dance halls, often without the protection of a chaperon. The referee, Miriam Van Waters, requested that the family appear in court the following week to discuss the matter.

At the hearing, it became clear that Patricia's behavior had been a source of conflict within the family for some time. To support a family of seven children, Alberti worked as a laborer and also depended on the wages of the two eldest children, Patricia and her older brother. Patricia had quit school the previous year to work in a department store. Although they needed her wages, her parents were increasingly upset by the independent manners she had demonstrated since starting this job. She had adopted the styles of her American coworkers by plucking her eyebrows and wearing makeup. And despite her father's objections, she insisted on going out every Saturday evening. "She goes about seven or eight and comes back at twelve, and sometimes twelve thirty and I don't know where she goes," he complained to the referee. Her mother admitted that Patricia often went out at night without her consent: "She told me she was going out. She said she was going to a dance. I said, 'I don't want you to go.' She says, 'I am going to have a good time.'" Mrs. Alberti also objected to her daughter's American companions. "They are not of our language," she explained in court. Like the Albertis, many immigrant parents blamed their daughters' delinquency on the influence of American culture and practices. In so doing, they reversed the analysis of middle-class reformers, who traced juvenile delinquency to immigrant family life and the inadequate training provided by immigrant parents.

Patricia's older brother had tried to carry out his expected role by accompanying his sister to dances. But on those occasions when he told her to stay home, she insisted on going to the dances alone. "So now," he explained, "I don't pay much attention to her and let her go about her own business." In her defense, Patricia claimed that she did not attend the "rough" dance halls and said that, although she did not always remain with her brother, "I never come home with any boys we don't know."

As the court referee, Van Waters helped to reinforce parental authority within the Alberti family. She instructed Patricia to obey her parents by not "painting her face" and by staying out of public dance halls, and she urged the brother to adhere to his duty as chaperon. "I think you have some responsibility for your sister's welfare," she told him, "and I think you will have to assume your share of giving her recreation and see it is the right kind." Her parents agreed to let Patricia attend safe and respectable amusements two evenings a month. The referee urged the family to work together with the probation officer who would be visiting the home regularly.[9]

Immigrant parents also used the court to attempt to enforce traditional courtship and marriage customs. Many of these immigrants came from cultures in which families still arranged marriages for their children. In Jewish shtetls and Mexican and Italian villages, for example, families had traditionally made decisions about their children's marriages based largely on considerations of status and economic circumstances. The practice of prearranged marriages had begun to decline in some areas with the coming of economic changes and greater geographic mobility of young people, but even among the more liberal families, parental approval of a match was still required.[10]

In the United States, however, many young women picked up American customs of dating and romance from coworkers and from Hollywood movies, to the great dismay of their parents. Their new environments allowed them to meet men from outside their local neighborhoods and family circle of friends. These young women asserted their right to date and marry whom they chose, regardless of family considerations. They emphasized the importance of love and affection in marriage over financial and status concerns.[11] Some even chose partners from different ethnic or religious backgrounds, which became a source of great friction in their homes, as the following case demonstrates.

Mr. and Mrs. Solomon, Jews originally from Russia, called for court intervention when their seventeen-year-old daughter Rachel began to date a non-Jewish boyfriend. The Solomons had migrated to Los Angeles the previous year from New Jersey, where they had first settled upon arriving in the country. They were very anxious for their daughter to marry someone of her own faith and refused to permit her Gentile boyfriend to visit their home. The Solomons had attempted to arrange a marriage for Rachel with a twenty-four-year-old Jewish man when she was sixteen years old. Subsequently they had selected several other men whom they considered suitable for her, but in the probation officer's words, "[Rachel] refuses to be dealt with in this manner." She, like other immigrant daughters, insisted on choosing her own mate and on making this decision based on love and affection rather than the economic and status concerns of her family.

In the short run, the court upheld the parents' wishes: Rachel was kept in Juvenile Hall for two weeks until she agreed to stop seeing her boyfriend. "I want you to know," the court referee told her, "no girl of seventeen can treat her mother the way you have treated her and have your own way. You can't marry this man if your mother does not wish you to." But once Rachel turned eighteen, she requested and received the court's permission to marry the young man, for California law permitted females eighteen years and older to marry without parental consent. The couple married that same day.[12]

Conflicts over dating and marriage brought Mexican parents and their daughters into court more often than any other issue. Many Mexican daughters challenged family authority by running away from home to marry or live with their boyfriends. Some hoped to overcome their parents' objections to a particular young man, while others aimed to escape an overly strict or unhappy home situation.[13] One Mexican mother in Los Angeles, interviewed by sociologist Emory S. Bogardus, expressed the concerns of many parents about this problem: "It is because they can run around so much and be so free, that our Mexican girls do not know how to act. So many girls run away and get married. This terrible freedom in this United States. The Mexican girls seeing American girls with freedom, they want it too, so they go where they like. They do not mind their parents; this terrible freedom. But what can the Mexican mothers do?"[14]

Mexican parents often linked the elopement of their daughters to the influence of American ways, but the practice also had roots in Mexican culture. In some Mexican villages, young couples would circumvent parental opposition to their marriage by resorting to a custom known as *robo* (which literally means robbery), in which a young man would stage a ritualized "stealing" of the young woman away from her family in order to marry her. After the elopement, the young man's father would pay a formal visit to the woman's family to apologize for his son's behavior and to secure their approval for the union. The custom both allowed the young people to have their way and yet preserved a degree of parental authority over the children's marriages.[15]

In Los Angeles, young Mexican couples continued to elope, but often they did not bother to seek the sanction of their parents. Others committed an even worse offense by living together without being married. Such affronts to patriarchal authority led a number of Mexican fathers to seek redress from the courts. One such case involved the Santos family, whose fifteen-year-old daughter Teresa ran off to marry Frank Torres, a young man from their neighborhood. Mr. and Mrs. Santos, who had recently migrated from Mexico with their eight children, lived in a small, sparsely furnished house. The father and his oldest sons worked picking fruit to support the family, and in the summers they were joined at this occupation by the mother and daughters.

Although poor, Mr. Santos possessed a strong sense of family justice and had no intention of allowing Frank Torres to run off with his daughter without his consent. He called on law enforcement authorities to have the young man arrested. Police discovered the couple several weeks later in the home of friends. They arrested Frank and sent Teresa to Juvenile Hall for questioning and examination. Court officials learned that Frank was still officially married to another woman who lived in Mexico. Although they had separated several years earlier, the couple still had not yet secured a divorce. Frank and Teresa said that they loved each other and wanted to marry legally as soon as Frank's divorce came through. Offended by the challenge to his authority, however, Santos at first refused to permit the marriage and told the court through an interpreter that "he wants her put some place for a while, he don't know how long, where she will be taken care of until they know what to do." Teresa was placed in a private home for several months, and during that time Frank helped to pay for her room and board. Once he received his divorce papers, he notified Teresa's family and received her father's approval for their marriage.[16]

Another Mexican father called on the court when his fourteen-year-old daughter Maria ran away to live with her boyfriend, Juan Cardoza, and did not even bother with a marriage ceremony. Mr. Sánchez, who lived with his second wife, daughter, and two other relatives, worked in a pottery to support the family. When he discovered Maria in Juan's home two days later, he marched both of them down to the probation office and filed a juvenile court petition against his daughter. According to the probation officer, Sánchez "was very anxious to have them marry and says he cannot have [Maria] in his home any more after disgracing him in the manner she has." In his eyes, his daughter had undermined his authority and dishonored the family name by her promiscuous behavior.

Maria, however, had other concerns. She told court officials that she was very much in love with Juan and thought that by running away she would be able to marry him. She also wanted to leave home because she did not get along with her stepmother. The court, though, prohibited the marriage because Maria was too young according to California law. Since Sánchez refused to take his daughter back home, the court placed her with a private family to do housework. Maria ran away from this placement several times in an attempt to rejoin Juan. After the third escape, the court had her committed to the House of the Good Shepherd. Not long after this, her grandmother and two uncles moved from Mexico to join the family in Los Angeles. After several months and with some urging from the grandmother, Sánchez eventually relented and agreed to accept Maria back into the home. According to the probation officer, "now that the family is united they are very desirous to have [Maria] make her home with them."[17]

Conflicts over the social autonomy of daughters may have been particularly intense within immigrant families, but they also disturbed native-born working-class families, both black and white. Like the immigrant groups, most of these native-born families were newcomers to the state of California. Only one-quarter of the native-born daughters whose place of birth was recorded were born in California. The others had moved with their families from all regions of the country. The largest share (34 percent) were from the Midwest; others came from the West (21 percent), Northeast (13 percent), and South (7 percent).[18]

These families had migrated to Los Angeles in the hopes of establishing a better life for themselves and their children. As they settled in southern California, the parents sought to maintain the strict moral, religious, and family values nurtured in small towns in other areas of the country.[19] Native-born parents may have been somewhat more accustomed to the liberal styles of young women in American cities than their immigrant counterparts, but they nevertheless expected their daughters to behave in a modest, respectable manner and to remain sexually chaste before marriage. Many linked the moral respectability of their daughters to the family's reputation and status and feared that one child's promiscuous behavior would threaten the standing of the whole family, as the following case demonstrates.

The Tates, a white working-class family, had moved out west with their five children from a small town in Pennsylvania three years before their contact with the court. They first settled in Oregon, but when plans did not work out there, they packed up again and moved to California. The family had better luck once settled in Los Angeles. Mr. Tate found work as a motorman while Mrs. Tate ran a rooming house, and with their combined income they managed to purchase an "up-to-date," six-room house. Their youngest daughter Lona, however, threatened the family's improved standing when, over the strong objections of her mother, she began to date a young Armenian man, Sam Abdalian, whom she had met at the laundry where she worked as a cashier. Lona created an even greater stir when she spent the night with Sam in his apartment and did not return home until the following day. To punish her daughter and keep her away from Sam, an angry Mrs. Tate had Lona placed temporarily in a private institution for wayward girls. Sam visited the Tate home and explained that even though he and Lona had done wrong, they loved each other and wanted to get married. Mrs. Tate apparently threatened to harm him if he came to the house again and declared, "No foreigner is going to marry my daughter!" She explained to court officials that she had already raised four decent children and was not about to let her youngest daughter disgrace the family any more than she already had.[20]

Another native-born white mother asked for the court's help when her daughter Helen continued to smoke, drink, and visit disreputable cafés late at night, despite her repeated objections. Mrs. Bishop was divorced from her husband and had recently moved with her daughter from the Midwest to Los Angeles, where they lived with her married son and his wife. Although her own life had not worked out as planned, Bishop had ambitious plans for her daughter. Eager to improve the family's status, she wanted Helen to enroll in a commercial course in order to "fit herself for a business life." But this Helen refused to do. Instead, she wanted to keep her present job as an usher at Grauman's Theater and to continue to enjoy the exciting night life that Los Angeles offered. An exasperated Bishop eventually turned Helen over to juvenile authorities when the young woman returned home one morning at 2 A.M. with her breath smelling of liquor. After a two-day detention in Juvenile Hall, the court released Helen to her mother, placed her under the supervision of a probation officer, and made arrangements for her to enroll in a business course at a local polytechnic institute. The case was dismissed a year later at the request of Mrs. Bishop, who reported that Helen had completed the course and found a "good office position."[21]

Another white, working-class couple became very distraught and angry upon discovering that their fourteen-year-old daughter had been sexually active. When Minnie Reynolds informed her parents that she might be pregnant, her father, a machinist by trade, took her to the juvenile detention center and signed a rape complaint against her male partner. Although the physician found no evidence of pregnancy, the parents, according to juvenile authorities, were "almost crazed with surprise and grief and asked to have her placed in the reform school, at once, that day, and positively refused to keep her in their home any longer."[22] After a month-long detention in Juvenile Hall, Minnie was placed in a private home to do domestic work and care for small children. In the eyes of her parents,

Minnie's sexual behavior had damaged her own and thus the family's reputation. By sending her away, the Reynoldses hoped to hide the disgrace
their daughter had brought to them. Their concern about respectability,
however, did not completely override their attachment to their daughter.
After several months, they relented and asked to have her sent back home.

Several native-born black families also used the court to control the
activities of their daughters. African Americans who had joined the migration to California came mostly from small towns and rural areas in the
South. They headed west in search of employment, a more hospitable
racial climate, and better opportunities for their children.[23] Many brought
with them strong religious and moral principles. One such person was
Mabel Faulkner, a mother who worked hard to raise her four children in a
proper Christian manner. Faulkner was separated from her husband, but
he lived and worked close by and contributed regularly to the support of
the family. She earned wages as a domestic worker and was also a preacher
for her church and held religious meetings on a streetcorner three nights a
week. Obviously a woman of strong religious convictions, Faulkner became very upset when she learned that her fourteen-year-old daughter
Celia had been skipping school to go to the movies and had become intimately involved with a teenage boy from the neighborhood. She notified
women officers in the police department and filed a juvenile court petition
against the girl. Court officials had Celia detained in Juvenile Hall for two
weeks, a punishment that her mother hoped would teach her to behave
properly in the future.[24]

Although parent-daughter conflicts over social and sexual autonomy
were common in many working-class families during this period, they
were particularly stressful in female-headed households. Single mothers,
native-born and immigrant, black and white, formed a disproportionately
large share of the parents who initiated court proceedings to settle conflicts with their adolescent daughters.[25] Thirty-four percent of all family
referrals came from single mothers, even though female-headed families
constituted only one-fifth (21 percent) of the families living in Los Angeles.[26] The economic and social changes that heightened generational
tensions between working-class parents and their daughters also exacerbated the economic vulnerability of single mothers. Urbanization, an intense rate of immigration, and an expanding wage-labor economy disrupted earlier survival strategies of single mothers and made them even
more dependent on the domestic and wage-labor contributions of their
adolescent children.[27]

The causes of single parenthood were varied. Of the single mothers who requested court assistance in Los Angeles County, 39 percent were widows and the rest were either divorced (25 percent) or separated (36 percent) from their husbands. They came from a range of ethnic and racial backgrounds. Fifty-one percent were native-born whites; 10 percent were native-born blacks; and 39 percent were immigrants. More than half of the immigrant mothers were of Mexican descent; the rest had migrated from Canada and various European countries.[28]

All of these women faced a precarious existence as they struggled to raise their children on their own in early twentieth-century Los Angeles. In a rapidly growing city with a wage-labor economy and a highly mobile population, single mothers could not depend as readily on the support of family and kin as they had in small towns and agrarian communities. Even though, in preindustrial communities, the loss of a husband might have forced some single mothers into poorhouses and onto charity rolls, others had managed to survive by being absorbed into extended-family economies and households or by taking over their husband's craft or farm.[29] But in an economy in which working-class incomes just barely covered living expenses, most families could not bear the additional financial burden of supporting a mother and her dependent children.

It is not surprising, therefore, that nearly all of the single mothers who requested juvenile court intervention in Los Angeles lived alone with their children rather than in extended-family households. There is insufficient data to determine whether the percentage of female-headed families was increasing in Los Angeles during this period, but the census does suggest that, in general, the percentage of such households tended to increase with urbanization. The rates for the two largest cities in California, Los Angeles and San Francisco, were 21 percent and 20 percent, respectively, compared to 16 percent for the state as a whole.[30]

Mrs. Johnson, a single black mother, discovered that she could not depend on her family for support when she moved her six children from their home in New Orleans to Los Angeles after the death of her husband. According to the probation officer's report, "Mrs. [Johnson] states that her reason for coming here was that her father lived here and she thought he would be able to assist her in caring for her family. Upon her arrival, she found that he was not able to do so, however."[31] Without the expected support from her father, Johnson had to scrape together whatever income she could from local charities and from her work as a laundress to support her large family.

Although relatives could rarely take a whole family into their homes, they sometimes could and did assist in more limited ways by helping to raise dependent children and by providing occasional financial support. When one single mother who moved from Chicago to Los Angeles with her three children could not afford to support her family on the meager wages she earned as an unskilled factory laborer, her half-sister agreed to adopt one of the sons.[32] A Mexican-born mother, whose husband had died and left her with six children to support, sent her thirteen-year-old daughter to live with a sister and brother-in-law who resided nearby.[33]

Some single mothers, however, did not have nearby relatives to whom they could turn for assistance. This situation may have been particularly common in a rapidly growing city like Los Angeles, where the vast majority of inhabitants were recent migrants.[34] More than three-quarters of the single mothers involved with the Los Angeles Juvenile Court in 1920 were newcomers to the area, either from foreign countries or from other regions within the United States. Some women who had lost their husbands and lacked family networks in Los Angeles had to resort to institutionalizing their children. When her husband died, leaving her with no adult relatives nearby, Flora López was compelled to enter the paid labor force and to place her young daughter in the Boyle Heights Orphanage for several years until she could once more support her.[35]

Often unable to rely on relatives for adequate assistance, single mothers also received little in the way of financial aid or child care assistance from public or private charitable sources. The federal government did not begin to address the plight of single mothers until the 1930s with passage of New Deal legislation to aid families with dependent children. Although most states passed mothers' pension laws between 1910 and 1920, these assisted only a small number of female-headed households because of their stringent eligibility requirements. The California law, passed in 1913, made pensions available to widows only. Insisting that the state would not support "deserting" husbands and fathers, legislators ignored in the process the needs of divorced, separated, and unmarried mothers and their children. The law further stipulated that, to receive aid, a family must have lived in California for at least three years, a requirement that many widows in Los Angeles could not meet.[36]

In addition to the formal eligibility requirements established by the state, the Los Angeles County Outdoor Relief Department, which was responsible for processing county applications for aid, adopted a policy of refusing mothers' pensions to Mexican widows. County officials claimed that Mexican immigrants had a dangerous propensity for "leaning" on the state. The "feudal background" of Mexican immigrants, according to officials, made it difficult for them "to understand and not abuse the principle of a regular grant of money from the state."[37] Thus Mexican widows who were otherwise eligible were denied pensions from the state and were forced to seek assistance from other sources.

The Los Angeles County Charities Office and the few private charities in the area were the only options left for the many single mothers who did not qualify for state pensions. These charities, however, typically dispensed aid on a piecemeal, emergency basis—when families were at the brink of starvation and desperation.[38] The paltry assistance given and the humiliating way in which it was dispensed discouraged many needy mothers from even applying for aid. In view of the severe limitations of both county and state aid, it is not surprising that few single mothers received outside financial assistance. Less than a quarter (24 percent) of the mothers who sought juvenile court intervention with their daughters in 1920 had received any form of private or public assistance during the time they had lived in the county.

With limited kin support and scarce public assistance, most single mothers were forced not only to seek paid employment for themselves, but also to send their adolescent children into the work force in order to meet the economic needs of their families. The demands of wage work seriously complicated their ability to care for and supervise their children. In an attempt to reconcile these conflicting needs, some single mothers struggled to devise ways of earning an income while remaining at home. One Mexican mother, for example, took in two boarders in an effort to support her five children.[39] Other female breadwinners worked in their homes as seamstresses or laundresses.[40] Another mother, who had moved from Michigan to Los Angeles, found a job managing a small apartment house so that she could remain at home to supervise her fourteen-year-old daughter during the day.[41]

Most single mothers, however, had no choice but to work outside the home. In 1920, when only one-ninth of all married women in the United States were wage-earners, over half (57 percent) of the single mothers who sought the assistance of the Los Angeles Juvenile Court were employed in the paid labor force.[42] Despite long hours and hard work, most working mothers earned barely enough to support a single person, let alone a family with dependent children, because the labor market confined female workers to the least-skilled, lowest-paid jobs. Largely as a result of sex-based job segregation, female workers during this period earned only approximately 60 percent of the wages men earned.[43] The occupational outlook was particularly grim for working mothers. Because employers preferred young, single women for the higher-status jobs in offices and department stores, working mothers were concentrated in the lowest-paid, most menial forms of female employment.[44] Most of the single mothers from the Los Angeles Juvenile Court cases held such jobs as domestics, laundresses, janitors, or unskilled laborers in canneries and food processing plants.

The typical wages of working mothers in Los Angeles fell far short of what was needed to support a family. Under California's minimum wage law, the minimum wage for women workers in 1920 was sixteen dollars per week. Set by the California Industrial Welfare Commission, this wage was based on the cost of living for a single woman. Although it was more progressive than many other state minimum wage laws, the California statute still did not cover major sectors of female employment, principally domestic work, a common occupation for single mothers and particularly for African American mothers, who were largely excluded from factory, clerical, and retail work. Even those women who attained the minimum wage of sixteen dollars per week still earned only approximately half of the estimated income needed to support a family of four. Obviously, it was rare that a single mother could support her family on her earnings alone.[45]

In addition to their own paid employment, therefore, single mothers also relied heavily on the wage-earning and domestic labor of their older children to hold the families together. Due to the lack of public assistance and facilities for child care, adolescent daughters frequently had to assume the major responsibility for supervising younger children and performing household tasks while their mothers worked. One single mother of four, who worked as a domestic from seven in the morning until seven at night, explained to court officials the central role her teenage daughter played in managing the household: "She is my housekeeper. . . . I go to work early and come home late. She had to get the meals and keep house and send the children to school. My husband has been dead 8 years and I tried to keep them together and it has been hard."[46]

In most female-headed homes, family survival also dictated that adolescent daughters leave school to enter the paid labor force as soon as legally permissible under child labor laws. The California child labor law, passed in 1913, prohibited the employment of minors under sixteen years of age; in cases of great family need, county officials could grant work permits to minors between twelve and fifteen years of age.[47] Although by 1920 a growing number of working-class fathers earned enough to keep their adolescent children out of the work force, single mothers still counted on the economic contributions of their high school–age children. In nearly every female-headed household in this sample, the daughters had left school to become wage-earners at age sixteen or earlier to assist in the support of their families.

In many cases, the survival of a single mother's household depended on the combined wage-earning and household labor of both mother and daughter, as the following case illustrates. A Hungarian widow who worked as a janitor left home early in the morning, leaving her seventeen-year-old daughter to care for the three younger children. When she returned in the afternoon, she took over the domestic duties from her daughter, who then left for an evening job with the telephone company. Since she received no outside support from public or private charities, this mother had been able to hold her family together only through a careful coordination of both her own and her daughter's earnings and domestic labor.[48]

At a time when single working-class mothers were particularly dependent on the domestic and wage-earning contributions of their daughters, these young women were beginning to demand greater economic and social independence from their families. Single mothers faced a serious dilemma as they sent their teenage daughters into the work force: they needed the additional economic contributions of their daughters but were very apprehensive of the independence encouraged by wage-earning. Many white, black, and immigrant mothers objected to the late-night entertainments, the makeup and new styles of dress, and the casual relations their daughters formed with young men they met on the streets and at work. It was in their struggle to reconcile the family's economic needs with the proper supervision of teenage daughters that some single mothers turned to the juvenile court for assistance.

Several cases from the Los Angeles court records illuminate these struggles between mothers and their teenage daughters. A single mother of Mexican descent resorted to court intervention when she could no longer control the behavior of her wage-earning daughter. The mother of six children, Mrs. Pérez had been separated from her husband for four years. The family survived on the earnings of the two oldest children, sixteen-year-old Carmen and her eighteen-year-old brother, Louis, and the rent paid by two boarders. With this income, they managed to rent a five-room house in San Gabriel, California.

Carmen left school after the seventh grade and began working to help support her family. When she found a job in a cigar factory in Los Angeles, she persuaded her mother to let her move into an apartment in the city with two girlfriends so that she would be closer to her place of employment. After a month in Los Angeles, Carmen and one of her girlfriends quit their jobs at the cigar factory because they considered the work too dull and tedious; they found new jobs as waitresses at a café, where they worked from three in the afternoon until twelve midnight. Not long after she started the job, Carmen began dating a young Greek man she met at the café.

When Pérez learned of her daughter's new job and her male acquaintance, she sent her oldest son to Los Angeles to retrieve the girl. Louis tracked Carmen down at the restaurant and demanded that she quit the job immediately and return to the family home in San Gabriel. When she refused, he contacted the police and had Carmen arrested and detained in Juvenile Hall on a charge of delinquency. He told probation officers that his mother wanted Carmen to move back to San Gabriel with her family and work in a factory near their home.[49]

A single black mother, Elizabeth Wright, faced a similar rebellion on the part of her sixteen-year-old daughter Mattie. To support her two children, the daughter and an eight-year-old son, Wright worked as a domestic. She had been separated from her husband for years and had been able to obtain child support only by taking him to court. Once Mattie turned sixteen, however, her father was no longer obligated to support her, and Wright had been compelled to place Mattie as a live-in domestic in a private home so that she could contribute to the family income. Apprehensive about having her daughter live away from home, Wright was careful to find her a well-supervised domestic position with a respectable family.

Mattie soon became dissatisfied with the position, however, and after several months she quit to take another domestic job that paid more money and permitted her more freedom to stay out at night with her friends. Away from the close supervision of her mother and her previous employer, Mattie went out dancing with young men in the evenings after work and on several occasions stayed out all night. She tried to conceal her night life from her mother. As Wright explained to the court, "I did not know she was staying out nights. She told me she was going back out where she worked. She would not let the lady she worked for and I get together. The lady wanted to tell me [Mattie] was not doing the right thing. . . . She said [Mattie] was too nice a girl to be going the gate she was going, men and girls calling her up." At first, Wright scolded Mattie and tried to make her change her ways. When the girl continued "staying out nights," her exasperated mother finally notified a local police officer and had Mattie taken to Juvenile Hall. Wright explained to court officials that she came from a good family and had always tried to raise her daughter properly. Unable to do this any longer on her own, she called on the juvenile court for assistance.[50]

A young woman's personal ambitions could sometimes threaten the very economic survival of the family, as well as upsetting its traditional roles and expectations. In one such case, Florence Walker, a single mother of three children, called on the Los Angeles Juvenile Court for help in retrieving her eighteen-year-old daughter Lydia, who had left home a month earlier to become a dancer with the Broadway Beauties Travelling Chorus Show. Lydia had toured with the show for several weeks, performing in various towns in the Southwest, until the company went broke and she and the other dancers were dismissed. After the show disbanded, Walker expected Lydia to return home and resume her previous job with the telephone company, but Lydia had other plans. She decided to move to San Francisco with her girlfriend and audition with dance companies there. When a week had passed with no word from Lydia, Walker panicked and decided to notify the juvenile authorities of her daughter's absence. She told the probation officer that she was "very much worried lest the girl should have fallen into the hands of the white slavers."[51]

In response to Walker's request for help, the chief probation officer of the Los Angeles Juvenile Court notified authorities in San Francisco to look out for Lydia. The police there found and arrested her several days later as she was leaving the post office. Investigators discovered that, far from being a victim of white slavery, Lydia had been struggling to succeed as a dancer during her brief stay in the city. She was auditioning for a show at a theater in Oakland and was teaching dance classes in the evenings to earn money to support herself. Her arrest by San Francisco police put an abrupt end to these plans.

Walker had appealed to the court because her daughter's acts of independence seriously compromised the family's economic well-being. Walker's husband, a piano maker by trade, had been confined to an insane asylum in Illinois for the previous ten years, leaving her the sole supporter of three children. Several years before her involvement with the juvenile court, Walker had moved her children from their home in Chicago to Los Angeles, where she hoped to make a better life for her family. However, economic opportunities for working mothers were paltry even in a thriving city like Los Angeles. Walker found a job in a food-processing plant where she earned ten dollars a week, barely enough to support a single person, let alone a family of four. The family's economic straits required that Lydia leave school and go to work as soon as she reached age sixteen. First employed as a factory laborer, the young woman found a higher-paying job several months later as a telephone operator for the Southern California Telephone Company, where she earned fifteen dollars a week, making her the principal wage-earner in the family.

As the major contributor to the family income, Lydia began to demand privileges from her mother, such as staying out late and going to dance halls with her friends. She took an even bolder step when she quit her job with the telephone company to join the traveling chorus show. Bored with the tedium of office and factory, Lydia set her sights on the more exciting opportunities available in the entertainment industry. As a dancer with the Broadway Beauties, she not only did something she enjoyed but also earned more money (thirty dollars a week).

Persuaded in part by the higher salary, Lydia's mother had at first agreed to allow her daughter to join the company. She soon discovered, however, that she was losing control over the girl. While Lydia lived at home, she had dutifully turned her entire paycheck over to her mother. Once on the road, she still sent money home but began withholding a certain amount for herself, leading her mother to write several letters complaining about the insufficient funds she received from Lydia. At home, her mother had tried to prevent Lydia from wearing makeup and going to dances unchaperoned. Out on the road with the dance company, however, Lydia herself determined where she would go and how she would dress. This experience also provided Lydia with opportunities for sexual experimentation. It was while she was on tour with the Broadway Beauties that she had her first sexual relationship.

When Lydia was returned forcibly to Los Angeles, her mother requested that she be placed under court supervision and instructed to obey her mother's orders—specifically, to give up dancing and contribute to the support of the family by working once more at the telephone office. Walker also evidently decided to use the court to settle several other conflicts she had been having with her daughter. She asked the probation officer to "caution the girl that she must keep early hours and she must refrain in the future from any use of make-up, such as rouge and pencil which she has been using against the mother's desires for some time in the past."[52]

Working-class parents also used the juvenile court to discipline their disobedient sons, but they defined delinquency differently for sons than for daughters. An examination of the kinds of offenses with which boys were charged sheds light on the different expectations that working-class parents had for their sons and their daughters. Both immigrant and native-born parents reported boys to the court authorities and, as with the girls' cases, single mothers were overrepresented. More than one-third (36 percent) of the parental referrals in boys' cases came from single mothers. Parents were more likely to report younger, school-age sons than older ones. Fifty percent of the boys turned in by their parents were between the ages of eight and thirteen, compared with 20 percent of the girls.[53] The chief complaints made against younger sons were truancy and running away from home. One single mother, struggling to support her two children on the wages she earned as a domestic worker, sent her fourteen-year-old son to court for refusing to attend school. The mother, according to the probation officer, "works very hard and is trying to assist in every possible way to have her two sons get an education and become fitted for life's work."[54] Another mother complained that her thirteen-year-old son, in addition to skipping school, often left home for days at a time and had recently been caught stealing jewelry from a neighbor's home. According to the probation officer, "She states that she has no way of controlling the boy, and feels that if he can be placed somewhere under strict supervision that something might be made of him."[55]

Working-class parents were noticeably less likely to initiate court intervention against older sons than they were against daughters of the same age. Only 24 percent of the boys turned in by their parents were between the ages of sixteen and twenty-one, compared with 41 percent of the girls.[56] Working-class parents clearly granted older adolescent sons more autonomy over their labor, social activities, and romantic relations than daughters received. They expected sons as well as daughters to contribute to the family economy through wage-earning but gave them more control over their earnings and their free time. Daughters, particularly those in immigrant families, were expected to turn over all their wages to their parents and might receive a small allowance for their own spending. Sons were often given greater control over their wages; they routinely kept a portion for their own spending or paid their parents room and board from their earnings. Parents allowed their sons to roam the streets and neighborhoods with friends in the evenings after work and were also far less concerned about their romantic and sexual encounters than they were in the case of their daughters.[57]

Working-class parents most frequently reported older sons to court authorities for leaving home or for failing to contribute adequately to the family economy, but only rarely did they link these charges with inappropriate moral behavior, as they frequently did with daughters. One Jewish father, employed as a junk peddler, hauled his seventeen-year-old son into court for running away to live on his own in San Diego. Much to the father's alarm, the son no longer contributed part of his wages to the family. As the man explained to the judge: "I got four big boys older than he is and they all help me out. There are nine in the family. I can't make a living for all of them."[58] A widowed mother, raising two sons on her own, charged her teenage son with staying out late and "spending his money on foolishness." Instead of paying room and board to his mother as he was expected to, the son spent his wages on urban amusements and dates with his girlfriend.[59] Another mother reported her son for running away from home and taking fifty dollars from her, which he supposedly spent with his companions at various beach resorts.[60] In none of these cases did the parents express concern about the moral conduct displayed by their sons while they lived away from home or attended amusement parks and dance halls. Instead, they were primarily concerned that such behavior threatened the family's slim resources. As long as sons lived up to their economic responsibilities at home, they were granted considerable autonomy over other aspects of their lives.

Only one case involving an adolescent boy recalled the types of charges parents frequently brought against daughters. A Mrs. Smith reported her seventeen-year-old stepson John to court authorities for "staying out late" and "frequenting public dance halls." According to the probation officer, the mother expected her son to return home immediately after work and to "account to her for all his time and all his money, and she will help him to become what she thinks he ought to be." The officer described Smith as a concerned mother but thought her restrictions unreasonable for a young man of John's age. "It was found," he reported to the judge, "that the trouble was more in the home and in the stepmother than in the boy. She treated him as a little child."[61] The absence of similar cases suggests that most working-class parents apparently agreed that such limits were unnecessary for their wage-earning sons.

It was also very rare for working-class parents to report their sons to court authorities for sexual misconduct, as they frequently did with daughters. In very few of the boys' cases had parents complained of sexual misconduct (8 percent, compared with 60 percent of the girls' cases). The type as well as the number of sexual offenses also differed dramatically by gender. Parents did not reprimand teenage sons for promiscuous hetero-sexual activity, as they did with daughters. Rather, the most common sexual charge made against sons was for molesting younger sisters or stepsisters.[62] A few families also notified court authorities because they suspected their sons were involved in homosexual relationships.[63] Apparently, as far as parents were concerned, incest and homosexuality constituted the only sexual offenses of young men that were serious enough to warrant court intervention.

· · ·

Parents had a mixed record of success when they sought the assistance of the juvenile court to control disobedient daughters. Although some were able to use the court effectively, others found that court decisions and policies seriously conflicted with their own needs and desires. Parents usually had clear and specific ideas of what they wanted when they reported their daughters to the authorities. Most did not intend to relinquish the care and control of their children to the court; rather, they expected court officials to bolster their parental authority and to help them raise their daughters on their own terms. They thought that a stern reprimand by the referee and sometimes a brief detention in Juvenile Hall would make their daughters more submissive to parental orders. One mother wrote the following to court officials about her daughter, who was sent to Juvenile Hall for staying out late at night: "I am very glad to know that there is such a place as the juvenile court to look after matters of that kind as it sure does save many a young girl from ruin. I will be glad to have [Edith] come home again and hope that she will be obedient. If you can help me in any way to give her a good scare on that subject I would be much obliged."[64]

In numerous cases, court officials did help to strengthen parental authority in the home. Mrs. Bishop, whose case was discussed above, successfully used the court to restrain her daughter Helen, who insisted on drinking, attending cafés, and working in a movie theater despite her mother's objections. When Helen appeared in court, referee Van Waters reprimanded her for disobeying her mother: "I want you to understand, [Helen], you are not entitled to do as you please. . . . You have to obey and do as your mother says just exactly as she says and you are not to have friends she does not approve of and neither are you to go places she does not approve of."[65] At Bishop's request, the referee placed Helen under the supervision of a probation officer and instructed her to stay out of cafés and to quit her current job and enroll in a commercial course.

When one immigrant mother brought her teenage daughter into court for skipping work at the telephone company to attend movies and evening entertainments with friends, the referee again reinforced parental authority with a stern lecture. "If we let you go home," she told the girl, "I want you to understand you are to speak to your mother and obey her. You write down here what you are willing to do about going to work and obeying her in the home." With the referee's prodding, the girl made the following written pledge: "I hereby promise to all ways [sic] obey my Mother and be good to her. I am willing to go back and work for the telephone company."[66]

A few parents called for more drastic measures than a stern lecture or a short-term detention in Juvenile Hall. They wanted the court to place their daughters in a reformatory for a longer period of confinement. Families requested institutionalization for specific reasons, often to restrain rebellious daughters or to punish them for sexual misconduct. Mrs. Sutter, for example, asked the court to place her seventeen-year-old daughter Jean in the House of the Good Shepherd in order to keep her away from the "Mexican boys" she ran around with in the neighborhood. The court kept Jean in the institution for five months, until her mother was able to find a job for her daughter in the same establishment where she herself worked.[67] Other parents saw institutional commitment as a way to hide the shame of a "ruined" daughter. In two previously discussed cases, Mr. Reynolds and Mr. Sánchez had called on the court to confine and punish daughters who had disgraced the family name by engaging in sex before marriage.[68] But even when they requested institutionalization, most parents still expected to retain authority over their daughters. They meant for the confinement to be temporary, and they expected to be the ones who would determine when their daughters would return home. Both the Sánchez and the Reynolds families called for the release of their daughters after several months.

In some instances, mothers and fathers disagreed about the need to remove their daughters from the home. In the case of the Franzes and their daughter Marguerite, Mr. Franz agreed to have his daughter placed in the state reformatory for girls because she refused to perform the economic and household duties he expected of her, but Mrs. Franz at first pleaded with the court to let Marguerite return home. She explained that she would miss her daughter and needed her help. In the end, court officials persuaded Mrs. Franz to have Marguerite sent to the state reformatory, though her reasons were different from her husband's. She decided that the reformatory would provide Marguerite with a better home life and protect her from her father's abuse. As she told the court, "I like you to put her in Whittier [juvenile reformatory] where she got a good home; she got nothing home, and there a good home. And her papa talk bad to her, and it makes me sick if she cry for me to take her away."[69]

Court officials expressed still other reasons for sending Marguerite to the reform school. They were far more concerned about her sexual delinquency than about her refusal to work. The pelvic exam administered in Juvenile Hall revealed that Marguerite was not a virgin; she admitted that she had engaged in sex with an older man in the neighborhood in exchange for money. Women officials considered the Franzes incapable of supervising their daughter properly and thought that without the control and training provided by the reformatory, Marguerite would present a moral danger to herself and the rest of society.

In the cases just described, court decisions happened to coincide with parental goals. In other cases, however, parents were less successful in obtaining a court decision that met their needs. Conflicts most frequently resulted when court officials ordered a daughter's removal from the home against the wishes of her parents. As already noted, most parents had initiated court intervention with the expectation that their daughters would be sent home with instructions to obey them. To their great dismay, many discovered that the court instead had ordered detention or institutional placement to correct female delinquency.

This was the situation that confronted Mrs. Walker, the single mother who had asked the court to find and reprimand her runaway daughter Lydia. She had asked court officials simply to send Lydia back home with instructions to give up her dancing career and resume her previous job with the telephone company. Against Walker's vigorous objections, however, the court held Lydia in Juvenile Hall for three months once they discovered she had been sexually active. Under questioning by her probation officer, Lydia admitted spending the night with a sailor when she first arrived in San Francisco. To the consternation of court officials, she stated she had no intention of marrying this man. In addition to her unorthodox sexual behavior, Lydia had contracted a case of venereal disease, and the court followed its regular policy of detaining all infected girls in the hospital at Juvenile Hall until they were considered cured.

Walker visited the probation office on several occasions to plead for her daughter's release. She explained that she and her young son desperately needed Lydia's financial support. In response, the probation officer told Walker to report to county charities for assistance, because Lydia would not be released until her diseased condition improved. Too ashamed to seek county aid, Walker took in boarders and solicited relatives for financial support.[70]

This case aptly demonstrates that parents and court officials frequently defined the nature and causes of female delinquency differently and, consequently, sought different solutions. Walker complained about Lydia's neglect of her family obligations, while court officials focused on the young woman's sexual misconduct. To be sure, parents were also very concerned about moral behavior and, as already shown, many requested court intervention to restrain sexually active daughters. But such behavior was not always the only focus of concern for parents, whereas for the court it was.

Parents were just as troubled when a daughter withheld wages, refused to obey, or ran away from home. Her sexual activity was but one element in a configuration of behavior problems that worried them. The juvenile court, on the other hand, following a long tradition in the criminal justice system, identified sexual immorality as the primary form of delinquency for young women. Court procedures were designed to identify evidence of sexual misconduct. All girls who were arrested, no matter what their offense, faced compulsory pelvic examinations to determine if they were virgins and compulsory testing and treatment for venereal disease. In keeping with these policies, Lydia was tested and detained in Juvenile Hall hospital for three months until she was considered no longer infectious. The detention of daughters proved particularly harmful to single mothers like Mrs. Walker, for it deprived them of a crucial source of income and household assistance. The court's concern about sexual promiscuity and venereal disease often took precedence over the needs of working-class families.

Once the central problem—as defined by the court—was solved, the referee turned to Walker's concerns about her daughter. Lydia was placed on probation and allowed to return home after her release from the hospital. In the final court hearing, the referee instructed Lydia to obey her mother's orders: "to assist in the support of the family" and "to refrain from using any make-up on her face." As Walker requested, Lydia was to be kept under the supervision of a probation officer to see that she remained at home. In keeping with the court's preoccupation with sexual promiscuity and venereal disease, Lydia was also ordered to "entertain no more sailors in her home or otherwise."[71]

Working-class parents also encountered problems in court when their lifestyles and methods of child rearing did not conform to the standards envisioned by juvenile officials. By the very act of seeking court assistance, they opened their family lives to the scrutiny of officials and risked having their daughters removed from their care. The Taylors, for example, had originally called on the court for help with their pregnant teenage daughter, Pauline. They agreed to have her placed in the Truelove Home for unmarried mothers, but after she gave birth and agreed to give the child up for adoption, they wanted her sent back home. The court, however, had other plans for Pauline. Her probation officer strongly urged the referee not to allow Pauline to return to her parents, for "she did not receive the proper care when she was there and the present trouble is the direct result of neglect on the part of the parents." As a result of this recommendation, the court sent Pauline to live with her married sister and brother-in-law.

About a month and a half later, the probation officer discovered that Pauline had returned to her parents' home without the court's permission. When the officer went to retrieve the girl, her father insisted that she remain with him and his wife, but the court overruled the parents' wishes and placed their daughter in a private home to work as a domestic, because "the father and mother both work and [Pauline] has no supervision in her home." Pauline was not permitted to return to her parents until almost two years after her initial removal from their home. Although they were the ones who had initiated the court proceedings, the Taylors painfully discovered that they could not control the court's decisions concerning their own daughter.[72]

Single mothers had a particularly difficult time living up to court standards of family life and thus frequently faced the disapproval of court officials. They were most often chastised for taking paid employment outside of the home and for their failure to supervise their daughters adequately. These single mothers were caught in a double bind: they relied more heavily than other parents on court assistance with disobedient daughters, but they were also more vulnerable to court criticism for poor child-rearing methods. Such was the dilemma faced by Mrs. Balassa, a single mother who had migrated from Hungary to Los Angeles fifteen years earlier. A widow with five children, Balassa worked as a janitor to support her family and also depended on the wages her seventeen-year-old daughter Martha earned at the job she held in the evenings. In addition to wage-earning, Martha was expected to care for the younger children during the day while her mother worked.[73]

Balassa originally requested the court's help when Martha began to skip work to go out in the evenings with friends. Court officials detained Martha for a short period in Juvenile Hall and then sent her home with strict instructions to obey her mother. A year later, the probation officer learned that the teenager was again missing work and staying out late at night. Martha insisted on having some control over her earnings and social activities. She used part of her wages for evening entertainments and had become sexually intimate with a young man she was dating and hoped to marry. Balassa merely wanted the court to remind Martha of her family responsibilities. Referee Van Waters, however, had other plans. She had Martha committed to the House of the Good Shepherd, both to curb her sex delinquency and to remove her from her mother's poor supervision.

Balassa vigorously protested her daughter's removal and repeatedly visited the probation office and the House of the Good Shepherd to demand Martha's release. She explained to the referee that she was desperate for Martha's wages and her help at home: "Mrs. Anderson [the probation officer], she promised to look and maybe get me a little help from the county, but she didn't keep her word and I need [Martha] for the baby girl and I want her now. In the morning I have to go at half past eight and I don't think it is right to have my three year baby left with the boys." Van Waters refused to comply with the request and instead criticized Balassa for working outside the home and failing to care adequately for her daughter: "This girl was placed in your care. . . . How long did she stay good?" A representative from the House of the Good Shepherd confirmed the referee's assessment. She stated that "the mother is away and [Martha] would be left alone to her own resources. The mother failed in the attempt to supervise [Martha] when we placed her there before."[74]

Regardless of what the juvenile court officials might prefer, it was impossible for Balassa not to work when she had no male breadwinner and five children to support. Even after the probation officer offered to help, she had been refused financial aid from the county. She had provided her children with as much supervision as her straitened circumstances permitted. The court's actions in this case only made conditions worse for the entire Balassa family, as Martha's confinement deprived the family of her wages and her assistance in taking care of the younger children during the day.

The cases of the Balassas and other families discussed in this chapter demonstrate the serious conflicts over social and sexual autonomy that plagued working-class families during this period. In pursuit of personal ambitions, many daughters rebelled against the demands of the family economy and traditional social expectations of young women. In response, some working-class parents turned to the juvenile court for assistance in reasserting their authority. Thus, even as the state assumed greater authority over moral behavior, families still continued to play an important role in the regulation of sexual conduct. Even when they requested court assistance, however, parents could not always shape court decisions to meet their needs. They confronted an institution with considerable power to intervene in their lives to enforce dominant standards of child rearing and moral conduct.

. . . .

*I*n the late nineteenth and early twentieth centuries, middle-class white women organized impressive campaigns to gain moral protection, provided by the state, for young working-class women. Through an extensive network of women's clubs and reform organizations, they achieved substantial changes in the legal system, first by raising the age of consent in all states, and then through the establishment of special police forces, juvenile courts, detention centers, and reformatories for girls in which women officials had a large role. Most of these reformers saw their efforts as part of the larger struggle to overcome women's subordination in society; they intended for their legal reforms to shield young women and girls from sexual danger and exploitation. But in the end, the legal measures advocated by reformers did little to address the more common forms of sexual exploitation of working-class women and girls and, in fact, led to coercive and repressive measures against them.

This unintended consequence of social purity campaigns resulted both from the limits on women's ability to shape the operation of justice and from the class and racial biases that informed their efforts. Age-of-consent reformers managed to persuade lawmakers to enact legislation designed to punish male seducers, but they did not control the instruments of state power that enforced the law. The male police officers, judges, and legal officials responsible for enforcement generally had little sympathy with reformers' feminist goals. In their view, the law served to bolster the interests of fathers, husbands, and the state by preserving the chastity of daughters and future wives and preventing the propagation of "illegitimate" and "unfit" offspring. Male officials did not treat the young women who passed through the courts as "victims" but rather as immoral seductresses who had led unsuspecting men astray. In such hands, the law was used to humiliate and punish young women who did not conform to dominant standards of female respectability. In addition, because court officials reserved the harshest punishments for African American men, the law became a tool for reinforcing racial discrimination within the criminal justice system.

In the second phase of the moral reform effort, women in the Progressive movement not only called for state protection of young women through the juvenile justice system but also struggled to win control over the enforcement process through the appointment of women police officers, judges, and probation officers. For the first time in American history, women gained access to official positions within the criminal justice system, one of the main institutions of state power. But despite their success, middle-class women still confronted restrictions on their authority within the legal system. They were confined to handling girls' cases in juvenile court and thus could not control how male judges and law enforcement officials dealt with the cases of male moral offenders. Male officials tended to treat young men charged with sexual offenses leniently, whereas women officials exercised considerably more stringent controls over teenage girls for similar offenses. As a result, the juvenile court perpetuated a long-standing gender bias within the criminal justice system, in which women traditionally have been punished for illicit sexual behavior far more harshly than men.[1]

The limits on women's authority were particularly evident during World War I, in the social hygiene campaign to eliminate immorality and disease from the armed forces. The federal government used Progressive institutions and the services of women professionals to carry out a discriminatory program of compulsory examination and incarceration of women and girls suspected of moral offenses. Progressive women were unable to shape this campaign in accordance with their stated desire to protect and rehabilitate wayward female youths. When the failure of their goals became evident, some resigned, but others continued to lend their expertise to the government's biased and punitive campaign.

In addition to the external constraints on their authority, white purity activists were hampered in their efforts by their own race and class biases. Age-of-consent reformers reflected the racism of the dominant society by extending their protection only to white women and girls, ignoring the severe forms of sexual exploitation that African American women faced by virtue of their race. They also ignored African American women's concerns about the blatant racial discrimination shown in the handling of sex crimes, in particular the brutal treatment of black men and the racist stereotyping of them as rapists of white women. Progressives did broaden their protective campaign to include young immigrant women, and a few reformers reached across racial boundaries to address the needs of young black women. The concerns of African Americans remained marginal to Progressive efforts, however, because black women reformers were essentially excluded from the new professional positions within the juvenile justice system and thus had little voice in shaping public policies.

White reformers may have ignored African American women, but they quickly assumed a mantle of moral authority with respect to the white working-class girls they aimed to safeguard. Protection campaigns, whatever their ultimate goals, were rooted in a middle-class ideology of female sexual modesty and restraint. The age-of-consent reformers of the late nineteenth century envisioned teenage girls as morally pure, innocent, and passionless. Progressive women viewed sexual awakening as a normal part of female adolescence, but they believed that this energy had to be directed into other channels, such as athletics or schooling, until the young woman had reached the point of adulthood and marriage. Neither group of reformers was willing to tolerate positive assertions of sexuality on the part of working-class teenage girls. In fact, the underlying agenda of the protection campaigns was an attempt to mold young women according to middle-class standards of female respectability. Those who did not conform to these standards were defined as helpless victims or as troubled delinquents—in either case, young women who required strict supervision and control by the state.

Thus, even after the new group of women professionals had gained some enforcement power within the juvenile courts and police departments, they still administered a system that punished young women for sexual misconduct. These middle-class women did devote greater attention to the particular problems of adolescent girls, and they challenged the harsh, gender-biased attitudes of male legal officials toward female moral offenders. But at the same time, they never doubted that the young women in question should be disciplined and rehabilitated, and they did not hesitate to use their legal authority toward that end.

For working-class daughters, though, sexuality had a more complex set of meanings than middle-class ideology allowed. The teenage girls who were apprehended by legal authorities had formed sexual relationships in a range of social contexts. Some were seeking intimacy and pleasure with steady boyfriends; others were rebelling against rigid family and social conventions; a number were looking for adventure and excitement to enliven a difficult, hard-pressed existence; and still others used sex as a strategy for survival in the face of poverty, abuse, and family hardship.

Working-class girls were clearly exploited in the sexual realm. Gender and class discrimination meant that engaging in sex outside of marriage entailed serious risks for them. They were sexually abused by boyfriends and male relatives, faced out-of-wedlock pregnancies, underwent illegal, often dangerous abortions, and suffered social ostracism and rejection by their families.

Yet the measures promoted in the social purity campaigns did little to address the sources of sexual exploitation. Middle-class reformers did attempt to hold young women's male partners accountable for out-of-wedlock pregnancies and sexual assaults, but their main objective was to protect adolescent girls by restricting their sexual expression. They did not try to empower these young women, economically and socially, to challenge the sexual exploitation they faced. Instead, age-of-consent laws and the juvenile court system merely perpetuated the stigma and supported the punishment of working-class females who engaged in unorthodox sexual behavior.

Although the new laws were created and enforced by middle-class reformers and professionals, working-class parents also played a critical role in the policing of adolescent female sexuality. As this study has shown, many parents, working in conjunction with court officials, used the legal system to restrain rebellious daughters. The concern that working-class parents voiced about their daughters' sexuality, however, should not be interpreted as a sign that they had merely absorbed middle-class notions of morality, but rather as a reflection of their own economic circumstances, family structures, and cultural and religious beliefs.

In demonstrating the agency of working-class families, it is important not to overestimate their power and influence within the legal system. Parents could initiate cases, but they could not necessarily count on court decisions to fit their needs, for they were not equal partners in the negotiation process. Some parents used the legal system effectively, but others found themselves subjected to scrutiny and criticism because their lifestyles and child-rearing practices did not conform to court standards. Officials had extensive powers of intervention in the lives of working-class families, and if they judged parents to be negligent or incompetent, they had the legal authority to remove children from the home.

During the 1920s, the intense public anxiety about female promiscuity that had fueled moral protection campaigns began to subside as a result of several developments. The new sexual mores first evident among working-class daughters in American cities were increasingly adopted by middle-class teenagers in a somewhat tamer form and consequently appeared less threatening. Middle-class teenage girls displayed a more liberal sexual style by wearing shorter skirts, makeup, and bobbed hair and by experimenting with new social customs. Instead of receiving male admirers at home, young women went out on "dates" to movies and dance halls, and they often engaged in "petting," which included a range of erotic encounters just short of intercourse, from kissing to fondling. Sex surveys indicate that middle-class women who came of age in the 1920s engaged in premarital intercourse more often than those born in preceding decades. Generally, intercourse was confined to relationships with their "steadies" or men they expected to marry, but this development nevertheless marked an important shift in middle-class sexual behavior.[2]

Furthermore, a new ideology that endorsed heterosexual pleasure became increasingly pronounced among middle-class Americans in the 1920s. Physicians, psychologists, educators, and other social experts rejected the Victorian emphasis on sexual restraint and repression and promoted heterosexual desire as a positive good—something important to individual happiness and successful marriages. They advocated a new ideal of "companionate marriage" that urged spouses to be both amiable companions and pleasing sexual partners for one another. Sexual liberals acknowledged, even encouraged, female sexual expression but nonetheless set clear limits on women's behavior. It was all right for women to arouse male desire but not to initiate or control romantic relations; women could be sexually alluring but had to channel their desires into heterosexual relations and marriage. Within the context of this new sexual ethic, the frigid female and the lesbian came to seem more threatening and deviant than the promiscuous girl, because they rejected male sexual advances altogether.[3]

But even though the social panic over the heterosexual activity of young women may have subsided, the legal mechanisms of control that had resulted from moral protection campaigns remained firmly in place. The extensive system of courts, special police, detention centers, and reformatories established by purity reformers continued to monitor and regulate the sexuality of young women and girls throughout most of the twentieth century. The class and gender biases inherent in this system also persisted. It was still poor and working-class teenage girls who were disproportionally accused of sexual misconduct. And the double standard of morality that punished young women more often and more severely than men for similar sexual offenses persisted long after the reform movements had run their course.[4]

APPENDIX: A NOTE ON COURT RECORDS

. . . .

CHAPTERS 2 AND 3

The analysis of statutory rape prosecutions in Chapters 2 and 3 are based on two bodies of court records: (1) all prosecutions for statutory rape in the Alameda County Superior Court for the decade 1910–20 (112 cases); and (2) all prosecutions for statutory rape in the Los Angeles Juvenile Court for the years 1910 (8 cases) and 1920 (23 cases).

The unusually rich and complete body of felony trial court records from the Alameda County Superior Court are particularly fruitful for examining the enforcement of age-of-consent legislation. The two major sources of information are the register of actions and the case files. The register lists the defendant's name, case number, charge, and a summary of the legal processing of each case. The case files contain the official complaint and verbatim trial transcripts from the preliminary hearings that took place in the lower courts.

For the Los Angeles County Juvenile Court, case files of delinquent youth for each decade year beginning with 1910 have been preserved on microfilm. A complete case file contains a verbatim trial transcript, detailed probation report, and summary of the legal processing of the case. Most of the 1920 case files are complete, but many of the 1910 files are not. I have therefore relied on the 1920 case files alone for statistical analyses but have used both sets of records for qualitative descriptions of the cases.

Not all of the Alameda and Los Angeles court records that I have used for statistical analyses contain full information on each case. I have therefore indicated in the footnotes the number of case records (N) that have information on the particular subject under discussion and have made the calculations on the basis of this number.

When discussing individual cases, I have changed the names of the young women, parents, male partners, and relatives, although I have attempted to retain their particular ethnic characteristics.

CHAPTERS 5 AND 6

The analyses of juvenile court cases in Chapters 5 and 6 are based on case files from the Los Angeles County Juvenile Court. I have analyzed the entire case load of delinquent girls who came before the court in 1910 (96 cases) and 1920 (220 cases). I have not included the cases of dependent girls—that is, those who were taken to the juvenile court as a result of neglect or abandonment by the guardians. Because many of the 1910 case files are incomplete, I have relied on the 1920 case files alone for statistical analyses but have used both sets of records for qualitative descriptions of the cases. Unless otherwise indicated, where I have made comparisons with cases involving boys, I have relied on an analysis of a 10 percent sample of all delinquent boys who appeared before the court in 1920 (166 cases).

Not all of the 1920 records contain full information on each case. I have therefore indicated in the footnotes the number of case records (N) that have information on the particular subject under discussion and have made the calculations on the basis of this number.

When discussing individual cases, I have changed the names of the young women, parents, male partners, and relatives, although I have attempted to retain their particular ethnic characteristics.

NOTES

. . . .

ABBREVIATIONS USED IN NOTES

CU   Columbia University Rare Book and Manuscript Library, New York, N.Y.

ESDP   Ethel Sturges Dummer Papers, Arthur and Elizabeth Schlesinger Library, Radcliffe College, Cambridge, Mass.

HL   Huntington Library, San Marino, California

LAPL   Los Angeles Public Library, Los Angeles, Calif.

MVWP   Miriam Van Waters Papers, Arthur and Elizabeth Schlesinger Library, Radcliffe College, Cambridge, Mass.

NA   National Archives, Washington, D.C.

SL   The Arthur and Elizabeth Schlesinger Library, Radcliffe College, Cambridge, Mass.

UCLA   University Research Library, Department of Special Collections, University of California, Los Angeles, Calif.

WCTU   Woman's Christian Temperance Union

YWCA   Young Women's Christian Association

INTRODUCTION

1. D'Emilio and Freedman, *Intimate Matters*, pp. 140–45; Stansell, *City of Women*, chap. 9; Hobson, *Uneasy Virtue*, chap. 3; Smith-Rosenberg, "Beauty, the Beast, and the Militant Woman."

2. D'Emilio and Freedman, *Intimate Matters*, chap. 7; Friedman, *Crime and Punishment*, pp. 134–39, 324–44; Boyer, *Purity in Print*; Mohr, *Abortion in America*; Reagan, "When Abortion Was a Crime"; Rosen, *Lost Sisterhood*.

3. Hill, *Women in Gainful Occupations*, p. 45; Kessler-Harris, *Out to Work*, chaps. 5–6; Peiss, *Cheap Amusements*, pp. 38–41; Weiner, *From Working Girl to Working Mother*, pp. 27–30; Amott and Matthaei, *Race, Gender, and Work*, chaps. 9–10. On African American women's employment, see Jones, *Labor of Love*, chaps. 3–5; Amott and Matthaei, *Race, Gender, and Work*, pp. 157–90.

4. Ewen, *Immigrant Women*, chap. 12; Peiss, *Cheap Amusements*, chaps. 2–6; Glenn, *Daughters of the Shtetl*, pp. 159–66; Erenberg, *Steppin' Out*; Kasson, *Amusing the Million*.

5. Peiss, *Cheap Amusements*, pp. 108–14; Peiss, "'Charity Girls' and City

Pleasures"; Lunbeck, "'A New Generation of Women'"; Meyerowitz, *Women Adrift*, pp. 101–16.

6. Historians have offered various interpretations of moral reform movements. Some scholars have characterized them as conservative reactions to the disruptive economic and social changes of the period. See Boyer, *Urban Masses and Moral Order*, pts. 3 and 4; Filene, *Himself/Herself*, pp. 80–93; Connelly, *Response to Prostitution*; Schlossman and Wallach, "Crime of Precocious Sexuality."

Feminist historians have offered different interpretations of social purity reform. Some have viewed purity movements as women's efforts to challenge male sexual privilege and to overcome women's subordination in the home and society. See, for example, Freedman, "Sexuality in Nineteenth-Century America," pp. 208–9; Smith-Rosenberg, "Beauty, the Beast, and the Militant Woman"; Degler, *At Odds*, chap. 12; Rosen, *Lost Sisterhood*, chap. 4.

According to other feminist scholars, social purity reformers did indeed set forth a critique of male sexuality, but they did so by advocating a rigid moral code that denied women's sexual self-determination and reinforced distinctions between "good" and "bad" female behavior. See DuBois and Gordon, "Seeking Ecstasy on the Battlefield"; Ryan, "Power of Women's Networks"; Hobson, *Uneasy Virtue*. For a similar interpretation of social purity movements in Britain, see Walkowitz, *Prostitution and Victorian Society* and "Male Vice and Female Virtue."

7. For scholars who have relied on a social control framework to explain moral reform, see Boyer, *Urban Masses and Moral Order*; Filene, *Himself/ Herself*, pp. 69–93. Among scholars of the juvenile justice system who have used this interpretation, see Platt, *Child Savers*; Schlossman and Wallach, "Crime of Precocious Sexuality"; Shelden, "Sex Discrimination in the Juvenile Justice System." For a recent study that emphasizes the agency of working-class people within the juvenile justice system, see Schneider, *In the Web of Class*.

8. Gordon, "Feminism and Social Control" and *Heroes of Their Own Lives*; Pleck, "Challenges to Traditional Authority"; Pascoe, *Relations of Rescue*.

9. For this interpretation of daughters' roles within the working-class family, see Tentler, *Wage-Earning Women*, chap. 4; Yans-McLaughlin, *Family and Community*. For alternative interpretations, see Peiss, *Cheap Amusements*, pp. 67–72; Ewen, *Immigrant Women*, pp. 105–9.

10. Hartmann, "Family as the Locus of Gender," p. 111.

11. The literature on moral reform has focused almost exclusively on developments in the Northeast and Midwest. A notable exception is Pascoe's *Relations of Rescue*, which addresses female moral reform in the West.

CHAPTER ONE

1. A copy of the petition can be found in *Union Signal*, January 13, 1887, p. 12. See also WCTU of Northern California, *Annual Report*, 1888, p. 85; ibid., 1889, pp. 113–14; Spencer, *History of the Woman's Christian Temperance Union*, pp. 38, 47–48; Gullett, "Feminism, Politics, and Voluntary Groups," pp. 44–50.

2. WCTU of Northern California, *Annual Report*, 1889, pp. 113–14; Spencer, *History of the Woman's Christian Temperance Union*, pp. 47–48, 68.

3. On the social purity movement in the United States, see Pivar, *Purity Crusade*; D'Emilio and Freedman, *Intimate Matters*, pp. 147–56; Gordon, *Woman's Body, Woman's Right*, chap. 6. For an analysis of a similar social purity movement in Canada, see Valverde, *Age of Light, Soap, and Water*. An earlier period of moral reform took place in the United States in the 1830s and 1840s in northeastern cities and towns. On this movement, see Hobson, *Uneasy Virtue*, pp. 49–76; Smith-Rosenberg, "Beauty, the Beast, and the Militant Woman"; Boylan, "Women in Groups."

4. Bordin, *Woman and Temperance*, chaps. 1, 6; Bordin, *Frances Willard*; Mary Earhart Dillon, "Frances Willard," in James, James, and Boyer, eds., *Notable American Women*, 3:615–17; Scott, *Natural Allies*, pp. 93–103.

5. Meyerowitz, *Women Adrift*, pp. 44–55; Pivar, *Purity Crusade*, pp. 103–10; Freedman, *Their Sisters' Keepers*, chap. 7.

6. Bordin, *Woman and Temperance*, pp. 110–11; DeCosta, *White Cross*; Frances Willard, "Social Purity Work for 1887," *Union Signal*, January 13, 1887, p. 12; Rev. C. E. St. John, "The White Cross—Its Origin and Mission," *Philanthropist*, January 1888, pp. 1–3.

7. On women's role in abolitionism, see Hersh, *Slavery of Sex*; Yellin, *Women and Sisters*; Melder, *Beginnings of Sisterhood*, chaps. 5, 6; Midgley, *Women against Slavery*.

8. For an analysis of the racist dimensions of sexual reform campaigns in Canada, see Valverde, "When the Mother of the Race Is Free."

9. Walkowitz, "Male Vice and Female Virtue," p. 425. On efforts to raise the age of consent in England, see also Gorham, "'Maiden Tribute to Modern Babylon' Re-examined"; Pivar, *Purity Crusade*, pp. 132–35; Walkowitz, *City of Deadful Delight*, chap. 3.

10. "Mr. Stead's Case," *New York Daily Tribune*, November 29, 1885; "Mr. Stead and His 'Party,'" *New York Daily Tribune*, December 20, 1885.

11. Georgia Mark, "The Age of Consent," *Union Signal*, December 3, 1885, p. 4.

12. Blackstone, *Commentaries on the Laws of England*, 4:212; Mark, "Age of Consent"; Grossberg, *Governing the Hearth*, pp. 106–7.

13. Aaron M. Powell to Elizabeth Gay, January 5, 1886, Sidney Howard Gay Collection, CU.

14. "Legal Protection for Young Girls," *Philanthropist*, January 1886, p. 4.

15. *Union Signal*, January 13, 1887, p. 12; National WCTU, *Minutes*, 1886, pp. xxxvi–xxxvii; Willard, *Glimpses of Fifty Years*, pp. 419–24.

16. The quote from Stanton is found in the preface she wrote for Helen Gardener's book, *Pray You, Sir, Whose Daughter?* (New York: R. F. Renno and Co., 1892), p. viii. For a sampling of articles from the *Woman's Journal* dealing with the age of consent, see "Protection of Young Girls" (March 20, 1886), "Suffrage Needed for Protection" (April 24, 1886), "Legislation for Women in 1886" (September 18, 1886), "Shameful Vote in Kansas Senate" (February 23, 1889), "Age of Protection in Michigan" (April 20, 1895), "The Age of Protection" (February 15, 1896), "To Protect California Girls" (September 14, 1902).

17. The legislative activity on the age-of-consent issue by state suffrage organizations is recorded in the separate chapters on each state, usually under the section "Legislative Action and Laws," in Anthony and Harper, eds., *History of Woman Suffrage*, 4:465–1011.

18. Willard, *Glimpses of Fifty Years*, pp. 422–24; Frances Willard, "Three Weeks of Campaigning," *Union Signal*, February 17, 1887, pp. 4–5; National WCTU, *Minutes*, 1888, pp. 143–44.

19. On the use of the seduction narrative by early nineteenth-century moral reformers, see Hobson, *Uneasy Virtue*, pp. 56–61. For other discussions of the seduction narrative, see Meyerowitz, *Women Adrift*, pp. 49–50; Kunzel, *Fallen Women, Problem Girls*, pp. 19–25.

209. Gardener, *Is This Your Son, My Lord?*; Adelaide Washburn, "Helen Hamilton Gardener," in James, James, and Boyer, eds., *Notable American Women*, 2:12.

21. Gardener, *Pray You, Sir, Whose Daughter?*

22. Thomas, "The Double Standard."

23. Frances Willard, "A Woman's Plea for Purity," *Philanthropist*, February 1887, p. 2.

24. National WCTU, *Minutes*, 1885, p. 74; Willard, *Glimpses of Fifty Years*, p. 421.

25. "Masculine Immorality," *Arena* 3 (February 1891): 382.

26. National WCTU, *Minutes*, 1885, p. 74.

27. Helen H. Gardener, "What Shall the Age of Consent Be?," *Arena* 11 (January 1895): 196–98.

28. Emily Blackwell, "Age of Consent Legislation," *Philanthropist*, February 1895, p. 1–2.

29. On the sexual relations of young working-class women and girls, see Chap. 2. See also Brumberg, "'Ruined Girls'"; Hobson, *Uneasy Virtue*, pp. 59–61.

30. Hill, *Women in Gainful Occupations*, pp. 36–45; Peiss, *Cheap Amusements*, pp. 35–38; Stansell, *City of Women*, pp. 11–18, 105–29, 155–68. For a historical overview of women's role in the labor force, see Kessler-Harris, *Out to Work*; Tentler, *Wage-Earning Women*; Amott and Matthaei, *Race, Gender, and Work*.

31. On women's paid labor in the nineteenth century, see Stansell, *City of Women*, chaps. 6, 8; Kessler-Harris, *Out to Work*, chap. 2; Amott and Matthaei, *Race, Gender, and Work*, chap. 9. The statistics on female employment are found in Hill, *Women in Gainful Occupations*, p. 45.

32. Weiner, *From Working Girl to Working Mother*, pp. 4–7; Hill, *Women in Gainful Occupations*, pp. 67–69. In 1910, 61 percent of women workers were single, 15 percent were widowed or divorced, and 24 percent were married.

33. Hill, *Women in Gainful Occupations*, p. 45; Weiner, *From Working Girl to Working Mother*, pp. 27–30; Kessler-Harris, *Out to Work*, chaps. 5, 6; Peiss, *Cheap Amusements*, pp. 38–41; Davies, *Women's Place*, pp. 59–61; Amott and Matthaei, *Race, Gender, and Work*, chaps. 9–10.

34. For an excellent discussion of working-class amusements in the nineteenth century, see Peiss, *Cheap Amusements*, chap. 1; see also Rosenzweig, *Eight Hours for What We Will*.

35. Ewen, *Immigrant Women*, chap. 12; Peiss, *Cheap Amusements*, chaps. 2–6; Erenberg, *Steppin' Out*; Kasson, *Amusing the Million*; May, *Screening Out the Past*. On urban youth culture in nineteenth-century New York City, see Stansell, *City of Women*, pp. 89–101.

36. Brumberg, "'Ruined Girls'"; Hobson, *Uneasy Virtue*, pp. 59–61.

37. On the changes in sexual mores among young, working-class women, see Peiss, *Cheap Amusements*, pp. 108–14; Peiss, "'Charity Girls' and City Pleasures"; Lunbeck, "'A New Generation of Women'"; Meyerowitz, *Women Adrift*, pp. 101–16. On premarital pregnancy rates, see D'Emilio and Freedman, *Intimate Matters*, pp. 199–200; Smith and Hindus, "Premarital Pregnancy in America"; Smith, "Dating of the American Sexual Revolution."

38. Holly quoted in Gardener, "A Battle for Sound Morality," pt. 2, p. 5; Willard, "A Woman's Plea for Purity."

39. Holly quoted in Gardener, "A Battle for Sound Morality," pt. 2, p. 6.

40. Lerner, ed., *Black Women in White America*, pp. 172–88; Jones, *Labor of Love*, pp. 149–50. On rape as a tool of racial terror and control, see Davis, "Rape, Racism, and the Myth of the Black Rapist"; Hine, "Rape and the Inner Lives of Black Women in the Middle West"; Hall, "'The Mind That Burns in Each Body.'"

41. Lerner, ed., *Black Women in White America*, pp. 155–56; see also pp. 151–55, 158–59.

42. Ibid., pp. 155–56.

43. Salem, *To Better Our World*, pp. 18–31; Gordon, "Black and White Visions of Welfare," pp. 568–70, 578–79; White, "Cost of Club Work," pp. 254–60.

44. Terrell quoted in Salem, *To Better Our World*, p. 51. On social purity work in the NACW and other black women's organizations, see *Woman's Era* 2 (July 1895): 2; 2 (August 1895): 1; 3 (July 1896): 5. See also Salem, *To Better Our World*, pp. 18–31, 36–37, 44–51; Hamilton, "National Association of Colored Women," pp. 10–26, 69–75; Jenkins, "History of the Black Woman's Club Movement," pp. 65–67, 95–99; Moses, "Domestic Feminism Conservatism"; White, "Cost of Club Work," pp. 254–60.

45. Hamilton, "National Association of Colored Women," pp. 110–11; Salem, *To Better Our World*, pp. 20–21; Fannie Barrier Williams, "The Intellectual Progress of the Colored Women of the United States since the Emancipation Proclamation" (1893),in Loewenberg and Bogin, eds., *Black Women in Nineteenth-Century American Life*, pp. 274–75.

46. Cooper, *A Voice from the South*, pp. 24–25.

47. *Woman's Era* 1 (March 1894): 1; ibid. 2 (November 1895): 14; Salem, *To Better Our World*, pp. 44–48, 90–92; Hamilton, "National Association of Colored Women," pp. 74–75; Jenkins, "History of the Black Woman's Club Movement," pp. 49–50, 80–83; Peebles-Wilkins, "Black Women and American Social Welfare," pp. 983–84.

48. *Woman's Era* 2 (January 1896): 3.

49. Hamilton, "National Association of Colored Women," pp. 70, 100–101; Gordon, "Black and White Visions of Welfare," p. 579; *Woman's Era* 2 (July 1895): 1; ibid. 2 (January 1896): 3.

50. I found evidence of only one black women's group—the Woman's Club of Omaha, Nebraska—that supported the age-of-consent campaign. See *Woman's Era* 2 (August 1895): 7.

51. Hall, *Revolt against Chivalry*, chap. 5; Hall, "'The Mind That Burns in Each Body'"; NAACP, *Thirty Years of Lynching in the United States, 1889–1918*; Davis, "Rape, Racism, and the Myth of the Black Rapist"; Hodes, "Sexualization of Reconstruction Politics"; Wells, "A Red Record" and "Southern Horrors."

52. On the antilynching campaign, see Lerner, ed., *Black Women in White America*, pp. 193–215; Salem, *To Better Our World*, pp. 51–52; Thompson, *Ida B. Wells-Barnett*, pp. 25–84; Wells, *Crusade for Justice*, chaps. 6–26.

53. Willard quoted in Bordin, *Frances Willard*, p. 216.

54. "Resolutions," *Union Signal*, December 6, 1894, p. 18; Wells, "A Red Record," p. 236. On the conflict between black clubwomen and the WCTU over this issue of lynching, see Wells, "A Red Record," pp. 226–39; Thompson, *Ida B. Wells-Barnett*, pp. 56–61; Bordin, *Frances Willard*, pp. 216–17; *Woman's Era* 1 (June 1894): 6–7; ibid. 2 (July 1895): 12; ibid. 2 (August 1895): 16–17.

55. *Woman's Era* 2 (July 1895): 12.

56. Ibid. 2 (August 1895): 16.

57. Ibid. 1 (June 1894): 6–7.

58. Ibid.

59. National WCTU, *Minutes*, 1887, pp. clxxi–clxxv; Anthony and Harper, eds., *History of Woman Suffrage*, vol. 4 (see separate chaps. on each state, pp. 465–1011). During the 1880s, Montana, Nebraska, and Delaware raised the age of consent to fifteen; Arizona, California, Connecticut, North Dakota, South Dakota, Illinois, Maine, Massachusetts, Michigan, Missouri, Nevada, Rhode Island, Vermont, Wisconsin, and Wyoming raised the age to fourteen; and Iowa and Utah raised the age to thirteen.

60. Anthony and Harper, eds., *History of Woman Suffrage*, 4:649–51; National WCTU, *Minutes*, 1887, p. clxxv.

61. Gardener, "Shame of America," pp. 194–95; "Shameful Vote in Kansas Senate," *Woman's Journal*, February 23, 1889, p. 57; "Another Vicious 'Age of Consent' Bill," *Philanthropist*, March 1891, p. 4.

62. The two quotes are found in Nellie M. Richardson, "Report of the WCTU State Superintendent of Legislation and Petitions," *Arena* 14 (September 1895): 22, 27. On opponents' objections to women's political activity, see also Will Allen Dromgoole, "The Age of Consent in Tennessee," *Arena* 11 (January 1895): 212.

63. On opponents' use of the blackmail argument, see also "The Age of Consent," *Union Signal*, June 10, 1886, p. 3; "Mental Maturity the Age of Consent," *Woman's Journal*, March 27, 1886, p. 100; "How to Protect Men!," *Woman's Journal*, December 14, 1895, p. 396; "Opposing Views by Legislators on the Age of Consent: A Symposium," *Arena* 13 (July 1895): 216; Helen M. Stoddard, "Review of Age of Consent Legislation in Texas," *Arena* 14 (November 1895): 410; John Yeiser, "The Campaign in Nebraska," *Arena* 14 (September 1895): 27.

64. "Opposing Views by Legislators on the Age of Consent," p. 219.

65. Mapes, "Higher Enlightenment," p. 106.

66. Ada C. Bittenbender, "Report Criticized," *Union Signal*, January 6, 1887, p. 5. See also Mapes, "Higher Enlightenment," p. 106; Stoddard, "Review of Age of Consent Legislation," p. 410; Gardener, "A Battle for Sound Morality," pt. 3, p. 217.

67. Roberts, "Physical Maturity of Women," pp. 149–50.

68. Mapes, "Higher Enlightenment," p. 107.

69. A. C. Tompkins, "The Age of Consent from a Physio-Psychological Standpoint," *Arena* 13 (July 1895): 223. For other examples of legislators' use of racist arguments to oppose a higher age of consent, see Dromgoole, "Age of Consent in Tennessee," p. 211; Stoddard, "Review of Age of Consent Legisla-

tion," p. 410. On stereotypes of black female sexuality, see Lerner, ed., *Black Women in White America*, pp. 164–71; White, *Ar'n't I a Woman?*, pp. 27–46; Collins, *Black Feminist Thought*, pp. 77–78.

70. Tompkins, "Age of Consent," p. 223.

71. Richardson, "Report of the WCTU State Superintendent," p. 21; Stoddard, "Review of Age of Consent Legislation," p. 410.

72. Quoted in Anthony and Harper, eds., *History of Woman Suffrage*, 4:866. On the efforts to lower the age of consent in New York and Kansas, see also "Scheme to Lower the Age of Consent," *Philanthropist*, January 1889, p. 5; "Shameful Vote in Kansas Senate"; "Another Vicious 'Age of Consent' Bill."

73. Mott, *History of American Magazines*, pp. 401–16.

74. Gardener, "Shame of America," pp. 192–98. The four-part series of articles entitled "A Battle for Sound Morality" followed.

75. Gardener, "A Battle for Sound Morality."

76. Ibid., pt. 1, pp. 357–68.

77. "Brief of Dr. George W. Brush, on Bill Increasing Age of Consent to Eighteen Years in New York," *Arena* 13 (August 1895): 357–64; "Address of Dr. Ancil Martin, Arizona," *Arena* 13 (August 1895): 365–68; Gardener, "A Battle for Sound Morality," pt. 1, p. 356.

78. Bordin, *Woman and Temperance*, pp. 76–83; Scott, *Southern Lady*, pp. 135–50.

79. Bordin, *Woman and Temperance*, pp. 81–82, 111.

80. Tompkins, "Age of Consent," p. 223. For other examples of the use of racial arguments by legislators to oppose a higher age of consent, see Dromgoole, "Age of Consent in Tennessee," p. 211; Stoddard, "Review of Age of Consent Legislation," p. 410.

81. Many southern states enacted a statute, separate from the rape statute, to make sex with an underage female a criminal offense. The offense was typically referred to as "carnal knowledge of a female child."

82. Dromgoole, "Age of Consent in Tennessee," pp. 209–12; Stoddard, "Review of Age of Consent Legislation," pp. 408–11. On the campaign in Florida, Georgia, and Kentucky, see Anthony and Harper, eds., *History of Woman Suffrage*, 4:478–79, 581–86, 673–74. On the campaigns in Mississippi, Arkansas, and North Carolina, see Gardener, "A Battle for Sound Morality," pt. 4, pp. 401–8, 412–13.

83. These included California, Connecticut, Louisiana, North and South Dakota, Maryland, Maine, Massachusetts, Michigan, Montana, Ohio, Oregon, Rhode Island, Tennessee, and Vermont (Anthony and Harper, eds., *History of Woman Suffrage*, vol. 4).

84. *Woman's Bulletin*, June 1912, p. 15; ibid., February 1914, pp. 21–22; Spencer, *History of the Woman's Christian Temperance Union*, pp. 87–88, 104.

85. Anthony and Harper, eds., *History of Woman Suffrage*, 4:578–79, 6:133.

CHAPTER TWO

1. Alameda County Superior Court, Oakland, Calif., Case No. 6009 (1915). Cases are hereafter referred to as Alameda Case No. 6009 (1915).

2. Parents and relatives initiated close to half (46 percent, N=92) of the statutory rape cases heard before the Alameda court from 1910 to 1920; another 13 percent were initiated by the young women themselves and 38 percent by law enforcement officials. Families initiated more than half (57 percent, N=23) of such cases before the Los Angeles Juvenile Court; the remaining 43 percent were reported primarily by law enforcement officials. See Appendix for further information on the statistical calculations in this chapter.

3. In this and other chapters that draw on original case files, I have changed the names of the young women, male partners, family members, and others involved in the cases but have attempted to retain their ethnic distinctions.

4. The official complaint in statutory rape cases did not indicate if force was used. To determine whether a sexual encounter was consensual or forcible, I relied on how the young women themselves described their experiences in the transcripts of the court hearings.

5. For the Alameda County cases, N=106; for the Los Angeles County cases, N=22.

6. U.S. Bureau of the Census, *Tenth Census of the United States, 1880: Population*, 1:416, and *Fourteenth Census of the United States, 1920: Population*, 3:118; Johnson, *Second Gold Rush*, pp. 13–15; Fogelson, *Fragmented Metropolis*, chap. 4.

7. Johnson, *Second Gold Rush*, pp. 13–19; Bagwell, *Oakland*, pp. 69–73; Hinkel and McCann, *Oakland*, 2:812–902.

8. Bean and Rawls, *California*, pp. 188–93, 278–90; Clark, "Improbable Los Angeles," pp. 270–81; Fogelson, *Fragmented Metropolis*, chaps. 3–6; McWilliams, *Southern California*, pp. 113–37.

9. U.S. Bureau of the Census, *Twelfth Census of the United States, 1900: Population*, vol. 1, pt. 1, California; *Thirteenth Census of the United States, 1910: Population*, vol. 2, *Reports by States*, California; *Fourteenth Census of the United States, 1920: Population*, vol. 3, *Composition and Characteristics of the Population by States*, California; Bagwell, *Oakland*, pp. 81–90; Johnson, *Second Gold Rush*, pp. 16–17; Fogelson, *Fragmented Metropolis*, pp. 75–83.

10. U.S. Bureau of the Census, *Thirteenth Census of the United States, 1910: Abstract of the Census, Supplement for California*, p. 610.

11. Rosenbaum, *Free to Choose*, pp. 57–64; Vorspan and Gartner, *History of the Jews of Los Angeles*, pp. 117–19, 124–29.

12. Cinel, *From Italy to San Francisco*, chaps. 1, 6, 7; DiLeonardo, *Varieties of Ethnic Experience*, pp. 47–95; DiLeonardo, "Myth of the Urban Village"; Kirschner, "Italian in Los Angeles."

13. Hallinan, "Portuguese of California"; Pap, *Portuguese-American*, pp. 66–78, 130–55.

14. On Mexican immigrants, see Camarillo, *Chicanos in a Changing Society*; Griswold del Castillo, *La Familia*; Gamio, *Mexican Immigrant*; Romo, *East Los Angeles*; Ruiz, *Cannery Women*; Sánchez, *Becoming Mexican American*; Taylor, "Mexican Women in Los Angeles Industry."

15. Beaseley, *Negro Trail Blazers*; Bond, "Negro in Los Angeles"; Bunch, "Past Not Necessarily Prologue"; Crouchett, Bunch, and Winnacker, eds., *Visions toward Tomorrow*; De Graff, "The City of Black Angels."

16. On middle-class sexuality, see D'Emilio and Freedman, *Intimate Matters*, pp. 66–72; Barker-Benfield, *Horrors of the Half-Known Life*; Welter, "Cult of True Womanhood"; Cott, "Passionlessness"; Socolow, *Eros and Modernization*.

17. For this interpretation of working-class sexuality in nineteenth-century New York City, see Stansell, *City of Women*, pp. 85–101, 175–80. D'Emilio and Freedman also posit a sharp distinction between the sexual norms and attitudes of middle-class Americans and those of immigrants, workers, and African Americans (*Intimate Matters*, pp. 74–75, 183–88).

18. Tilly and Scott, *Women, Work, and Family*, pp. 31–42; Glenn, *Daughters of the Shtetl*, pp. 8–16, 79–89; Yans-McLaughlin, *Family and Community*, pp. 82–98; Tilly, Scott, and Cohen, "Women's Work," pp. 452–70.

19. D'Emilio and Freedman, *Intimate Matters*, pp. 4–6; Gutiérrez, *When Jesus Came*, pp. 241–43; Stone, *Family, Sex, and Marriage*, pp. 498–501; Noonan, *Contraception*, pp. 36–46, 131–39.

20. Smout, "Aspects of Sexual Behavior"; Thomas, "Double Standard."

21. Griswold del Castillo, *La Familia*, pp. 26–29; Gutiérrez, *When Jesus Came*, chaps. 5–7; Peristiany, ed., *Honor and Shame*; Pitt-Rivers, "Honor"; Schneider, "Of Vigilance and Virgins"; Yans-McLaughlin, *Family and Community*, pp. 82–84, 92–94.

22. Rothman, *Hands and Hearts*, pp 46–49; Smout, "Aspects of Sexual Behavior," pp. 210–13; Tilly and Scott, *Women, Work, and Family*, pp. 38–40; Engel, "Peasant Morality and Pre-Marital Relations," pp. 700–701.

23. DiLeonardo, *Varieties of Ethnic Experience*, pp. 48–54; Sánchez, *Becoming Mexican American*, pp. 26–27, 33–35; Yans-McLaughlin, *Family and Community*, pp. 52–54, 170–74; Glenn, *Daughters of the Shtetl*, pp. 16–26.

24. Cinel, *From Italy to San Francisco*, p. 189; Griswold del Castillo, *La Familia*, pp. 29, 76; Ewen, *Immigrant Women*, pp. 208–9; Glenn, *Daughters of the Shtetl*, pp. 82, 147, 157; Sánchez, *Becoming Mexican American*, pp. 31–35; Yans-McLaughlin, *Family and Community*, pp. 82–83.

25. Griswold del Castillo, *La Familia*, p. 29; Gutiérrez, *When Jesus Came*, p. 211; Engel, "Peasant Morality and Pre-Marital Relations," p. 699; Tilly and Scott, *Women, Work, and Family*, pp. 39–40.

26. Tilly and Scott, *Women, Work, and Family*, pp. 39–40; Stansell, *City of Women*, p. 61.

27. Gutman, *Black Family in Slavery and Freedom*, pp. 63–75, 449.

28. Levine, *Labor's True Woman*, pp. 129–53; Jameson, "High-Grade and Fissure," chap. 8, and "Imperfect Unions"; Weeks, *Sex, Politics, and Society*, pp. 75–76. On the family wage, see May, "Historical Problem of the Family Wage," pp. 276–81.

29. Hamilton, "National Association of Colored Women," pp. 10–26; Gordon, "Black and White Visions of Welfare," pp. 568–70, 578–79; Jenkins, "History of the Black Woman's Club Movement," pp. 65–67; Salem, *To Better Our World*, pp. 20–31, 44–51; White, "Cost of Club Work," pp. 254–60.

30. Hill, *Women in Gainful Occupations*, p. 45; Loranger and Tyler, "Working Women in the Los Angeles Area"; California Industrial Welfare Commission, *Biennial Report*, 1913–14, 1919–20.

31. Jones, *Labor of Love*, chaps. 3–5; Amott and Matthaei, *Race, Gender, and Work*, pp. 157–70.

32. For a discussion of similar changes among wage-earning daughters in New York and Chicago, see Ewen, *Immigrant Women*, pp. 104–9; Peiss, *Cheap Amusements*, chap. 2; Meyerowitz, *Women Adrift*, pp. 1–20.

33. Herman, "Idora Park"; Bagwell, *Oakland*, p. 148; McWilliams, *Southern California*, pp. 129–33; Sánchez, *Becoming Mexican American*, pp. 171–87; Case, *History of Long Beach and Vicinity*, 1:521–25; Long Beach Municipal Convention and Publicity Bureau, "Long Beach Amusement Zone," [n.d.], Long Beach Public Library, Pike File. For an excellent discussion of working-class women's leisure, see Peiss, *Cheap Amusements*. See also Ewen, *Immigrant Women*, pp. 208–17; Glenn, *Daughters of the Shtetl*, pp. 159–66.

34. Kessler-Harris, *Out to Work*, pp. 137–38; Ruiz, *Cannery Women*, pp. 11, 33; Yans-McLaughlin, *Family and Community*, p. 171; Ewen, *Immigrant Women*, pp. 212–13.

35. Alameda Case No. 5558 (1913). Karen Dubinsky has shown that parents in Ontario used the legal system to control the sexual behavior of their daughters (*Improper Advances*, chaps. 3, 5).

36. Alameda Case No. 7550 (1920).

37. Alameda Case No. 5920 (1914).

38. Alameda Case No. 6858 (1918).

39. *Oakland Tribune*, August 26, 1911, clipping located in Oakland Police Department Scrapbooks, Oakland Public Library, Oakland, Calif.; Connelly, *Response to Prostitution*, pp. 125–26.

40. *Oakland Tribune*, February 9, 1912, clipping located in Oakland Police Department Scrapbooks, Oakland Public Library.

41. Alameda Case No. 5501 (1913); Alameda Case No. 5502 (1913).

42. Alameda Case No. 5023 (1911).

43. Alameda Case No. 7595 (1920).

44. Los Angeles County Juvenile Court, Case No. 2351 (1910). Cases are hereafter referred to as Los Angeles Case No. 2351 (1910).

45. Los Angeles Case No. 16363 (1920).

46. Alameda Case No. 6081 (1915).

47. Los Angeles Case No. 17608 (1920).

48. Ibid.

49. For the Alameda cases, N=106; for the Los Angeles cases, N=22.

50. For these cases, N=105.

51. For these cases, N=86.

52. For these cases, N=23.

53. Alameda Case No. 5732 (1914).

54. Alameda Case No. 5201 (1912).

55. Alameda Case No. 6153 (1915).

56. Los Angeles Case No. 1937 (1910).

57. Los Angeles Case No. 16190 (1920).

58. Los Angeles Case No. 2184 (1910).

59. Peiss, *Cheap Amusements*, p. 52; Kessler-Harris, *Out to Work*, p. 230; Tentler, *Wage-Earning Women*, p. 19.

60. For an analysis of the practice of "treating" among working-class youth in New York City in the early twentieth century, see Peiss, *Cheap Amusements*, pp. 108–14. On a similar practice in nineteenth-century New York, see Stansell, *City of Women*, pp. 97–100.

61. Alameda Case No. 5564 (1913).

62. Los Angeles Case No. 16266 (1920).

63. Los Angeles Case No. 16059 (1920).

64. Alameda Case No. 6672 (1917).

65. Alameda Case No. 7550 (1920).

66. Alameda Case No. 7678 (1920).

67. Los Angeles Case No. 16196 (1920).

68. Alameda Case No. 5670 (1914).

69. Alameda Case No. 6153 (1915).

70. Los Angeles Case No. 16077 (1920).

71. Alameda Case No. 6882 (1918). See Reagan, "When Abortion Was a Crime."

72. For an insightful analysis of the system of sexual exchange among working-class youth and its consequences for young women in nineteenth-century New York, see Stansell, *City of Women*, pp. 97–100.

73. Alameda Case No. 5657 (1914).

74. For these cases, N=106. To discuss forcible assaults on underage females, I have used only the cases from the Alameda County Superior Court. The Los Angeles Juvenile Court sent cases of statutory rape that involved men over eighteen years old to the county's criminal court. Because I did not

have access to these records, it was not possible to follow the legal processing of the cases.

75. For similar findings in a study of rape and sexual assault in Ontario, see Dubinsky, *Improper Advances*, chap. 2.

76. For these cases, N=30.

77. Alameda Case No. 6402 (1916). For discussion of sexual assaults by family members during this period, see Gordon and O'Keefe, "Incest as a Form of Family Violence"; Gordon, "Incest and Resistance"; Pleck, *Domestic Tyranny*, pp. 81–82; Stansell, *City of Women*, p. 182; Clark, *Women's Silence, Men's Violence*, pp. 100–103.

78. Alameda Case No. 5572 (1913).

79. On the sexual exploitation of domestic workers by male employers, see Dudden, *Serving Women*, pp. 214–17; Katzman, *Seven Days a Week*, pp. 216–18; Gillis, "Servants"; Clark, *Women's Silence, Men's Violence*, pp. 104–8.

80. Alameda Case No. 5352 (1912).

81. Alameda Case No. 7612 (1920).

82. Gordon and O'Keefe, "Incest as a Form of Family Violence," p. 28; Stansell, *City of Women*, p. 182.

83. Alameda Case No. 6402 (1916).

84. On this issue, see Gordon, "Incest and Resistance."

85. Alameda Case No. 6859 (1918).

86. Alameda Case No. 6574 (1917).

87. Alameda Case No. 5572 (1913).

88. Alameda Case No. 6402 (1916).

89. Bordin, *Woman and Temperance*, pp. 7–9; Pleck, *Domestic Tyranny*, pp. 88–107. A handful of reformers did address sexual abuse of girls within the family: women's rights advocates Lucy Stone and Henry Blackwell, who edited the *Woman's Journal*, and the women who founded and ran the Protective Agency for Women and Children in Chicago (Pleck, *Domestic Tyranny*, pp. 95–98, 101–6).

CHAPTER THREE

1. Alameda County Superior Court, Oakland, Calif., Case No. 6042 (1915). Cases are hereafter referred to as Alameda Case No. 6042 (1915). In all chapters that draw on original case files, I have changed the names of the young women, male partners, family members, and others involved in the cases but have attempted to retain their ethnic distinctions.

2. For an excellent discussion of the operation of the criminal justice system in Alameda County in the late nineteenth and early twentieth centuries, see Friedman and Percival, *Roots of Justice*.

3. For these cases, N=112. See Appendix for further information on the calculations in this chapter.

4. Alameda Case No. 5530 (1913).

5. Alameda Case No. 5670 (1914); Case No. 5676 (1914); Case No. 5705 (1914); Case No. 5706 (1914).

6. Alameda Case No. 5540 (1913).

7. Alameda Case No. 5624 (1913).

8. Alameda Case No. 6672 (1917). For another example of resistance by female witnesses, see Alameda Case No. 5663 (1914).

9. Alameda Case No. 6332 (1916).

10. Alameda Case No. 5773 (1914). For other cases in which questions about the witnesses' consent were permitted, see Alameda Case No. 5515 (1913); Case No. 5731 (1914); Case No. 5734 (1914); Case No. 5844 (1914); Case No. 6859 (1918); Case No. 6332 (1916); Case No. 6346 (1916).

11. Alameda Case No. 6734 (1917); Case No. 5501 (1913); Case No. 5707 (1914).

12. Alameda Case No. 5821 (1914). On the harassment of women and girls in rape and seduction trials in Ontario in the late nineteenth and early twentieth centuries, see Dubinsky, *Improper Advances*, pp. 22–31, 77–79.

13. Alameda Case No. 7231 (1919).

14. Alameda Case No. 5657 (1914).

15. For feminist analyses of acquaintance rape, see Estrich, *Real Rape*; Warshaw, *I Never Called It Rape*; Parrot and Bechhofer, eds., *Acquaintance Rape*.

16. Alameda Case No. 5657 (1914).

17. Alameda Case No. 5844 (1914).

18. Alameda Case No. 6859 (1918). On the treatment in rape trials of the issue of women's resistance to sexual assault, see Friedman, *Crime and Punishment*, pp. 216–17; Estrich, *Real Rape*, pp. 29–41.

19. Nemeth, "Character Evidence in Rape Trials"; Estrich, *Real Rape*, pp. 47–53; Wigmore, *Student's Textbook*, pp. 59–64, 88–91; Wigmore, *Treatise on the System of Evidence*, 1:125–32.

20. *Lee v. State*, 132 Tenn. 658 (1915).

21. Wigmore, *Student's Textbook*, p. 63; see also Wigmore, *Treatise on the System of Evidence*, 1:130.

22. Wigmore, *Student's Textbook*, pp. 63–64; Wigmore, *Treatise on the System of Evidence*, 1:131–32.

23. Alameda Case No. 5657 (1914).

24. Alameda Case No. 6346 (1916).

25. Alameda Case No. 5706 (1914). For other cases in which questions about prior sexual acts were permitted, see Alameda Case No. 4979 (1911); Case No. 5676 (1914); Case No. 5732 (1914); Case No. 5695 (1914); Case No. 6428 (1916); Case No. 6631 (1917).

26. Alameda Case No. 5920 (1914).

27. Alameda Case No. 6546 (1917).

28. Alameda Case No. 4979 (1911). For a discussion of the differential treatment of "chaste" and "unchaste" females in rape trials, see Friedman, *Crime and Punishment*, p. 217; Estrich, *Real Rape*, p. 49.

29. Alameda Case No. 6084 (1915).

30. Alameda Case No. 5562 (1913).

31. Spencer, *History of the Woman's Christian Temperance Union*, pp. 67–68.

32. "The Amended Penal Code—First Successful Case of Prosecution," *Philanthropist*, February 1888, p. 4; Anna Rice Powell to Elizabeth Gay, March 21, 1898, Sidney Howard Gay Collection, CU; "For the Better Legal Protection of Young Girls," *Philanthropist*, March 1891; "The Protective Agency for Women and Children of Chicago," *Union Signal*, October 6, 1887, p. 8; Protective Agency for Women and Children, *Annual Reports*, 1887–91. On the Protective Agency for Women and Children in Chicago, see Pleck, "Feminist Responses," pp. 465–69; Pleck, *Domestic Tyranny*, pp. 95–98.

33. *Berkeley Reporter*, March 21, 1906, p. 1.

34. "Protective Agency for Women and Children of Chicago."

35. *Woman's Bulletin*, June 1912, p. 15; ibid., February 1914, pp. 21–22; Gibson, *Record of Twenty-five Years*, pp. 181–83.

36. On the recall campaign, see "The Recall League of San Francisco," *Woman's Bulletin*, April 1913, p. 13; Weiss, "Feminine Point of View."

37. "Recall League of San Francisco," p. 13.

38. Quoted in Weiss, "Feminine Point of View," p. 18. On the movement to put women on juries in the United States, see Friedman, *Crime and Punishment*, pp. 419–21.

39. Weiss, "Feminine Point of View," pp. 17–23.

40. On Curtis D. Wilbur, see Bates, ed., *History of the Bench and Bar*, p. 556; Curtis D. Wilbur File, California State Library, Sacramento, Calif. On Sidney Reeve, see McGroarty, *Los Angeles*, 2:113–14. On the Progressive Era juvenile court movement, see Rothman, *Conscience and Convenience*, chaps. 6–8; Schlossman, *Love and the American Delinquent*, chap. 4.

41. Los Angeles Case No. 17619 (1920).

42. Los Angeles Case No. 17299 (1920).

43. Los Angeles Case No. 16196 (1920).

44. Kerr, *Consolidated Supplement*, sec. 264, p. 2066.

45. Los Angeles Case No. 15969 (1920).

46. Rothman, *Conscience and Convenience*, pp. 218–19; Schlossman, *Love and the American Delinquent*, pp. 60–66.

47. Friedman and Percival, *Roots of Justice*, pp. 224–28; Friedman, *Crime and Punishment*, pp. 406–9.

48. For these cases, N=112.

49. Friedman and Percival, *Roots of Justice*, pp. 179–81; Friedman, *History of American Law*, p. 576.

50. For these cases, N=75.

51. For these cases, N=50.

52. For these cases, N=23.

53. Alameda Case No. 5688 (1914).

54. Alameda Case No. 5563 (1913).

55. For these cases, N=50.

56. For these cases, N=23.

57. Alameda Case No. 5620 (1913).

58. Alameda Case No. 5688 (1914).

59. Alameda Case No. 5501 (1913).

60. Alameda Case No. 6929 (1918). For other cases in which judges discussed the "immoral" character of the female witness as an important factor in granting probation, see Alameda Case No. 5707 (1914); Case No. 5540 (1913); Case No. 5732 (1914); Case No. 5799 (1914); Case No. 6042 (1915); Case No. 6084 (1915); Case No. 6929 (1918); Case No. 7231 (1919); Case No. 7550 (1920).

61. Alameda Case No. 6008 (1915).

62. Alameda Case No. 6672 (1917).

63. Alameda Case No. 5821 (1914).

CHAPTER FOUR

1. On the antiprostitution crusade during the Progressive Era, see Hobson, *Uneasy Virtue*, chaps. 6–8; Rosen, *Lost Sisterhood*; Connelly, *Response to Prostitution*.

2. On the eugenics movement in the early twentieth century, see Haller, *Eugenics*; Pickens, *Eugenics and the Progressives*; Kevles, *In the Name of Eugenics*.

3. Brandt, *No Magic Bullet*, chap. 1; Pivar, "Women, Sexuality, and the Social Hygiene Movement."

4. Connelly, *Response to Prostitution*, chap. 6; Rosen, *Lost Sisterhood*, chap. 7.

5. Clifford G. Roe, *The Great War on White Slavery* (New York: n.p., 1911); Ernest A. Bell, *Fighting the Traffic in Young Girls* (Chicago: n.p., 1910); Reginald Wright Kauffman, *The House of Bondage* (New York: Moffat, Yard and Co., 1910); Mrs. C. I. Harris, *Modern Herodians or Slaughterers of Innocents* (Portland, Oreg.: Wallace Printing Co., 1909); Theodore A. Bingham, *The Girl Who Disappears* (Boston: Gorham Press, 1911).

6. Connelly, *Response to Prostitution*, chap. 6; Rosen, *Lost Sisterhood*, chap. 7.

7. Quoted in Haller, *Eugenics*, p. 45; see also Rosen, *Lost Sisterhood*, pp. 21–23. On the great social anxiety about feeble-mindedness during the Progressive Era, see Haller, *Eugenics*, chap. 7.

8. Goddard and Hill, "Delinquent Girls," p. 51.

9. For those recommending permanent custodial care, see Goddard and Hill, "Delinquent Girls"; Lamb, "Study of Thirty-five Delinquent Girls"; Evans and Dewson, "Feeble-mindedness and Juvenile Delinquency"; Ordahl and Ordahl, "Study of Delinquent and Dependent Girls"; Sessions, "Delinquent Girl as a Community Problem"; Walker, "Factors Contributing to the Delinquency of Defective Girls." For those recommending sterilization, see Sears, "Wayward Girl"; Walker, "Factors Contributing to the Delinquency of Defective Girls." On sterilization laws and the growth of institutions for the feeble-minded, see Haller, *Eugenics*, pp. 129, 133–37.

10. Other scholars who have discussed the changing conceptions of female sexuality during this period are Lunbeck, "'A New Generation of Women'"; Meyerowitz, *Women Adrift*, chaps. 3, 6; Alexander, "'Girl Problem'"; Kunzel, *Fallen Women, Problem Girls*, chaps. 1–2.

11. On Progressive women reformers, see Blair, *Clubwoman as Feminist*; Boris, "Reconstructing the 'Family'"; Fitzpatrick, *Endless Crusade*; Gordon, ed., *Women, the State, and Welfare*; Koven and Michel, "Womanly Duties"; Ladd-Taylor, *Mother-Work*; Muncy, *Creating a Female Dominion*; Neverdon-Morton, *Afro-American Women of the South*; Sklar, "Hull House"; Sklar, "Historical Foundations of Women's Power"; Skocpol, *Protecting Soldiers and Mothers*.

12. There is a vast literature on the Progressive movement. See, for example, Buenker, Burnham, and Crunden, *Progressivism*; Hays, *Response to Industrialism*; Hofstadter, *Age of Reform*; Haber, *Efficiency and Uplift*; Painter, *Standing at Armageddon*; Rodgers, "In Search of Progressivism"; Rothman, *Conscience and Convenience*; Wiebe, *Search for Order*.

13. Breckinridge and Abbott, *Delinquent Child and the Home*.

14. Woods and Kennedy, eds., *Young Working Girls*, p. v; True, *Neglected Girl*.

15. G. Stanley Hall discussed female adolescent and sexual development in the following works: *Adolescence*, 1: chap. 7, 2: chap. 17; "Budding Girl"; "Education and the Social Hygiene Movement." On conceptions of female adolescence during this period, see Alexander, "'Girl Problem,'" chaps. 2–4; Bissell Brown, "Golden Girls," chap. 2; Dyhouse, *Girls Growing Up*, chap. 4.

16. Hall, "Budding Girl," pp. 3–4.

17. Ibid.; Hall, "Education and the Social Hygiene Movement." For discus-

sions of the sexual bias in Hall's views of female adolescence, see Bissell Brown, "Golden Girls," chap. 2; Dyhouse, *Girls Growing Up*, chap. 4.

18. Hall, "Budding Girl," p. 33.

19. Woods and Kennedy, eds., *Young Working Girls*, pp. 8–9.

20. True, *Neglected Girl*, p. 58.

21. On Progressives' environmental analysis of social problems, see Boyer, *Urban Masses and Moral Order*, chap. 15; Freedman, *Their Sisters' Keepers*, chap. 6; Fitzpatrick, *Endless Crusade*, chaps. 3, 5, 7; Rothman, *Conscience and Convenience*, pp. 47–56.

22. Breckinridge and Abbott, *Delinquent Child and the Home*, p. 89.

23. Woods and Kennedy, eds., *Young Working Girls*, p. 23.

24. Ibid., pp. 26–27.

25. New York City Committee of Fourteen, *Department Store Investigation Report of the Subcommittee* (New York, 1915), Committee of Fourteen Papers, New York Public Library; Louise DeKoven Bowen, "The Department Store Girl: Based upon Interviews with Two Hundred Girls" (Chicago, 1911), Juvenile Protective Association Records, University Library, University of Illinois at Chicago, Chicago, Ill.

26. Woods and Kennedy, eds., *Young Working Girls*, p. 102; see also True, *Neglected Girl*, chap. 5.

27. Woods and Kennedy, eds., *Young Working Girls*, p. 108; True, *Neglected Girl*, p. 70.

28. Breckinridge and Abbott, *Delinquent Child and the Home*, pp. 55–69.

29. Breckinridge and Abbott briefly address the problems of African American youth (*Delinquent Child and the Home*, pp. 56–62). See also Addams, *New Conscience*, pp. 118–19, 169–70; Louise DeKoven Bowen, "The Colored People of Chicago" (Chicago, 1913), Juvenile Protective Association Records, University Library, University of Illinois at Chicago, Chicago, Ill.; Salem, *To Better Our World*, pp. 86–87.

30. Breckinridge and Abbott, *Delinquent Child and the Home*, p. 105.

31. Woods and Kennedy, eds., *Young Working Girls*, p. 66.

32. Ibid., pp. 66–68. On reformers' attempts to enforce a middle-class standard of family life, see Boris, "Reconstructing the 'Family'"; Muncy, *Creating a Female Dominion*, pp. 109–23; Gordon, *Heroes of Their Own Lives*, pp. 55–58.

33. Woods and Kennedy, eds., *Young Working Girls*, p. 41. On the issue of overcrowding, see also True, *Neglected Girl*, p. 78; Breckinridge and Abbott, *Delinquent Child and the Home*, chap. 7. The term "confused family groupings" is from Breckinridge and Abbott, p. 118.

34. Breckinridge and Abbott, *Delinquent Child and the Home*, p. 115.

35. Woods and Kennedy, eds., *Young Working Girls*, p. 37. On wage earning as a source of power for working-class daughters, see Peiss, *Cheap Amusements*, chap. 2; Ewen, *Immigrant Women*, p. 106.

36. Woods and Kennedy, eds., *Young Working Girls*, p. 48. On immigrant parents, see Breckinridge and Abbott, *Delinquent Child and the Home*, pp. 65–68.

37. Breckinridge and Abbott, *Delinquent Child and the Home*, p. 96. On reformers' objections to wage-earning mothers, see Michel, "Limits of Maternalism."

38. Michel, "Limits of Maternalism"; Boris, "Reconstructing the 'Family.'"

39. Paul Boyer, for example, distinguishes between the repressive or "coercive" strategies pursued by late nineteenth-century vice crusaders and the constructive or "environmental" strategies pursued by settlement workers. The former, argues Boyer, attempted to eliminate urban vice through legal repression, whereas the latter worked to discourage vice and delinquency by altering the urban industrial environment with the construction of parks, playgrounds, and decent housing. In a similar vein, Estelle Freedman, in her study of women's prison reform, argues that "prevention became the watchword of the Progressives." In contrast to their nineteenth-century predecessors, she argues, women penal reformers of the Progressive Era tended to favor "extra-institutional, preventive services" over institutionalization. See Boyer, *Urban Masses and Moral Order*, pp. 233–74; Freedman, *Their Sisters' Keepers*, pp. 126–30.

40. Boyer, *Urban Masses and Moral Order*, pp. 233–74; Freedman, *Their Sisters' Keepers*, pp. 126–30; Peiss, *Cheap Amusements*, chap. 7; Dye, *As Equals and Sisters*, chap. 3; Meyerowitz, *Women Adrift*, chap. 3; Connelly, *Response to Prostitution*, pp. 28–39; Ladd-Taylor, *Mother-Work*, chap. 5.

41. Quote found in "Improvements at Whittier," *Los Angeles Examiner*, April 7, 1912, Friday Morning Club Scrapbook No. 1, Friday Morning Club Collection, HL.

42. On nineteenth-century women's penal reform, see Freedman, *Their Sisters' Keepers*, chaps. 1–3; Rafter, *Partial Justice*, chaps. 1–2.

43. On the development of "scientific" social work among women reformers, see Fitzpatrick, *Endless Crusade*; Freedman, *Their Sisters' Keepers*, chaps. 6–7; Kunzel, "Professionalization of Benevolence"; Muncy, *Creating a Female Dominion*; Rafter, *Partial Justice*, chap. 3.

44. On reformers' promotion of scientific diagnosis in the rehabilitation of young female offenders, see Miner, *Slavery of Prostitution*, pp. 165–77; Miner, "Problem of Wayward Girls and Delinquent Women," pp. 606–9; Van Waters, "The Juvenile Court as a Social Laboratory," Box 37, File 465, MVWP; Van Waters, "Juvenile Court Procedure."

45. On the policewoman movement, see Owings, *Women Police*; Hamilton, *The Policewoman*; Feinman, *Women in the Criminal Justice System*, chap. 4; Saunders, "Study of the Work of the City Mother's Bureau"; Van Winkle, "Policewoman as a Socializing Agency"; Pigeon, "Policewomen in the United States"; Darwin, "Policewomen"; Abbott, "Training for the Policewoman's

Job." On early efforts to hire policewomen in Los Angeles, see Owings, *Women Police*, pp. 101–4; Saunders, "Study of the Work of the City Mother's Bureau," p. 17; Feinman, *Women in the Criminal Justice System*, pp. 82–84; Los Angeles Police Department, *Annual Report*, 1912, pp. 40–41, and *Annual Report*, 1914, pp. 26–27. The quote from Wells is found in Darwin, "Policewomen," p. 1372.

46. Owings, *Women Police*, pp. 104–6; Feinman, *Women in the Criminal Justice System*, pp. 82–86.

47. Quote found in Feinman, *Women in the Criminal Justice System*, p. 82. On the protective work of policewomen, see also Hamilton, *The Policewoman*, p. 9; Van Winkle, "Policewoman as a Socializing Agency," pp. 198–99; Darwin, "Policewomen."

48. Abbott, "Training for the Policewoman's Job," p. 30.

49. Estelle Lawton Lindsey, "Policewomen Take Up Cudgel to Protect Girls from Loose Men," *Los Angeles Record*, May 5, 1913; Los Angeles Police Department, *Annual Report*, 1913, p. 21, and *Annual Report*, 1914, p. 26.

50. Los Angeles Police Department, *Annual Report*, 1913, p. 21.

51. On the history of the juvenile court and juvenile justice in the Progressive Era, see Rothman, *Conscience and Convenience*, chaps. 6, 7; Schlossman, *Love and the American Delinquent*; Mennel, *Thorns and Thistles*; Platt, *Child Savers*; Ryerson, *Best-Laid Plans*; Tiffin, *In Whose Best Interest*; Schneider, *In the Web of Class*.

52. Schlossman, *Love and the American Delinquent*, pp. 61–62; Rothman, *Conscience and Convenience*, pp. 218–19; Miner, *Slavery of Prostitution*, pp. 165–67; Miner, "Community's Responsibility," p. 13.

53. Quotation found in "Our Juvenile Court Problem, the Delinquent Girl—Need for a Woman Judge," *Women Lawyers' Journal* 2 (February 1913): 59. See also "The Juvenile Court and the Girl," *Women Lawyers' Journal* 2 (August 1912): 42; "Give Us Women as Judges for Girls," *Women Lawyers' Journal* 2 (November 1912): 51; "This Court's All Women," *Los Angeles Times*, November 4, 1915; "Urge Trial by Woman Judge of All Girl Cases," *Los Angeles Herald*, October 2, 1914, Friday Morning Club Scrapbook No. 3, Friday Morning Club Collection, HL.

54. "The Ideal Woman Judge for Children," *Women Lawyers' Journal* 2 (May 1913): 67; Estelle B. Freedman, "Mary Margaret Bartelme," in Sicherman et al., eds., *Notable American Women: The Modern Period*, pp. 60–61.

55. Quotation found in Los Angeles County Probation Department, *Annual Report*, 1917, p. 2. See also "Orfa Jean Shontz, Referee, Juvenile Court, Los Angeles," *Women Lawyers' Journal* 6 (January 1917): 30; "This Court's All Women"; "Dr. Van Waters Made Referee," *Los Angeles Times*, April 4, 1920; Robert M. Mennel, "Miriam Van Waters," in Sicherman et al., eds., *Notable American Women: The Modern Period*, pp. 709–11.

56. Quotations are found in "Orfa Jean Shontz, Referee, Juvenile Court, Los Angeles," p. 30. See also Hiller, *Juvenile Court of Los Angeles County*, pp. 19–20; "Ideal Woman Judge for Children," p. 67.

57. Leonard, ed., *Woman's Who's Who of America*, p. 566; Miner, *Slavery of Prostitution*, chap. 6; Miner, "Problem of Wayward Girls and Delinquent Women," pp. 135–36; Miner, "Community's Responsibility," pp. 9–10.

58. Grace Abbott, "Abstract of Juvenile Court Laws," in Breckinridge and Abbott, *Delinquent Child and the Home*, pp. 257–59; Towne, "Place of the Juvenile Court Detention Home in the Community"; Rippen, "Municipal Detention for Women."

59. On the importance of individual method and scientific diagnosis in the rehabilitation of young female offenders, see Miner, *Slavery of Prostitution*, pp. 165–77; Miner, "Problem of Wayward Girls and Delinquent Women," pp. 132–35; Van Waters, "The Juvenile Court as a Social Laboratory," Box 37, File 465, MVWP; Van Waters, "Juvenile Court Procedure."

60. Rothman, *Conscience and Convenience*, chap. 2; Schlossman, *Love and the American Delinquent*, chap. 4; Freedman, *Their Sisters' Keepers*, chaps. 6, 7.

61. Breckinridge and Abbott, *Delinquent Child and the Home*, pp. 27, 41. See also Dewson, "Probation and Institutional Care of Girls"; Francis, "Delinquent Girl"; Amigh, "Section on Juvenile Delinquents."

62. Breckinridge and Abbott, *Delinquent Child and the Home*, pp. 40–41; Shelden, "Sex Discrimination in the Juvenile Justice System," pp. 67–70; Schlossman and Wallach, "Crime of Precocious Sexuality," pp. 72–73. The differences in institutional commitments for males and females who appeared before the Los Angeles County Juvenile Court will be discussed in the next chapter.

63. Wilson, *Fifty Years' Work with Girls*; Kunzel, *Fallen Women, Problem Girls*; Poggi, "Study of the Social Activities of the Catholic Church," pp. 41–46.

64. Schlossman and Wallach, "Crime of Precocious Sexuality," p. 70; Van Waters, "Where Girls Go Right"; Reeves, *Training Schools for Delinquent Girls*. On the movement to establish Progressive reformatories for adult women, see Freedman, *Their Sisters' Keepers*, and Rafter, *Partial Justice*. The first effort to establish reformatories for girls took place in the mid-nineteenth century and is discussed in Brenzel, *Daughters of the State*.

65. Quotation is found in Van Waters, *Youth in Conflict*, p. iii; Mary Dewees, "Martha Platt Falconer," in Sicherman et al., eds., *Notable American Women: The Modern Period*, pp. 594–96. The papers of Miriam Van Waters contain notes for a biography of Falconer that she planned to write but never completed (see Box 41, File 506, MVWP).

66. Falconer, "Work of the Girls' Department"; Falconer, "Culture of Family Life"; Falconer, "Reformatory Treatment for Women"; Dewees, "Martha Platt

Falconer," p. 595; notes from an uncompleted biography of Falconer, pp. 1–3, Box 41, File 506, MVWP; Elliot, *Correctional Education*, pp. 9–11.

67. Falconer, "Work of the Girls' Department," p. 392; Van Waters, "Where Girls Go Right," p. 371; notes from an uncompleted biography of Falconer, pp. 1–2, Box 41, File 506, MVWP; Elliot, *Correctional Education*, pp. 9–11. For other discussions of Progressive developments in correctional treatment of delinquent girls, see Dewson, "Probation and Institutional Care of Girls"; Berry, "State's Duty to the Delinquent Girl"; Morse, "Methods Most Helpful to Girls"; Burleigh and Harris, *Delinquent Girl.*

68. Falconer, "Work of the Girls' Department," p. 392. See also Elliot, *Correctional Education*, p. 22; Burleigh and Harris, *Delinquent Girl*, p. 8; Morse, "Methods Most Helpful to Girls," p. 310; Berry, "State's Duty to the Delinquent Girl," pp. 85–86.

69. Falconer, "Work of the Girls' Department," p. 393; Burleigh and Harris, *Delinquent Girl*, pp. 36–42. See also Berry, "State's Duty to the Delinquent Girl," p. 87; Elliot, *Correctional Education*, p. 98; Sessions, "Parole Work."

70. Van Waters, "Where Girls Go Right." Miriam Van Waters was not the official superintendent of the El Retiro reformatory, but she designed the plan for the school and played an important role in its administration throughout the 1920s.

71. See, for example, Mennel, *Thorns and Thistles*, pp. 171–80; regarding reformatories for adult women, see Freedman, *Their Sisters' Keepers.*

72. Carby, "Policing the Black Woman's Body"; Du Bois, ed., *Efforts for Social Betterment*, pp. 47–64, 100–103, 121–29; Salem, *To Better Our World*, pp. 109–12; Shaw, "Black Club Women," pp. 14–19; Peebles-Wilkins, "Black Women and American Social Welfare," pp. 39–41; Hamilton, "National Association of Colored Women," pp. 71–72.

73. Anne Firor Scott, "Janie Porter Barrett," in Hine, ed., *Black Women in America*, pp. 90–91; Sadie Daniel St. Clair, "Janie Porter Barrett," in James, James, and Boyer, eds., *Notable American Women*, 1:96–97; Salem, *To Better Our World*, pp. 109–11; Delores Nicholson, "Janie Porter Barrett," in Smith, ed., *Notable Black American Women*, pp. 56–59.

74. Reeves, *Training Schools for Delinquent Girls*, pp. 42–43, 87–88; Du Bois, ed., *Efforts for Social Betterment*, pp. 102–3; Salem, *To Better Our World*, pp. 109–11.

75. Du Bois, ed., *Efforts for Social Betterment*, pp. 127–28; Salem, *To Better Our World*, pp. 111–12; "Petition from Committee for Colored Probation Officers," December 2, 1914, Los Angeles County Board of Supervisors' Archives, Detention Home File. See also "Petition from Colored Citizens' Civic and Commercial Club to the Honorable Board of Supervisors," September 15, 1921, Los Angeles County Board of Supervisors' Archives, Probation File.

76. Du Bois, ed., *Efforts for Social Betterment*, p. 127.

77. Adrienne Lash Jones, "Jane Edna Hunter" and "Phyllis Wheatley Clubs and Homes," in Hine, ed., *Black Women in America*, pp. 592–94, 920–23; Salem, *To Better Our World*, pp. 134–40; Shaw, "Black Club Women," pp. 15–16.

78. Du Bois, ed., *Efforts for Social Betterment*, pp. 102–3, 124–25; Salem, *To Better Our World*, pp. 109–11; Peebles-Wilkins, "Black Women and American Social Welfare," pp. 39–40.

79. Brandt, *No Magic Bullet*, chap. 2; Pivar, "Cleansing the Nation." For a comprehensive study of the CTCA, see Bristow, "Creating Crusaders."

80. Ibid.

81. Warren Olney Jr. to Raymond Fosdick, August 4, 1917, RG 165, Box 585, NA; Lane, "Girls and Khaki," p. 1; Miner, "Prevention of Delinquency," p. 59; Additon, "Work among Delinquent Women and Girls," p. 155; Brandt, *No Magic Bullet*, pp. 80–81.

82. Raymond Fosdick to Warren Olney Jr., August 14, 1917, RG 165, Box 585, NA; Fosdick to Julia Lathrop, September 14, 1917, RG 102, Box 153, NA; Miner, "Prevention of Delinquency"; Lane, "Girls and Khaki," pp. 2–4; Brandt, *No Magic Bullet*, pp. 81–92.

83. Miner, "Prevention of Delinquency," p. 59. See also Miner, "Report of the Committee on Protective Work With Girls," April 1918, RG 102, Box 153, NA; Lane, "Girls and Khaki," pp. 2–3.

84. Maude E. Miner, "Report of the Committee on Protective Work for Girls," April 1918, RG 102, Box 153, NA.

85. Public Affairs Committee, Monthly Bulletin no. 14 (June 1918), Friday Morning Club Scrapbook No. 5, Friday Morning Club Collection, HL.

86. Maude E. Miner to Raymond Fosdick, February 14, 1918, RG 165, Box 429, NA; "War Work Plans of the Social Morality Committee," [n.d.], p. 3, Social Morality Committee Files, National YWCA Archives, New York, N.Y.; "Report: Social Morality Committee, War Work Council, National YWCA," June 1917–July 1919, Reel 154.5, Social Morality Committee Files, ibid. See also "Social Morality Work of the Young Women's Christian Association," [n.d.], pp. 11–19, Social Morality Committee Files, ibid.

87. "Report: Social Morality Committee, War Work Council, National YWCA," and "Announcement," *Association Monthly* (September 1919): 388, both in Social Morality Committee Files, National YWCA Archives, New York, N.Y.; Brandt, *No Magic Bullet*, pp. 81–83.

88. Maude E. Miner, "Report," April 1, 1918, RG 165, Box 442, NA.

89. Maude E. Miner to Raymond Fosdick, April 9, 1918, RG 165, Box 443, NA.

90. Brandt, *No Magic Bullet*, pp. 84–85; Pivar, "Cleansing the Nation," pp. 33, 38.

91. Miner is quoted in Brandt, *No Magic Bullet*, p. 86. See also Maude E. Miner to Raymond Fosdick, April 9, 1918, RG 165, Box 443, NA.

92. Quoted in Brandt, *No Magic Bullet*, p. 86. Moral reformer Katharine C. Bushnell wrote a pamphlet opposing the CTCA policy (Bushnell, "Plain Words to Plain People," Woman's Rights Collection, Folder 36, SL).

93. Rippen, "Social Hygiene and the War," pp. 126–28; Additon, "Work among Delinquent Women and Girls," pp. 152–54.

94. Dietzler, *Detention Houses and Reformatories*, pp. 35–40; Falconer, "Part of the Reformatory," p. 2; Brandt, *No Magic Bullet*, p. 88.

95. Falconer, "Segregation of Delinquent Women and Girls," pp. 161–62; Falconer, "Part of the Reformatory"; Falconer, "Work of the Section on Reformatories."

96. Dietzler, *Detention Houses and Reformatories*, pp. 74–76; Brandt, *No Magic Bullet*, p. 89. The quote is from Franklin Hichborn, "The Anti-Vice Movement in California," pt. 2, p. 369 (reprint from *Social Hygiene* 6 [July 1920], located in John Randolph Haynes Papers, Box 73, File 68, UCLA).

97. Falconer, "Segregation of Delinquent Women and Girls," p. 164.

98. Dietzler, *Detention Houses and Reformatories*, pp. 27–34, 69; Brandt, *No Magic Bullet*, pp. 88–89.

CHAPTER FIVE

1. Los Angeles County Juvenile Court, Case No. 16814 (1920). Cases are hereafter referred to as Los Angeles Case No. 16814 (1920). In all chapters that draw on original case files, I have changed the names of the young women, male partners, family members, and others involved in the cases but have attempted to retain their ethnic distinctions.

2. "Miss Orfa Jean Shontz," *Woman's Bulletin* 4 (October 1916): 30; "Orfa Jean Shontz, Referee, Juvenile Court, Los Angeles," *Women Lawyers' Journal* 6 (January 1917): 30; Orfa Jean Shontz File, California Biography Files, LAPL; Fletcher, ed., *Who's Who in California*, p. 832; Binheim, ed., *Women of the West*, p. 83. On the position of female referee, see Chapter 4.

3. On Van Waters's life in general, see Rowles, *Lady at Box 99*; Robert Mennel, "Miriam Van Waters," in Sicherman et al., eds., *Notable American Women: The Modern Period*, pp. 709–11; McGroarty, *History of Los Angeles County*, 2:136–38; Freedman, "In the Matter of the Removal of Miriam Van Waters." On Van Waters's role in the Los Angeles juvenile justice system, see Odem, "City Mothers and Delinquent Daughters," pp. 186–93.

4. Rowles, *Lady at Box 99*; Mennel, "Miriam Van Waters."

5. Miriam Van Waters to Ethel Sturges Dummer, November 19, 1921, Box 38, File 819, ESDP; Van Waters to Dummer, October 1922, ibid.; Rowles, *Lady at Box 99*, pp. 106–17; "College Girl Works Wonders," *Los Angeles Times*, February 3, 1918; Van Waters, "Where Girls Go Right."

6. Van Waters, "The Socialization of Juvenile Court Procedure," p. 65, Box 37, File 465, MVWP.

7. Van Waters, "Cause and Cure," talk delivered at the California Conference of Social Agencies, Riverside, Calif., May 8, 1920, Box 36, File 464, MVWP; Van Waters to Ethel Sturges Dummer, June 12, 1920, Box 37, File 818, ESDP; Van Waters, "Where Girls Go Right."

8. Van Waters, "The Juvenile Court as a Social Laboratory," p. 12, Box 37, File 465, MVWP.

9. Rowles, *Lady at Box 99*, pp. 124–25; Miriam Van Waters to her parents, February 14, 1918, Box 5, File 46, MVWP; Van Waters, "Speeches in Connection with Juvenile Hall Work," 1919, Box 33, File 427, MVWP.

10. Rowles, *Lady at Box 99*, pp. 106–17; "College Girl Works Wonders," *Los Angeles Times*, February 3, 1918, p. 14; Miriam Van Waters to Ethel Sturges Dummer, September 16, 1927, Box 38, File 822, ESDP; Van Waters to Dummer, December 11, 1921, Box 38, File 819, ESDP.

11. Miriam Van Waters to her parents, April 3, 1921, Box 5, File 49, MVWP; Van Waters to Ethel Sturges Dummer, December 29, 1922, Box 38, File 820, ESDP.

12. Miriam Van Waters to her father, November 28, 1921, Box 5, File 49, MVWP.

13. Miriam Van Waters to Ethel Sturges Dummer, December 4, 11, 1921, Box 38, File 819, ESDP.

14. Van Waters, "Where Girls Go Right," pp. 361–76; Van Waters, "El Retiro, the New School for Girls," 1920, Box 17, John Randolph Haynes Papers, UCLA; Los Angeles County Probation Committee, *Report on Juvenile Hall and El Retiro*, pp. 21–27; "Industrial Home Ordered," *Los Angeles Times*, April 1, 1919; Van Waters to Ethel Sturges Dummer, July 17, 1921, Box 38, File 819, ESDP.

15. Ethel Sturges Dummer to Miriam Van Waters, July 30, 1920, Box 37, File 818, ESDP; Van Waters, "Where Girls Go Right."

Dummer continued to offer Van Waters both emotional and financial support over the next ten years. She corresponded regularly, encouraging Van Waters in her work, and visited El Retiro and the Colony on several occasions. Dummer sent money to help El Retiro through times of financial crisis. She also provided financial support for Van Waters's career by hiring a stenographer to assist her with the *Survey* article and paying her salary when she took time off to write *Youth in Conflict*. See Van Waters to Dummer, November 19, 1921, Box 38, File 819, ESDP; Van Waters to Dummer, 1924, Box 6, File 52, MVWP.

16. Miriam Van Waters to Ethel Sturges Dummer, January 8, 1922, and March 6, 1921, Box 38, File 819, ESDP.

17. Miriam Van Waters to Ethel Sturges Dummer, October 28, 1923, Box 38, File 820, ESDP.

18. Miriam Van Waters to Ethel Sturges Dummer, September 14, 1920, and October 17, 1920, Box 37, File 818, ESDP; "El Retiro Girls Stay," *Los Angeles Times*, September 17, 1920; Van Waters to Dummer, May 9, 1921, Box 38, File 819, ESDP.

19. For these cases, N=101.

20. For these cases, N=185. Thirty-one percent is a conservative estimate because the court records did not consistently record information on mothers' employment. On married women's employment, see Hill, *Women in Gainful Occupations*, p. 75; Weiner, *From Working Girl to Working Mother*, p. 89, table 6.

21. Los Angeles County Probation Department, *Annual Report*, 1920, pp. 3–4. The statistics on race and ethnicity are taken from this 1920 report, which included all girls who appeared in court, both the delinquent and dependent, a total of 361. I have relied on this source instead of the case files because the 1920 case files do not consistently record the girls' places of birth and ethnic backgrounds.

22. For these cases, N=61.

23. For these cases, N=209.

24. The federal government did not address the plight of single mothers until the 1930s, with the passage of New Deal legislation to aid families with dependent children. Most states had enacted mothers' pension laws between 1910 and 1920, but they assisted only a small number of female-headed families due to stringent eligibility requirements. The California law, for example, provided pensions for widows only and neglected the needs of divorced, separated, and unmarried mothers and their children. Vandepol, "Dependent Children," pp. 231–32; Leff, "Consensus for Reform," pp. 413–15; California State Board of Control, *Report of the Children's Department*, 1916–18.

25. For these cases, N=209.

26. Los Angeles County, *Laws of California*, pp. 7–9.

27. For these cases, N=218. To determine the percentage of girls apprehended for sexual offenses, it was necessary to examine the court transcript and probation officer's report for each case, in addition to the official petition. Offenses listed on the petition often did not include charges of sexual immorality that were discussed in the other documents.

28. Los Angeles Case No. 17666 (1920).

29. Los Angeles Case No. 16534 (1920).

30. Los Angeles Case No. 16364 (1920).

31. Los Angeles Case No. 15919 (1920).

32. Los Angeles Case No. 17154 (1920).

33. Los Angeles Case No. 1937 (1910).

34. On amusements and recreations in early twentieth-century Los Angeles, see McWilliams, *Southern California*, pp. 129–33; Case, *History of Long*

Beach and Vicinity, 1:521–25; Long Beach Municipal Convention and Publicity Bureau, "Long Beach Amusement Zone," [n.d.], "Pike" File, Long Beach Public Library.

35. Los Angeles Case No. 17465 (1920).

36. On African American women's employment, see Hill, *Women in Gainful Occupations*, pp. 109–19; Jones, *Labor of Love*, pp. 127–34, 160–80; Amott and Matthaei, *Race, Gender, and Work*, pp. 154–68.

37. Los Angeles Case No. 15868 (1920).

38. For these cases, N=214.

39. Los Angeles Case No. 16007 (1920).

40. For these cases, N=216.

41. Los Angeles Case No. 15784 (1920).

42. Los Angeles Case No. 16509 (1920).

43. Los Angeles Case No. 17123 (1920).

44. Los Angeles Case No. 16196 (1920).

45. For these cases, N=217.

46. Los Angeles Case No. 16743 (1920).

47. Los Angeles Case No. 17608 (1920).

48. Los Angeles Case No. 16743 (1920).

49. Los Angeles Case No. 17624 (1920).

50. Los Angeles Case No. 16007 (1920).

51. Los Angeles Case No. 16509 (1920).

52. Los Angeles Case No. 16743 (1920).

53. Los Angeles Case No. 16814 (1920).

54. Los Angeles Case No. 17465 (1920).

55. Los Angeles Case No. 16314 (1920).

56. Los Angeles Case No. 16889 (1920).

57. Los Angeles Case No. 1937 (1910).

58. Los Angeles Case No. 17465 (1920).

59. Los Angeles Case No. 16936 (1920).

60. Van Waters, "The Socialization of Juvenile Court Procedure," p. 67, Box 37, File 465, MVWP. Van Waters discusses the need for a full examination of the social, physical, and mental aspects of delinquent youth in several other publications, including "Juvenile Court Procedure"; "The Juvenile Court as a Social Laboratory," Box 37, File 465, MVWP; *Youth in Conflict*, chap. 7.

61. "College Girl Works Wonders," *Los Angeles Times*, February 3, 1918; Van Waters, "The Socialization of Juvenile Court Procedure," pp. 66–68, Box 37, File 465, MVWP.

62. Los Angeles Case No. 1900 (1910).

63. Los Angeles County Probation Committee, "Rules Governing Juvenile Hall and Juvenile Hall Hospital," June 1915, Box 16, John Randolph Haynes Papers, UCLA; Los Angeles County Probation Committee, *Report on Juve-*

nile Hall and El Retiro, pp. 17–19; Dr. Muriel Dranga Cass to Dr. Miriam Van Waters, Superintendent of Juvenile Hall, March 17, 1920, Box 141, John Randolph Haynes Papers, UCLA; Miriam Van Waters, "Report of the Superintendent to the Probation Committee," March 24, 1920, ibid.; Mary L. Trowbridge, Secretary of Probation Committee, to Jonathan S. Dodge, Chairman, Board of Supervisors, November 17, 1919, Detention Home File, Los Angeles County Board of Supervisors Archives, Los Angeles, Calif. On the social hygiene campaign to combat venereal disease, see Brandt, *No Magic Bullet*, chaps. 1–3.

64. For these cases, N=217.

65. Los Angeles County Probation Committee, "Rules Governing Juvenile Hall and Juvenile Hospital," June 1915, Box 16, John Randolph Haynes Papers, UCLA; Dr. Muriel Dranga Cass to Dr. Miriam Van Waters, Superintendent of Juvenile Hall, March 17, 1920, Box 141, ibid.; Ackerman, "Juvenile Hall Superintendent," pp. 26–29, UCLA.

66. Rothman, *Conscience and Convenience*, chap. 2; Schlossman, *Love and the American Delinquent*, chap. 4; Rafter, *Partial Justice*, chap. 3.

67. N=220 for girls' cases; N=166 for boys' cases. Lower rates of probation for girls in juvenile court have been documented for other cities (Chicago, Memphis, Milwaukee) during this period. See Breckinridge and Abbott, *Delinquent Child and the Home*, pp. 40–41; Shelden, "Sex Discrimination in the Juvenile Justice System"; Schlossman and Wallach, "Crime of Precocious Sexuality."

68. For these cases, N=220.

69. Van Waters, *Youth in Conflict*, p. 115.

70. Los Angeles Case No. 1938 (1910).

71. For these cases, N=220.

72. On the state reformatory for girls in Ventura, see "Girl's Training School Bill," *Woman's Bulletin* 1 (July 1912): 22; "California School for Girls," in California State Board of Charities and Corrections, *Biennial Report*, 1912–14, pp. 88–92; "Improvements at Whittier," *Los Angeles Examiner*, April 7, 1912, and "Legislative Committee of Club Reports," *Los Angeles Tribune*, February 26, 1913, both in Friday Morning Club Scrapbook No. 1, Friday Morning Club Collection, HL. On the El Retiro School for Girls, see "Industrial Home Ordered," *Los Angeles Times*, April 1, 1919; Miriam Van Waters to her parents, May 17, 1919, Box 5, File 46, MVWP; Van Waters, "Where Girls Go Right"; Los Angeles County Probation Committee, *Report on Juvenile Hall and El Retiro*, pp. 21–27.

73. In making the calculations of the court's institutional placements, I have counted all the institutional placements used by the court for the girls arrested in 1920. Numerous girls were sent to more than one institution during the time of their involvement with the court. I have therefore counted each of the

different institutional placements for every girl. The total number of institutional placements is 93.

74. "Helen Sweeting Case," Box 17, John Randolph Haynes Papers, UCLA; "Definite Act May Wait Board Conference," *Los Angeles Express*, January 31, 1919, "Ventura School Charge Proved, Say Women," *Los Angeles Herald*, January 21, 1919, and "Decision in Ventura Row Expected Monday," *Los Angeles Herald*, February 6, 1919, all three located in Box 17, John Randolph Haynes Papers, UCLA; "Club Women to Hear Report on School," *Los Angeles Herald*, February 10, 1919, and "Heated Charges Hurled by Advocates of Shakeup in California Institution," [no paper or date given], both in Friday Morning Club Scrapbook No. 5, Friday Morning Club Collection, HL.

75. Miriam Van Waters to Ethel Sturges Dummer, October 28, 1923, Box 38, File 820, ESDP; Van Waters to Dummer, July 17, 1921, Box 38, File 819, ESDP; Van Waters, "Where Girls Go Right."

76. Poggi, "Study of the Social Activities of the Catholic Church," pp. 41–46; Wilson, *Fifty Years' Work with Girls*, pp. 335–40; Los Angeles County Probation Department, *Annual Report*, 1920, p. 10.

77. Poggi, "Study of the Social Activities of the Catholic Church," pp. 41–46; "Report by Dr. John R. Haynes of His Visit to the Convent of the Good Shepherd in the City of Los Angeles," September 24, 1913, Box 17, John Randolph Haynes Papers, UCLA; Bureau of Catholic Charities, *Annual Report*, January 1, 1921–January 1, 1922, pp. 5, 12.

78. Written by an El Retiro inmate, [n.d.], Box 15, File 165, MVWP. Not all of these papers written by El Retiro inmates are dated, but those that are were written on April 23, 1926.

79. Written by El Retiro inmate, April 23, 1926, ibid.

80. Written by El Retiro inmate, [n.d.], ibid.

81. Written by El Retiro inmate, [n.d.], ibid.

82. Los Angeles Case No. 16889 (1920).

83. Los Angeles Case No. 1938 (1910).

84. Los Angeles Case No. 17315 (1920).

85. Los Angeles Case No. 16295 (1920).

86. Los Angeles Case No. 16189 (1920).

87. Los Angeles Case No. 17153 (1920).

88. Los Angeles Case No. 17608 (1920).

89. Ibid.

90. Los Angeles Case No. 17015 (1920).

91. Los Angeles Case No. 16936 (1920). For other examples of the double standard, see Los Angeles Case Nos. 17143, 16944, 16945, 17338, 16355, and 17620 (all 1920).

92. Los Angeles Case No. 16936 (1920).

93. Los Angeles Case No. 15969 (1920).

94. Los Angeles Case No. 16196 (1920).

95. N=218 for girls' cases; N=166 for boys' cases.

96. N=220 for girls' cases; N=166 for boys' cases.

97. For these cases, N=23.

98. Los Angeles Case Nos. 17153 and 17299 (1920).

99. Los Angeles Case No. 17608 (1920).

CHAPTER SIX

1. Los Angeles County Juvenile Court, Case No. 2491 (1910). Cases are hereafter referred to as Los Angeles Case No. 2491 (1910).

2. For these cases, N=209. In all chapters that draw on original case files, I have changed the names of the young women, male partners, family members, and others involved in the cases.

3. For scholars who have interpreted the juvenile justice system as a form of social control of working-class youth, see Platt, *Child Savers*; Shelden, "Sex Discrimination in the Juvenile Justice System"; Schlossman and Wallach, "Crime of Precocious Sexuality." For excellent critiques of social control theory, see Gordon, "Feminism and Social Control" and *Heroes of Their Own Lives*. For a recent reassessment of the social control analysis of the juvenile court, see Schneider, *In the Web of Class*.

4. For these cases, N=98.

5. On the changes in social and sexual mores among young working-class women, see Peiss, *Cheap Amusements*, chaps. 3–6; Peiss, "'Charity Girls' and City Pleasures"; Lunbeck, "'A New Generation of Women'"; Meyerowitz, *Women Adrift*, pp. 101–16. On parents' use of the legal system in Canada to control daughters' sexuality, see Dubinsky, *Improper Advances*, chaps. 3, 5.

6. On the ethnic background of the Los Angeles population, see Fogelson, *Fragmented Metropolis*, pp. 77–83. On the family and community lives of Mexican immigrants in Los Angeles and California, see the following: Camarillo, *Chicanos in a Changing Society*; Griswold del Castillo, *La Familia*; Gamio, *Mexican Immigrant*; Romo, *East Los Angeles*; Ruiz, *Cannery Women*; Sánchez, *Becoming Mexican American*; Bogardus, *Mexican in the United States*. On other immigrant groups, see Cinel, *From Italy to San Francisco*; DiLeonardo, *Varieties of Ethnic Experience*; Kirschner, "Italian in Los Angeles"; Vorspan and Gartner, *History of the Jews of Los Angeles*.

Other studies that have been particularly helpful on the roles of daughters and women in immigrant families but do not deal specifically with immigrants in California include: Ewen, *Immigrant Women*; García, "Chicana in American History"; Glenn, *Daughters of the Shtetl*; Lamphere, *From Working Daugh-*

ters to Working Mothers; Smith, *Family Connections*; Yans-McLaughlin, *Family and Community*.

I have found the definitions of patriarchal families by Linda Gordon and Judith Smith particularly useful. See Gordon, *Heroes of Their Own Lives*, pp. 55–56; Smith, *Family Connections*, pp. 23–24.

7. DiLeonardo, *Varieties of Ethnic Experience*, chap. 2; Sánchez, *Becoming Mexican American*, pp. 33–35; Yans-McLaughlin, *Family and Community*, pp. 23, 170–72; Smith, *Family Connections*, pp. 24–34; Glenn, *Daughters of the Shtetl*, chap. 1.

8. Los Angeles Case No. 1938 (1910).

9. Los Angeles Case No. 16314 (1920).

10. Cinel, *From Italy to San Francisco*, p. 176; Glenn, *Daughters of the Shtetl*, p. 37; Sánchez, *Becoming Mexican American*, pp. 30–32; Smith, *Family Connections*, pp. 90–94.

11. Bogardus, *Mexican in the United States*, pp. 28–30; Ewen, *Immigrant Women*, pp. 227–29; Glenn, *Daughters of the Shtetl*, pp. 156–59; Sánchez, *Becoming Mexican American*, pp. 141–50; Smith, *Family Connections*, pp. 93–94.

12. Los Angeles Case No. 16590 (1920).

13. Los Angeles Case Nos. 16102, 16103, and 16128 (1920).

14. Quoted in Bogardus, *Mexican in the United States*, p. 28.

15. On the practice of *robo*, see Sánchez, *Becoming Mexican American*, p. 31; Foster, *Tzintzuntzan*, pp. 67–74; González, *San José de Gracia*, p. 89.

16. Los Angeles Case No. 16103 (1920).

17. Los Angeles Case No. 17652 (1920).

18. For these cases, N=61. These percentages are based on the population of all delinquent girls, not just those reported by parents.

19. Studies of the native-born white working class in Los Angeles in the early twentieth century are scarce. See Kazin, "Great Exception Revisited"; McWilliams, *Southern California*, pp. 156–64; Viehe, "Black Gold Suburbs." On native-born African Americans in Los Angeles, see Beaseley, *Negro Trail Blazers*; Bass, *Forty Years*; Bond, "Negro in Los Angeles"; Bunch, "Past Not Necessarily Prologue"; De Graff, "City of Black Angels."

20. Los Angeles Case No. 16486 (1920).

21. Los Angeles Case No. 16364 (1920).

22. Los Angeles Case No. 17462 (1920).

23. On the African American community in Los Angeles, see Beaseley, *Negro Trail Blazers*; Bass, *Forty Years*; Bond, "Negro in Los Angeles"; Bunch, "Past Not Necessarily Prologue"; De Graff, "City of Black Angels."

24. Los Angeles Case No. 16116 (1920).

25. I am using the term *single mother* to include female guardians as well as natural mothers. Although most girls (82 percent) lived with their natural

mothers, 18 percent lived with either a foster mother or a female relative (typically an aunt or grandmother), usually because their own mothers had died.

26. For these cases, N=98. The data on female-headed families in Los Angeles is taken from the 1930 census. This data is not available for earlier census years, but the percentage for 1920 is likely to be very close to that of 1930. The 1930 census provided data on family heads for the city of Los Angeles, but not the county. One can assume that the percentage for the county is slightly lower than that for the city, because the percentage of female-headed families was greater in the two largest cities of California—Los Angeles (21 percent) and San Francisco (20 percent)—than for the state as a whole (16 percent). U.S. Bureau of the Census, *Fifteenth Census of the United States, 1930: Population*, 6:167–68.

27. Single mothers made use of other social welfare institutions such as child protection agencies. See Gordon, *Heroes of Their Own Lives*, chap.4; Gordon, "Single Mothers and Child Neglect, 1880–1920."

28. For these cases, N=33.

29. On survival strategies of single mothers in agrarian and preindustrial societies, see González, "Widowed Women of Santa Fe"; Gordon, *Heroes of Their Own Lives*, pp. 85–86; Tilly and Scott, *Women, Work, and Family*, pp. 51–53; Wilson, *Life after Death*, chaps. 3–4.

30. U.S. Bureau of the Census, *Fifteenth Census of the United States, 1930: Population*, 6:167–68.

31. Los Angeles Case No. 16924 (1920).

32. Los Angeles Case No. 17601 (1920).

33. Los Angeles Case No. 17267 (1920).

34. Fogelson, *Fragmented Metropolis*, pp. 78–80. Fogelson estimates that, among the native-born Americans in Los Angeles from 1910 through 1930, only 25 percent were born in California.

35. Los Angeles Case No. 17255 (1920).

36. On mothers' pensions, see Goodwin, "Experiment in Paid Motherhood"; Ladd-Taylor, *Mother-Work*, chap. 5; Leff, "Consensus for Reform," pp. 413–15; Vandepol, "Dependent Children," pp. 231–32; Skocpol, *Protecting Soldiers and Mothers*, chap. 8. On the California mothers' pension law, see Katz, "Socialist Women and Progressive Reform," pp. 121–27; California, *Statutes of California*, chap. 323, pp. 629–32; California State Board of Control, *Report of the Children's Department*, 1916–18.

37. California Department of Social Welfare, *First Biennial Report*, 1927–28, p. 55.

38. Los Angeles County Bureau of Efficiency, "Investigation of Outdoor Relief of the Los Angeles County Charities Office," 1915, Box 141, John Randolph Haynes Papers, UCLA.

39. Los Angeles Case No. 17267 (1920).

40. Los Angeles Case Nos. 16924 and 16118 (1920).

41. Los Angeles Case No. 16348 (1920).

42. For these cases, N=33. On married women's employment, see Hill, *Women in Gainful Occupations*, p. 75; Weiner, *From Working Girl to Working Mother*, p. 89, table 6.

43. Kessler-Harris, *Out to Work*, p. 230; Tentler, *Wage-Earning Women*, p. 19.

44. Tentler, *Wage-Earning Women*, pp. 142–47; Gordon, "Single Mothers and Child Neglect," pp. 182–84.

45. Katz, "Dual Commitments," pp. 581–91; Loranger and Tyler, "Working Women in the Los Angeles Area," pp. 8–13; California Industrial Welfare Commission, "What California Has Done to Protect Its Women Workers: Preliminary Report of the Industrial Welfare Commission," 1923, Box 9, Katherine Philips Edson Papers, UCLA; California Industrial Welfare Commission, *Biennial Report*, 1913–14; Nesbitt, *Study of a Minimum Standard of Living for Dependent Families in Los Angeles*.

46. Los Angeles Case No. 17465 (1920).

47. Los Angeles County, *Laws of California*, pp. 9–10.

48. Los Angeles Case No. 16372 (1920).

49. Los Angeles Case No. 16221 (1920).

50. Los Angeles Case No. 15868 (1920).

51. Los Angeles Case No. 17601 (1920).

52. Ibid.

53. In 1920, parents filed a total of 98 delinquency petitions against daughters and 72 against sons.

54. Los Angeles Case No. 15875 (1920).

55. Los Angeles Case No. 16158 (1920).

56. N=72 for boys' cases; N=98 for girls' cases.

57. On the different roles and expectations of working-class sons and daughters, see Tentler, *Wage-Earning Women*, pp. 89–91; Peiss, *Cheap Amusements*, pp. 62–72; Ewen, *Immigrant Women*, pp. 105–9.

58. Los Angeles Case No. 16375 (1920).

59. Los Angeles Case No. 16703 (1920).

60. Los Angeles Case No. 16312 (1920).

61. Los Angeles Case No. 15937 (1920).

62. Los Angeles Case Nos. 16129, 16830, and 16887 (1920).

63. Los Angeles Case No. 16004 (1920).

64. Los Angeles Case No. 2316 (1910).

65. Los Angeles Case No. 16364 (1920).

66. Los Angeles Case No. 16372 (1920).

67. Los Angeles Case No. 16798 (1920).

68. Los Angeles Case Nos. 17462 and 17652 (1920).
69. Los Angeles Case No. 1938 (1910).
70. Los Angeles Case No. 17601 (1920).
71. Ibid.
72. Los Angeles Case No. 17608 (1920).
73. Los Angeles Case No. 16372 (1920).
74. Ibid.

CONCLUSION

1. Freedman, *Their Sisters' Keepers*, pp. 12–15; Hobson, *Uneasy Virtue*, chap. 2; Rafter, *Partial Justice*.

2. Fass, *Damned and the Beautiful*, chap. 6; Smith, "Dating of the American Sexual Revolution"; D'Emilio and Freedman, *Intimate Matters*, pp. 256–65.

3. Simmons, "Modern Sexuality and the Myth of Victorian Repression"; D'Emilio and Freedman, *Intimate Matters*, pp. 265–70.

4. For a comprehensive study of the current treatment of female delinquency in the juvenile justice system, see Chesney-Lind and Shelden, *Girls, Delinquency, and Juvenile Justice*. See also Chesney-Lind, "Judicial Paternalism"; Allan Conway and Carol Bogdan, "Sexual Delinquency and the Persistence of a Double Standard," *Crime and Delinquency* 23 (April 1977): 131–35; Sue Davidson, ed., *Justice for Young Women: Close-Up on Critical Issues* (Tucson, Ariz.: New Directions for Young Women, 1982).

BIBLIOGRAPHY

. . . .

MANUSCRIPT COLLECTIONS

Cambridge, Massachusetts
The Arthur and Elizabeth Schlesinger Library, Radcliffe College
  Blackwell Family Papers
  Ethel Sturges Dummer Papers
  Helen Hamilton Gardener Papers
  Miriam Van Waters Papers
  Woman's Rights Collection

Chicago, Illinois
Chicago Historical Society
  Louise DeKoven Bowen Scrapbooks
  Chicago Woman's Club Collection
  Emily Washburn Dean Papers
Newberry Library
  Graham Taylor Collection
University of Chicago, Joseph Regenstein Library, Department of Special
  Collections
  Edith and Grace Abbott Papers
  Sophonisba Breckinridge Papers
University of Illinois at Chicago, University Library, Special Collections
  Department
  Jane Addams Papers
  Florence Crittenton Anchorage Papers
  Hull House Association Records
  Immigrants Protective League Records
  Juvenile Protective Association Records
  Travelers Aid Society of Chicago Records

Evanston, Illinois
Willard Memorial Library, National Woman's Christian Temperance Union
  Headquarters
  National Woman's Christian Temperance Union Papers

Long Beach, California
Long Beach Public Library
  Pike File

Los Angeles, California
Los Angeles City Archives
   Health Department Records
Los Angeles County Board of Supervisors' Archives
   Charities File
   Detention Home File
   El Retiro File
   Juvenile Court File
   Probation File
Los Angeles County Juvenile Court
   Juvenile Delinquency Case Files, 1910, 1920
Los Angeles Public Library
   California Biography Files
      Ernest K. Foster File
      Orfa Jean Shontz File
      Miriam Van Waters File
      Alice Stebbins Wells File
University of California, University Research Library, Department of Special
   Collections
   Ackerman, Rhea C. "Juvenile Hall Superintendent, 1936–1943" (oral
   history, 1971)
   Katherine Philips Edson Papers
   John Randolph Haynes Papers

New York, New York
Columbia University Rare Book and Manuscript Library
   Sidney Howard Gay Collection
National Young Women's Christian Association Archives
   National YWCA Social Morality Committee Files
New-York Historical Society
   Benjamin F. DeCosta Papers
New York Public Library
   Committee of Fifteen Papers
   Committee of Fourteen Papers

Northridge, California
Urban Archives Center, California State University
   League of Women Voters, Los Angeles Chapter Collection
   Young Women's Christian Association of Los Angeles Collection

Oakland, California
Alameda County Superior Court
   Criminal Case Files, 1880–90, 1910–20

Oakland Public Library, Oakland History Room
  Oakland Police Department Scrapbooks
  Newspaper Clippings File
  Herman, Ilene. "Idora Park" (unpublished paper, 1984)

Sacramento, California
California State Library
  California School for Girls, Inmate Register
  Curtis D. Wilbur File

San Francisco, California
California Historical Society
  League of Women Voters Collection

San Marino, California
Huntington Library
  California Civic League Minutes
  Friday Morning Club Collection

Stanford, California
Stanford University Library, Department of Special Collections
  Earl Barnes Papers
  Curtis D. Wilbur Papers

Swarthmore, Pennsylvania
Swarthmore College Library
  Friends Historical Library
    Janney Papers (Dr. Oliver Edward Janney)
  Peace Collection
    Anna Garlin Spencer Papers

Washington, D.C.
National Archives
  Records of the U.S. Public Health Service, RG 90
  Records of the War Department General and Special Staff, RG 165

NEWSPAPERS AND JOURNALS

Arena
California Outlook
Journal of Delinquency
Los Angeles Times

Los Angeles Record
New York Times
Oakland Tribune
Philanthropist
Social Hygiene
Survey
Union Signal
Vigilance
Woman's Bulletin
Woman's Era
Woman's Journal
Women Lawyers' Journal
Proceedings (National Conference of Charities and Correction)

ANNUAL REPORTS AND GOVERNMENT DOCUMENTS

American Purity Alliance. *Annual Report*, 1894–1909.

California. *The Statutes of California*. Sacramento: California State Printing Office, 1913.

California. Department of Institutions. *Biennial Report*, 1922–30.

California. Department of Social Welfare. *Biennial Report*, 1927–32.

California. Industrial Welfare Commission. *Biennial Report*, 1913–22.

California. State Board of Charities and Corrections. *Biennial Report*, 1908–20.

California. State Board of Charities and Corrections. *County Outdoor Relief in California*. Sacramento: California State Printing Office, 1916, 1918.

California. State Board of Control. *Report of the Children's Department*, 1914–20.

Chicago, Illinois. Vice Commission of Chicago. *The Social Evil in Chicago: A Study of Existing Conditions, with Recommendations*. Chicago: Gunthorp-Warren Printing Company, 1911.

Diocese of Monterey and Los Angeles. Bureau of Catholic Charities. *Annual Report*, 1921–22.

Los Angeles County. *Laws of California and Ordinances of the County and Cities of Los Angeles County Relating to Minors*. Los Angeles: Standard Printing Company, 1914.

Los Angeles County. Board of Supervisors. *Annual Report*, 1911–25.

Los Angeles County. Probation Committee. *Report on Juvenile Hall and El Retiro*. Los Angeles: n.p., 1929.

Los Angeles County. Probation Department. *Annual Report*, 1914–29.

Los Angeles County. *Report and Manual for Probation Officers of the*

Superior Court Acting as Juvenile Court. Los Angeles: Commercial
    Printing House, 1912.
Los Angeles, Calif. Police Department. *Annual Report*, 1912–22.
Los Angeles, Calif. Social Service Commission. *Annual Report*, 1913–25.
    (Before 1916, this was the Municipal Charities Commission.)
Massachusetts. *Report of the Commission for the Investigation of the White
    Slave Traffic, So Called*. H.Doc. 2281. Boston, 1914.
Minneapolis, Minnesota. Vice Commission of Minneapolis. *Report of the Vice
    Commission to His Honor James C. Haynes, Mayor*. Minneapolis, 1911.
National Woman's Christian Temperance Union. *Minutes* of Annual
    Conventions, 1885–1920. (Located in the Willard Memorial Library in
    Evanston, Ill.)
Oakland, Calif. Police Department. *Annual Report*, 1914.
Oakland, Calif. *A Review of the Municipal Activities in the City of Oakland,
    California, 1905–1915*, by Mayor Frank K. Mott. Oakland: n.p., 1915.
Protective Agency for Women and Children, Chicago, Illinois. *Annual
    Report*, 1887–1905.
U.S. Bureau of the Census. *Tenth Census of the United States, 1880:
    Population*. Vol. 1. Washington, D.C.: GPO, 1883.
——. *Twelfth Census of the United States, 1900: Population*. Vol. 1, pt. 1,
    California. Washington, D.C.: GPO, 1904.
——. *Thirteenth Census of the United States, 1910: Population*. Vol. 2,
    Reports by States. Washington, D.C.: GPO, 1913.
——. *Thirteenth Census of the United States, 1910: Abstract of the Census,
    Supplement for California*. Washington, D.C.: GPO, 1913.
——. *Fourteenth Census of the United States, 1920: Population*. Vol. 3,
    Composition and Characteristics of the Population by States. Washington,
    D.C.: GPO, 1922.
——. *Fifteenth Census of the United States, 1930: Population*. Vol. 6.
    Washington, D.C.: GPO, 1933.
U.S. Congress. Senate. *Report on the Condition of Women and Child Wage
    Earners in the United States*. S.Doc. 645, 61st Cong., 2d sess. Vol. 15,
    Relation Between Occupation and Criminality in Women. Washington,
    D.C., 1911.
Woman's Christian Temperance Union of Northern California. *Annual
    Reports*, 1887–1909.

BOOKS, ARTICLES, AND UNPUBLISHED STUDIES

Abbott, Edith. "Training for the Policewoman's Job." *Woman Citizen* 10
    (April 1926): 30.

Addams, Jane. *A New Conscience and an Ancient Evil*. New York: Macmillan, 1912.

Additon, Henrietta A. "Work among Delinquent Women and Girls." *Annals of the American Academy of Political and Social Science* 79 (September 1918): 152–59.

Alexander, Ruth. "'The Girl Problem': Class Inequity and Psychology in the Remaking of Female Adolescence, 1900–1930." Ph.D. diss., Cornell University, 1990.

Amigh, Mrs. O. L. "Section on Juvenile Delinquents." National Conference of Charities and Correction, *Proceedings* 30 (1903): 517.

Amott, Teresa L., and Julie A. Matthaei. *Race, Gender, and Work: A Multicultural History of Women in the United States*. Boston: South End Press, 1991.

Anthony, Susan B., and Ida Husted Harper, eds. *History of Woman Suffrage*, vols. 4, 5. Indianapolis, Ind.: Hollenbeck Press, 1902.

Arnold, Marybeth Hamilton. "'The Life of a Citizen in the Hands of a Woman': Sexual Assault in New York City, 1790–1820." In *Passion and Power: Sexuality in History*, edited by Kathy Peiss and Christina Simmons, pp. 35–56. Philadelphia, Pa.: Temple University Press, 1989.

Bagwell, Beth. *Oakland: The Story of a City*. Novato, Calif.: Presidio Press, 1982.

Bailey, Beth. *From Front Porch to Back Seat: Courtship in Twentieth-Century America*. Baltimore, Md.: Johns Hopkins University Press, 1988.

Baker, Joseph E. *Past and Present of Alameda County, California*. Chicago: S. J. Clarke Publishing Company, 1914.

Barker-Benfield, G. J. *The Horrors of the Half-Known Life: Male Attitudes toward Women and Sexuality in America*. New York: Harper and Row, 1976.

Bass, Charlotta. *Forty Years*. Los Angeles: C. A. Bass, 1960.

Bates, J. C., ed. *History of the Bench and Bar of California*. San Francisco: n.p., 1912.

Bean, Walton, and James J. Rawls. *California: An Interpretive History*. 5th ed. New York: McGraw-Hill, 1988.

Beaseley, Delilah. *Negro Trail Blazers of California*. Los Angeles: Times Mirror Printing and Binding House, 1919.

Bell, Ernest A. *Fighting the Traffic in Young Girls, or the War on the White Slave Trade*. Chicago: n.p., 1910.

Berry, Mary J. "The State's Duty to the Delinquent Girl." National Conference on the Education of Truant, Backward, Dependent, and Delinquent Children, *Proceedings* (1918): 82–83.

Bingham, Anne T. "Determinants of Sex Delinquency in Adolescent Girls

Based on Intensive Studies of 500 Cases." *Journal of the American Institute of Criminal Law and Criminology* 13 (February 1923): 494–586.

Binheim, Max, ed. *Women of the West*. Los Angeles: Publishers Press, 1928.

Bissell Brown, Victoria. "Golden Girls: Female Socialization in Los Angeles, 1880–1910." Ph.D. diss., University of California, San Diego, 1985.

Blackstone, William. *Commentaries on the Laws of England*, vol. 4. Chicago: University of Chicago Press, 1976. (Facsimile of the original first edition, published in 1765–69.)

Blair, Karen J. *The Clubwoman as Feminist: True Womanhood Redefined, 1868–1914*. New York: Holmes and Meier, 1980.

Blake, Evarts I., ed. *Greater Oakland*. Oakland, Calif.: Pacific Publishing Company, 1911.

Bogardus, Emory S. *The Mexican in the United States*. Los Angeles: University of Southern California Press, 1934.

Bond, J. Max. "The Negro in Los Angeles." Ph.D. diss., University of Southern California, 1936.

Bordin, Ruth. *Frances Willard: A Biography*. Chapel Hill: University of North Carolina Press, 1986.

——. *Woman and Temperance: The Quest for Power and Liberty, 1873–1900*. Philadelphia, Pa.: Temple University Press, 1981.

Boris, Eileen, "Reconstructing the 'Family': Women, Progressive Reform, and the Problem of Social Control." In *Gender, Class, Race, and Reform in the Progressive Era*, edited by Noralee Frankel and Nancy S. Dye, pp. 73–86. Lexington, Ky.: University Press of Kentucky, 1991.

Bowler, Alida. "A Study of 75 Delinquent Girls." *Journal of Delinquency* 2 (May 1917): 156–68.

Boyer, Paul. *Purity in Print: The Vice Society Movement and Book Censorship in America*. New York: Scribners, 1968.

——. *Urban Masses and Moral Order in America, 1820–1920*. Cambridge, Mass.: Harvard University Press, 1978.

Boylan, Anne. "Women in Groups: An Analysis of Women's Benevolent Organizations in New York and Boston, 1797–1840." *Journal of American History* 71 (December 1984): 497–523.

Brandt, Allan M. *No Magic Bullet: A Social History of Venereal Disease in the United States since 1880*. New York: Oxford University Press, 1985.

Breckinridge, Sophonisba P., and Edith Abbott. *The Delinquent Child and the Home: A Study of the Delinquent Wards of the Juvenile Court of Chicago*. 1912. Reprint. New York: Survey Associates, 1916.

Brenzel, Barbara. *Daughters of the State: A Social Portrait of the First Reform School for Girls in North America, 1865–1905*. Cambridge, Mass.: MIT Press, 1983.

Bristow, Nancy. "Creating Crusaders: The Commission on Training Camp Activities and the Progressive Social Vision during World War I." Ph.D. diss., University of California, Berkeley, 1989.

Brumberg, Joan Jacobs. " 'Ruined Girls': Changing Community Responses to Illegitimacy in Upstate New York, 1890–1920." *Journal of Social History* 18 (Winter 1984): 247–72.

Buenker, John D., John C. Burnham, and Robert M. Crunden. *Progressivism.* Cambridge, Mass.: Schenkman, 1977.

Bunch, Lonnie G. III. "A Past Not Necessarily Prologue: The Afro-American in Los Angeles." In *Twentieth-Century Los Angeles: Power, Promotion, and Social Conflict,* edited by Norman M. Klein and Martin J. Schiesl, pp. 101–30. Claremont, Calif.: Regina Books, 1990.

Burleigh, Edith, and Frances Harris. *The Delinquent Girl: A Study of the Girl on Parole in Massachusetts.* New York: New York School of Social Work, 1923.

Cahn, Frances, and Valeska Bary. *Welfare Activities of Federal, State, and Local Governments in California, 1850–1934.* Berkeley: University of California Press, 1936.

Camarillo, Albert. *Chicanos in a Changing Society: From Mexican Pueblos to American Barrios in Santa Barbara and Southern California, 1848–1930.* Cambridge, Mass.: Harvard University Press, 1979.

Carby, Hazel. "Policing the Black Woman's Body in an Urban Context." *Critical Inquiry* 18 (Summer 1992): 738–55.

Case, Walter H. *History of Long Beach and Vicinity,* vol. 1. Chicago: S. J. Clarke Publishing Company, 1927.

Chesney-Lind, Meda. "Judicial Paternalism and the Female Status Offender." *Crime and Delinquency* 23 (April 1977): 122–30.

Chesney-Lind, Meda, and Randall G. Shelden. *Girls, Delinquency, and Juvenile Justice.* Pacific Grove, Calif.: Brooks/Cole Publishing Company, 1992.

Cinel, Dino. *From Italy to San Francisco: The Immigrant Experience.* Stanford, Calif.: Stanford University Press, 1982.

Clark, Anna. *Women's Silence, Men's Violence: Sexual Assault in England, 1770–1845.* London: Pandora, 1987.

Clark, David. "Improbable Los Angeles." In *Sunbelt Cities: Politics and Growth since World War II,* edited by Richard M. Bernard and Bradley R. Rice, pp. 268–308. 1983. Reprint. Austin: University of Texas Press, 1988.

Collins, Patricia Hill. *Black Feminist Thought: Knowledge, Consciousness, and the Politics of Empowerment.* London: Routledge, 1991.

Connelly, Mark. *The Response to Prostitution in the Progressive Era.* Chapel Hill: University of North Carolina Press, 1980.

Cooper, Anna Julia. *A Voice from the South*. 1892. Reprint. New York: Oxford University Press, 1988.

Cott, Nancy F. "Passionlessness: An Interpretation of Victorian Sexual Ideology, 1790–1850." *Signs* 4 (Winter 1978): 219–36.

Crouchett, Lawrence P., Lonnie G. Bunch III, and Martha Kendall Winnacker, eds. *Visions toward Tomorrow: The History of the East Bay Afro-American Community, 1852–1977*. Oakland: Northern California Center for Afro-American History and Life, 1989.

Culp, Alice Bessie. "A Case Study of the Living Conditions of Thirty-Five Mexican Families with Special Reference to Mexican Children." Master's thesis, University of Southern California, 1921.

Darwin, Maud. "Policewomen: Their Work in America." *Nineteenth Century* 75 (June 1914): 1371–77.

Davies, Margery W. *Women's Place Is at the Typewriter: Office Work and Office Workers, 1870–1930*. Philadelphia, Pa.: Temple University Press.

Davis, Allen F. *Spearheads for Reform: The Social Settlement and the Progressive Movement, 1890–1914*. New York: Oxford University Press, 1967.

Davis, Angela. "Rape, Racism, and the Myth of the Black Rapist." In *Women, Race, and Class*, pp. 172–201. New York: Random House, 1981.

Davis, Katherine Bement. "Women's Education in Social Hygiene." *Annals of the American Academy of Political and Social Science* 79 (September 1918): 167–77.

DeCosta, Benjamin F. *The White Cross: Its Origins and Progress*. Chicago: Sanitary Publishing Company, 1887.

Degler, Carl N. *At Odds: Women and the Family in America from the Revolution to the Present*. New York: Oxford University Press, 1981.

De Graff, Lawrence. "The City of Black Angels: Emergence of the Los Angeles Ghetto, 1890–1930." *Pacific Historical Review* 39 (August 1970): 323–52.

D'Emilio, John, and Freedman, Estelle B. *Intimate Matters: A History of Sexuality in America*. New York: Harper and Row, 1988.

Dewson, Mary. "Probation and Institutional Care of Girls." In *The Child in the City*, edited by Sophonisba P. Breckinridge, pp. 355–69. Chicago: Manz Engraving Company/Hollister Press, 1912.

Dietzler, Mary Macy. *Detention Houses and Reformatories as Protective Social Agencies in the Campaign of the United States Government against Venereal Diseases*. Washington, D.C.: Government Printing Office, 1922.

DiLeonardo, Micaela. "The Myth of the Urban Village: Women, Work, and Family among Italian-Americans in Twentieth-Century California." In *The Women's West*, edited by Susan Armitage and Elizabeth Jameson, pp. 277–89. Norman: University of Oklahoma Press, 1987.

——. *The Varieties of Ethnic Experience: Kinship, Class, and Gender among California Italian-Americans.* Ithaca, N.Y.: Cornell University Press, 1984.

Dubinsky, Karen. *Improper Advances: Rape and Heterosexual Conflict in Ontario, 1880–1929.* Chicago: University of Chicago Press, 1993.

DuBois, Ellen Carol, and Linda Gordon. "Seeking Ecstasy on the Battlefield: Danger and Pleasure in Nineteenth-Century Feminist Sexual Thought." *Feminist Studies* 9 (Spring 1983): 7–25.

Du Bois, W. E. B., ed. *Efforts for Social Betterment among Negro Americans.* Atlanta University Publications, no. 14. Atlanta, Ga.: Atlanta University Press, 1909.

Dudden, Faye E. *Serving Women: Household Service in Nineteenth Century America.* Middletown, Conn.: Wesleyan University Press, 1983.

Dye, Nancy Schrom. *As Equals and Sisters: The Labor Movement and the Women's Trade Union League of New York.* Columbia: University of Missouri Press, 1980.

Dyhouse, Carol. *Girls Growing Up in Late Victorian and Edwardian England.* London: Routledge and Kegan Paul, 1981.

Ehrenreich, John H. *The Altruistic Imagination: A History of Social Work and Social Policy in the United States.* Ithaca, N.Y.: Cornell University Press, 1985.

Elliot, Mabel A. *Correctional Education and the Delinquent Girl.* Harrisburg, Pa.: n.p., 1928.

Engel, Barbara Alpern. "Peasant Morality and Pre-Marital Relations in Late Nineteenth-Century Russia." *Journal of Social History* 23 (Summer 1990): 695–714.

Erenberg, Lewis A. *Steppin' Out: New York Nightlife and the Transformation of American Culture.* Westport, Conn.: Greenwood Press, 1981.

Estrich, Susan. *Real Rape.* Cambridge, Mass.: Harvard University Press, 1987.

Evans, Elizabeth Glendower, and Dewson, Mary W. "Feeble-mindedness and Juvenile Delinquency." *Charities and the Commons* 20 (May 2, 1908): 183–91.

Ewen, Elizabeth. *Immigrant Women in the Land of Dollars: Life and Culture on the Lower East Side.* New York: Monthly Review Press, 1985.

Falconer, Martha P. "The Culture of Family Life versus Reformatory Treatment." National Conference of Charities and Correction, *Proceedings* 41 (1914): 108–10.

——. "The Part of the Reformatory in the Elimination of Prostitution." *Social Hygiene* 5 (January 1915): 1–9.

——. "Reformatory Treatment for Women." National Conference of Charities and Correction, *Proceedings* 41 (1914): 253–56.

——. "The Report of the Committee on the Council on Social Hygiene." *Social Hygiene* 1 (September 1915): 514–28.

——. "The Segregation of Delinquent Women and Girls as a War Measure." *Annals of the American Academy of Political and Social Science* 79 (September 1918): 160–66.

——. "Work of the Girls' Department, House of Refuge, Philadelphia, PA." National Conference of Charities and Correction, *Proceedings* 35 (1908): 391–94.

——. "Work of the Section on Reformatories and Houses of Detention." National Conference of Charities and Correction, *Proceedings* 45 (1918): 668–71.

Fass, Paula. *The Damned and the Beautiful: American Youth in the 1920s.* New York: Oxford University Press, 1977.

Feinman, Clarice. *Women in the Criminal Justice System.* 1980. Reprint. New York: Praeger, 1986.

Fernald, Grace. "Report of the Psychological Work in the California School for Girls." *Journal of Delinquency* 1 (March 1916): 22–32.

Fesler, Alice May. "A Study of the Relation of Inadequate Parental Control to Truancy among Girls." Master's thesis, University of Southern California, 1922.

Filene, Peter. *Himself/Herself: Sex Roles in Modern America.* 2d ed. Baltimore, Md.: Johns Hopkins University Press, 1986.

Fitzpatrick, Ellen. *Endless Crusade: Women Social Scientists and Progressive Reform.* New York: Oxford University Press, 1990.

Fletcher, Russell Holmes, ed. *Who's Who in California.* Los Angeles: Who's Who Publications Company, 1941.

Fogelson, Robert M. *The Fragmented Metropolis: Los Angeles, 1850–1930.* Cambridge, Mass.: Harvard University Press, 1967.

Foster, George. *Tzintzuntzan: Mexican Peasants in a Changing World.* 1967. Reprint. New York: Elsevier–New York, 1979.

Foucault, Michel. *The History of Sexuality: An Introduction.* New York: Random House, 1978.

Fout, John C., and Maura Shaw Tantillo, eds. *American Sexual Politics: Sex, Gender, and Race since the Civil War.* Chicago: University of Chicago Press, 1990.

Fowler, Rosalie. "A Case Study of the Causes of Delinquency among School Girls in Los Angeles." Master's thesis, University of Southern California, 1922.

Francis, Vida Hunt. "The Delinquent Girl." National Conference of Charities and Correction, *Proceedings* 33 (1906): 141–42.

Frankel, Noralee, and Nancy S. Dye, eds. *Gender, Class, Race, and Reform in the Progressive Era.* Lexington, Ky.: University Press of Kentucky, 1991.

Freedman, Estelle B. "In the Matter of the Removal of Miriam Van Waters: Female Deviance in Post–World War II America." Paper presented at the Berkshire Conference on the History of Women, Smith College, June 1, 1984.

——. *Their Sisters' Keepers: Women's Prison Reform in America, 1830–1930.* Ann Arbor: University of Michigan Press, 1981.

——. "Sexuality in Nineteenth-Century America: Behavior, Ideology, and Politics." *Reviews in American History* 10 (December 1982): 197–215.

Friedman, Lawrence M. *Crime and Punishment in American History.* New York: Basic Books, 1993.

——. *A History of American Law.* 2d ed. New York: Simon and Schuster, 1985.

Friedman, Lawrence M., and Robert Percival. *The Roots of Justice: Crime and Punishment in Alameda County, California, 1870–1910.* Chapel Hill: University of North Carolina Press, 1981.

Frost, Carrie A. "The Degenerate Girl." *Wisconsin Medical Journal* 12 (February 1914): 287–89.

Gamio, Manuel. *The Mexican Immigrant: His Life Story.* 1931. Reprint. New York: Arno Press, 1969.

García, Mario T. "The Chicana in American History: The Mexican Women of El Paso, 1880–1920." *Pacific Historical Review* 49 (May 1980): 315–37.

Gardener, Helen H. "A Battle for Sound Morality, or the History of Recent Age-of-Consent Legislation in the United States." Pt. 1, *Arena* 13 (August 1895): 353–71; pt. 2, *Arena* 14 (September 1895): 1–32; pt. 3, *Arena* 14 (October 1895): 205–20; pt. 4, *Arena* 14 (November 1895): 401–19.

——. *Pray You, Sir, Whose Daughter?* Boston: Arena Publishing Company, 1892.

——. *Is This Your Son, My Lord?* New York: Fenno, 1890.

——. "The Shame of America: The Age of Consent Laws in the United States." *Arena* 11 (January 1895): 192–215.

Gibson, Mary S. *A Record of Twenty-five Years of the California Federation of Women's Clubs, 1900–1925.* N.p.: California Federation of Women's Clubs, 1927.

Gillis, John. "Servants, Sexual Relations, and the Risks of Illegitimacy in London, 1801–1900." *Feminist Studies* 5 (Spring 1979): 142–73.

Glazer, Penina Migdal, and Miriam Slater. *Unequal Colleagues: The Entrance of Women into the Professions, 1890–1940.* New Brunswick, N.J.: Rutgers University Press, 1987.

Glenn, Susan A. *Daughters of the Shtetl: Life and Labor in the Immigrant Generation.* Ithaca, N.Y.: Cornell University Press, 1990.

Goddard, Henry H., and Helen F. Hill. "Delinquent Girls Tested by the Binet Scale." *Training School Bulletin* 8 (1911): 50–56.

González, Deena J. "The Widowed Women of Santa Fe: Assessments on the Lives of an Unmarried Population, 1850–1880." In *On Their Own: Widows and Widowhood in the American Southwest, 1848–1939*, edited by Arlene Scadron, pp. 65–90. Urbana: University of Illinois Press, 1988.

González, Luis. *San José de Gracia: Mexican Village in Transition*. Austin: University of Texas Press, 1972.

Goodwin, Joanne. "An Experiment in Paid Motherhood." *Gender and History* 4 (Autumn 1992): 323–42.

Gordon, Anna. *The Beautiful Life of Frances Willard*. Chicago: Woman's Temperance Publishing Association, 1898.

Gordon, Linda. "Black and White Visions of Welfare: Women's Welfare Activism, 1890–1945." *Journal of American History* 78 (September 1991): 559–90.

———. "Feminism and Social Control: The Case of Child Abuse and Neglect." In *What Is Feminism?: A Re-examination*, edited by Juliet Mitchell and Ann Oakley, pp. 63–84. New York: Pantheon Books, 1986.

———. *Heroes of Their Own Lives: The Politics and History of Family Violence*. New York: Viking, 1988.

———. "Incest and Resistance: Patterns of Father-Daughter Incest, 1880–1930." *Social Problems* 33 (April 1986): 253–67.

———. "Single Mothers and Child Neglect, 1880–1920." *American Quarterly* 37 (Summer 1985): 173–92.

———. "Voluntary Motherhood: The Beginnings of Feminist Birth Control Ideas in the United States." In *Clio's Consciousness Raised: New Perspectives on the History of Women*, edited by Mary S. Hartman and Lois W. Banner. New York: Harper and Row, 1974.

———. *Woman's Body, Woman's Right: A Social History of Birth Control in America*. 2d ed. New York: Penguin, 1977.

———, ed. *Women, the State, and Welfare*. Madison: University of Wisconsin Press, 1990.

Gordon, Linda, and Paul O'Keefe. "Incest as a Form of Family Violence: Evidence from Historical Case Records." *Journal of Marriage and the Family* 46 (February 1984): 27–34.

Gordon, Lynn. *Gender and Higher Education in the Progressive Era*. New Haven, Conn.: Yale University Press, 1990.

Gorham, Deborah. "The 'Maiden Tribute to Modern Babylon' Re-examined: Child Prostitution and the Idea of Childhood in Late-Victorian England." *Victorian Studies* 21 (Spring 1978): 353–79.

Griswold del Castillo, Richard. *La Familia: Chicano Families in the Urban Southwest, 1848 to the Present*. Notre Dame, Ind.: University of Notre Dame Press, 1984.

Grossberg, Michael. *Governing the Hearth: Law and the Family in*

Nineteenth-Century America. Chapel Hill: University of North Carolina Press, 1985.

Gullett, Gayle Ann. "Feminism, Politics, and Voluntary Groups: Organized Womanhood in California, 1886–1896." Ph.D. diss., University of California, Riverside, 1983.

Gusfield, Joseph. *Symbolic Crusade: Status Politics and the American Temperance Movement.* Westport, Conn.: Greenwood Press, 1963.

Gutiérrez, Ramón A. *When Jesus Came, the Corn Mothers Went Away: Marriage, Sexuality, and Power in New Mexico, 1500–1846.* Stanford, Calif.: Stanford University Press, 1991.

Gutman, Herbert G. *The Black Family in Slavery and Freedom, 1750–1925.* New York: Pantheon Books, 1976.

Haber, Samuel. *Efficiency and Uplift: Scientific Management in the Progressive Era, 1890–1920.* Chicago: University of Chicago Press, 1964.

Hall, G. Stanley. *Adolescence: Its Psychology and Its Relations to Physiology, Anthropology, Sociology, Sex, Crime, Religion, and Education.* 2 vols. 1904. Reprint. New York: D. Appleton and Company, 1915.

——. "The Budding Girl." In *Educational Problems*, 2:1–41. New York: n.p., 1911.

——. "Education and the Social Hygiene Movement." *Social Hygiene* 1 (December 1914): 29–35.

Hall, Jacquelyn Dowd. "'The Mind That Burns in Each Body': Women, Rape, and Racial Violence." In *Powers of Desire: The Politics of Sexuality*, edited by Ann Snitow et al., pp. 328–49. New York: Monthly Review Press, 1983.

——. *Revolt against Chivalry: Jessie Daniel Ames and the Women's Campaign against Lynching.* New York: Columbia University Press, 1974.

Haller, Mark H. *Eugenics: Hereditarian Attitudes in American Thought.* New Brunswick, N.J.: Rutgers University Press, 1963.

Hallinan, Tim Stirling. "The Portuguese of California." Ph.D. diss., University of California, Berkeley, 1968.

Hamilton, Alice. "Venereal Diseases in Institutions for Women and Girls." National Conference of Charities and Correction, *Proceedings* 37 (1910): 53–56.

Hamilton, Mary E. *The Policewoman: Her Service and Ideals.* New York: Frederick A. Stokes Company, 1924.

Hamilton, Tullia Brown. "The National Association of Colored Women, 1896–1920." Ph.D. diss., Emory University, 1978.

Harris, Barbara. *Beyond Her Sphere: Women and Professions in American History.* Westport, Conn.: Greenwood Press, 1978.

Harris, Mrs. C. I. *Modern Herodians, or Slaughterers of Innocents*. Portland, Oreg.: Wallace Printing Co., 1909.

Hartmann, Heidi. "The Family as the Locus of Gender, Class, and Political Struggle: The Example of Housework." In *Feminism and Methodology*, edited by Sandra Harding, pp. 109–34. Bloomington: Indiana University Press, 1987.

Hays, Samuel P. *The Response to Industrialism*. Chicago: University of Chicago Press, 1957.

Heitman, Emily Norma. "A Study of the Probation System for Juvenile Offenders in Los Angeles County." Master's thesis, University of Southern California, 1924.

Hersh, Blanche. *The Slavery of Sex: Feminist Abolitionists in Nineteenth-Century America*. Urbana: University of Illinois Press, 1978.

Hewitt, Nancy A., and Suzanne Lebsock. *Visible Women: New Essays on American Activism*. Urbana: University of Illinois Press, 1993.

Hill, Joseph A. *Women in Gainful Occupations, 1870–1920*. Washington, D.C.: Government Printing Office, 1929.

Hiller, Francis H. *The Juvenile Court of Los Angeles County, California*. Los Angeles: Rotary Club of Los Angeles, 1928.

Hine, Darlene Clark. "Rape and the Inner Lives of Black Women in the Middle West: Preliminary Thoughts on the Culture of Dissemblance." *Signs* 14 (Summer 1989): 912–20.

——, ed. *Black Women in America: An Historical Encyclopedia*. New York: Carlson Publishing, 1993.

Hinkel, Edgar J., and William E. McCann. *Oakland, 1852–1938: Some Phases of the Social, Political, and Economic History of Oakland, CA*. 2 vols. Oakland, Calif.: Oakland Public Library, 1939.

Hobson, Barbara Meil. *Uneasy Virtue: The Politics of Prostitution and the American Reform Tradition*. New York: Basic Books, 1987.

Hodes, Martha. "The Sexualization of Reconstruction Politics: White Women and Black Men in the South after the Civil War." In *American Sexual Politics: Sex, Gender, and Race since the Civil War*, edited by John C. Fout and Maura Shaw Tantillo. Chicago: University of Chicago Press, 1990.

Hofstadter, Richard. *The Age of Reform*. New York: Vintage Books, 1955.

James, Edward T., Janet Wilson James, and Paul S. Boyer, eds. *Notable American Women, 1607–1950: A Biographical Dictionary*. Cambridge, Mass.: Belknap Press of Harvard University Press, 1971.

Jameson, Elizabeth. "High-Grade and Fissure: A Working-Class History of the Cripple Creek, Colorado, Gold Mining District, 1890–1905." Ph.D. diss., University of Michigan, 1987.

——. "Imperfect Unions: Class and Gender in Cripple Creek, 1894–1904." In

Class, Sex, and the Woman Worker, edited by Milton Cantor and Bruce Laurie, pp. 166–202. Westport, Conn.: Greenwood Press, 1977.

Jenkins, Maude T. "The History of the Black Woman's Club Movement in America." Ph.D. diss., Teachers' College, Columbia University, 1984.

Johnson, Marilynn S. *The Second Gold Rush: Oakland and the East Bay in World War II.* Berkeley: University of California Press, 1993.

Jones, Jacqueline. *Labor of Love, Labor of Sorrow: Black Women, Work, and the Family from Slavery to the Present.* New York: Basic Books, 1985.

Kasson, John F. *Amusing the Million: Coney Island at the Turn of the Century.* New York: Hill and Wang, 1978.

Katz, Michael. *Poverty and Policy in American History.* New York: Academic Press, 1983.

Katz, Sherry. "Dual Commitments: Feminism, Socialism, and Women's Political Activism in California, 1890–1920." Ph.D. diss., University of California, Los Angeles, 1991.

———. "Socialist Women and Progressive Reform." In *California Progressivism Revisited,* edited by William Deverel and Thomas Sitton, pp. 117–43. Berkeley: University of California Press, 1994.

Katzman, David M. *Seven Days a Week: Women and Domestic Service in Industrializing America.* Urbana: University of Illinois Press, 1981.

Kaufmann, Reginald Wright. *The House of Bondage.* New York: Moffat, Yard and Co., 1910.

Kazin, Michael. "The Great Exception Revisited: Organized Labor and Politics in San Francisco and Los Angeles, 1870–1940." *Pacific Historical Review* 55 (August 1986): 371–402.

Kellogg, Mary Brockett. "An Analysis of Broken Homes as Disclosed by a Case Study of Child Welfare." Master's thesis, University of Southern California, 1923.

Kerr, James M. *Consolidated Supplement to Kerr's Cyclopedic California Codes.* San Francisco: Bender-Moss, 1913.

Kessler-Harris, Alice. *Out to Work: A History of America's Wage-Earning Women in the United States.* New York: Oxford University Press, 1982.

Kevles, Daniel J. *In the Name of Eugenics: Genetics and the Uses of Human Heredity.* New York: Knopf, 1985.

Kirshner, Olive Putnam. "The Italian in Los Angeles." Master's thesis, University of Southern California, 1920.

Koven, Seth, and Sonya Michel, eds. *Mothers of a New World: Maternalist Politics and the Origins of Welfare States.* London: Routledge, 1993.

———. "Womanly Duties: Maternalist Politics and the Origins of Welfare States in France, Germany, Great Britain, and the United States, 1880–1920." *American Historical Review* 95 (October 1990): 1076–1108.

Kunzel, Regina G. *Fallen Women, Problem Girls: Unmarried Mothers and the Professionalization of Social Work, 1890–1945*. New Haven, Conn.: Yale University Press, 1993.

——. "From Seduced Victims to Sex Delinquents: Evangelicals, Social Workers, and Unmarried Mothers, 1890–1945." Paper delivered at the annual meeting of the Pacific Coast Branch of the American Historical Association, San Francisco, August 12, 1988.

——. "The Professionalization of Benevolence: Evangelicals and Social Workers in the Florence Crittenton Homes, 1915–1945." *Journal of Social History* 22 (Fall 1988): 21–43.

Ladd-Taylor, Molly. *Mother-Work: Women, Child Welfare, and the State, 1890–1930*. Urbana: University of Illinois Press, 1994.

Lamb, Emily. "A Study of Thirty-five Delinquent Girls." *Journal of Delinquency* 4 (March 1919): 74–85.

Lamphere, Louise. *From Working Daughters to Working Mothers: Immigrant Women in a New England Industrial Community*. Ithaca, N.Y.: Cornell University Press, 1987.

Lane, Winthrop D. "Girls and Khaki." *Survey* 39 (December 1, 1917). (I have relied on a reprint of this article produced by the Commission on Training Camp Activities, located in RG 165, Box 442, NA.)

Leach, R. B. "The Age of Consent: A Symposium." *Arena* 12 (April 1895): 282–88.

Leff, Mark H. "Consensus for Reform: The Mothers' Pension Movement in the Progressive Era." *Social Service Review* 47 (September 1973): 397–417.

Leiby, James. *A History of Social Welfare and Social Work in the United States*. New York: Columbia University Press, 1978.

Leonard, John William, ed. *Woman's Who's Who of America*. New York: American Commonwealth Company, 1914.

Lerner, Gerda, ed. *Black Women in White America: A Documentary History*. New York: Pantheon Books, 1972.

Levine, Susan. *Labor's True Woman: Carpet Weavers, Industrialization, and Labor Reform in the Gilded Age*. Philadelphia, Pa.: Temple University Press, 1984.

Locke, Charles Edward. *White Slavery in Los Angeles: Some Startling Disclosures*. Los Angeles: Times Mirror Company Printer, 1913.

Loewenberg, Bert James, and Ruth Bogin, eds. *Black Women in Nineteenth-Century American Life: Their Words, Their Thoughts, Their Feelings*. University Park: Pennsylvania State University Press, 1976.

Loranger, Joyce, and Mary Tyler. "Working Women in the Los Angeles Area, 1920–39." Master's thesis, California State University, Dominquez Hills, 1984.

Lubove, Roy. *The Professional Altruist: The Emergence of Social Work as a Career, 1880–1930*. Cambridge, Mass.: Harvard University Press, 1965.

Lunbeck, Elizabeth. "'A New Generation of Women': Progressive Psychiatrists and the Hypersexual Female." *Feminist Studies* 13 (Fall 1987): 513–43.

Lynd, Robert S., and Helen Merrell Lynd. *Middletown: A Study in Modern American Culture.* 1929. Reprint. New York: Harcourt Brace Jovanovich, 1956.

McCulloch, Catharine Waugh. "Stop Ruin of Girls." *Chicago Record Herald,* January 8, 1905. Also published as a pamphlet by the Illinois Federation of Women's Clubs.

McGroarty, John S., ed. *History of Los Angeles County.* 3 vols. Chicago and New York: American Historical Society, 1923.

——. *Los Angeles: From the Mountains to the Sea.* 3 vols. Chicago and New York: American Historical Society, 1921.

McKibbon, Thomas Stuart. "The Origin and Development of the Los Angeles County Juvenile Court." Master's thesis, University of Southern California, 1932.

McWilliams, Carey. *Southern California: An Island on the Land.* 1946. Reprint. Salt Lake City, Utah: Gibbs M. Smith/Peregrine Smith, 1985.

Mapes, C. C. "Higher Enlightenment versus 'Age of Consent.'" *Medical Age: A Semi-Monthly Journal of Medicine and Surgery* 14 (February 26, 1896): 105–8.

May, Lary. *Screening Out the Past: The Birth of Mass Culture and the Motion Picture Industry.* New York: Oxford University Press, 1980.

May, Martha. "The Historical Problem of the Family Wage: The Ford Motor Company and the Five-Dollar Day." In *Unequal Sisters: A Multi-Cultural Reader in U.S. Women's History,* edited by Ellen Carol DuBois and Vicki L. Ruiz, pp. 275–91. New York and London: Routledge, 1990.

Melder, Keith. *Beginnings of Sisterhood: The American Woman's Rights Movement, 1800–1850.* New York: Schocken Books, 1977.

Mennel, Robert. *Thorns and Thistles: Juvenile Delinquency in the United States, 1825–1940.* Hanover, N.H.: Published for University of New Hampshire by University Press of New England, 1973.

Meyerowitz, Joanne. *Women Adrift: Independent Wage Earners in Chicago, 1880–1930.* Chicago: University of Chicago Press, 1988.

Michel, Sonya. "The Limits of Maternalism: Policies toward American Wage-Earning Mothers during the Progressive Era." In *Mothers of a New World: Maternalist Politics and the Origins of Welfare States,* edited by Seth Koven and Sonya Michel, pp. 277–320. London: Routledge, 1993.

Midgley, Clare. *Women against Slavery: The British Campaigns, 1780–1870.* London: Routledge, 1992.

Miller, Dan. "Alternatives to Incarceration: From Total Institutions to Total Systems." Ph.D. diss., University of California, Berkeley, 1980.

Miner, Maude E. "The Community's Responsibility for Safeguarding Girls."
    Address delivered under the auspices of the Educational Department of
    the Municipal Court of Philadelphia, February 6, 1920.
——. "Prevention of Delinquency in War Time." National Conference on the
    Education of Truant, Backward, Dependent, and Delinquent Children,
    Proceedings (1918): 56–63.
——. "The Problem of Wayward Girls and Delinquent Women." *Proceedings
    of the Academy of Political Science* 2 (1912): 604–12.
——. "Protective Work for Girls in War Time." National Conference of
    Charities and Correction, *Proceedings* 45 (1918): 656–65.
——. *Slavery of Prostitution: A Plea for Emancipation*. New York:
    Macmillan, 1916.
Mohr, James C. *Abortion in America: The Origins and Evolution of National
    Policy, 1800–1900*. Oxford: Oxford University Press, 1978.
Morse, Fannie French. "The Methods Most Helpful to Girls." National
    Conference of Charities and Correction, *Proceedings* 31 (1904): 306–11.
Moses, Wilson Jeremiah. "Domestic Feminism Conservatism, Sex Roles, and
    Black Women's Clubs, 1893–1896." In *Black Women in United States
    History*, edited by Darlene Clark Hine, 3:959–70. New York: Carlson
    Publishing, 1990.
Mott, Frank Luther. *A History of American Magazines, 1885–1905*.
    Cambridge, Mass.: Belknap Press of Harvard University Press, 1957.
Muncy, Robyn. *Creating a Female Dominion in American Reform*. New
    York: Oxford University Press, 1991.
Nathanson, Constance A. *Dangerous Passage: The Social Control of
    Women's Sexuality in Adolescence*. Philadelphia, Pa.: Temple University
    Press, 1991.
National Association for the Advancement of Colored People. *Thirty Years of
    Lynching in the United States, 1889–1918*. New York: NAACP, 1919.
Nelson, William. *The Americanization of the Common Law: The Impact of
    Legal Change on Massachusetts Society, 1760–1830*. Cambridge, Mass.:
    Harvard University Press, 1975.
Nemeth, Charles P. "Character Evidence in Rape Trials in Nineteenth-
    Century New York: Chastity and the Admissibility of Specific Acts."
    Women's Rights Law Reporter 6 (Spring 1980): 214–25.
Nesbitt, Florence. *Study of a Minimum Standard of Living for Dependent
    Families in Los Angeles*. Los Angeles: Community Welfare Federation,
    1927.
Neverdon-Morton, Cynthia. *Afro-American Women of the South and the
    Advancement of the Race, 1895–1925*. Knoxville: University of Tennessee
    Press, 1989.
New York City. Committee of Fifteen. *The Social Evil: With Special*

Reference to Conditions Existing in the City of New York. New York: G. P. Putnam's Sons, 1902.

New York City. Research Committee of the Committee of Fourteen. *The Social Evil in New York City: A Study in Law Enforcement.* New York: A. H. Kellogg Co., 1910.

Noonan, John T., Jr. *Contraception: A History of Its Treatment by the Catholic Theologians and Canonists.* Cambridge, Mass.: Belknap Press, 1965.

Odem, Mary E. "City Mothers and Delinquent Daughters: Female Juvenile Justice Reform in Early Twentieth-Century Los Angeles." In *California Progressivism Revisited,* edited by William Deverel and Thomas Sitton, pp. 175–99. Berkeley: University of California Press, 1994.

———. "Delinquent Daughters: The Sexual Regulation of Female Minors in the United States, 1880–1920." Ph.D. diss., University of California, Berkeley, 1989.

———. "Single Mothers, Delinquent Daughters, and the Juvenile Court in Early Twentieth-Century Los Angeles." *Journal of Social History* 25 (September 1991): 27–43.

Odem, Mary E., and Steven Schlossman. "Guardians of Virtue: The Juvenile Court and Female Delinquency in Early Twentieth-Century Los Angeles." *Crime and Delinquency* 37 (April 1991): 186–203.

Ordahl, Louise, and George Ordahl. "A Study of Delinquent and Dependent Girls." *Journal of Delinquency* 3 (March 1918): 41–73.

Otis, Margaret. "The Binet Tests Applied to Delinquent Girls." *Psychological Clinic* 7 (October 15, 1913): 127–34.

Owings, Chloe. *Women Police: A Study of the Development and Status of the Women Police Movement.* New York: Frederick H. Hitchcock, 1925.

Painter, Nell Irvin. *Standing at Armageddon.* New York: Norton, 1987.

Pap, Leo. *The Portuguese-American.* Boston: Twayne Publishers, 1981.

Parrot, Andrea, and Laurie Bechhofer, eds. *Acquaintance Rape: The Hidden Crime.* New York: John Wiley and Sons, 1991.

Pascoe, Peggy A. *Relations of Rescue: The Search for Female Authority in the American West, 1874–1939.* New York: Oxford University Press, 1990.

Peebles-Wilkins, Wilma. "Black Women and American Social Welfare: The Life of Fredericka Douglass Sprague Perry." In *Black Women in United States History,* edited by Darlene Clark Hine, 4:979–90. New York: Carlson Publishing, 1990.

Peiss, Kathy. " 'Charity Girls' and City Pleasures: Historical Notes on Working-Class Sexuality, 1880–1920." In *Powers of Desire: The Politics of Sexuality,* edited by Ann Snitow, Christine Stansell, and Sharon Thompson, pp. 74–87. New York: Monthly Review Press, 1983.

———. *Cheap Amusements: Working Women and Leisure in Turn-of-the-Century New York.* Philadelphia, Pa.: Temple University Press, 1986.

Peiss, Kathy, and Christina Simmons, eds. *Passion and Power: Sexuality in History*. Philadelphia, Pa.: Temple University Press, 1989.

Peristiany, John G., ed. *Honor and Shame: The Values of Mediterranean Society*. Chicago: University of Chicago Press, 1966.

Pickens, Donald. *Eugenics and the Progressives*. Nashville, Tenn.: Vanderbilt University Press, 1968.

Pigeon, Helen D. "Policewomen in the United States." *Journal of Criminal Law and Criminology* 18 (November 1927): 372–77.

Pitt-Rivers, Julian. "Honor." In *International Encyclopedia of the Social Sciences*, pp. 503–11. New York: Macmillan, 1968.

Pivar, David. "Cleansing the Nation: The War on Prostitution, 1917–1921." *Prologue: A Journal of the National Archives* 40 (Spring 1980): 29–40.

——. *Purity Crusade: Sexual Morality and Social Control, 1868–1900*. Westport, Conn.: Greenwood Press, 1973.

——. "Women, Sexuality, and the Social Hygiene Movement, 1920–1931." Paper delivered at the annual meeting of the Organization of American Historians, Los Angeles, April 5, 1984.

Platt, Anthony. *The Child Savers: The Invention of Delinquency*. Chicago: University of Chicago Press, 1969.

Pleck, Elizabeth H. "Challenges to Traditional Authority in Immigrant Families." In *The American Family in Social-Historical Perspective*, 3d ed., edited by Michael Gordon, pp. 504–17. New York: St. Martin's Press, 1983.

——. *Domestic Tyranny: The Making of American Social Policy against Family Violence from Colonial Times to the Present*. New York: Oxford University Press, 1987.

——. "Feminist Responses to 'Crimes against Women,' 1868–1896." *Signs* 8 (Spring 1983): 451–70.

Poggi, Mary Josephine. "A Study of the Social Activities of the Catholic Church in Los Angeles." Master's thesis, University of Southern California, 1916.

Powell, Aaron M., ed. *The National Purity Congress: Its Papers, Addresses, Portraits*. New York: American Purity Alliance, 1896.

Pyle, W. H. "A Study of Delinquent Girls." *Psychological Clinic* 8 (October 15, 1914): 143–48.

Rafter, Nicole Hahn. *Partial Justice: Women in State Prisons, 1800–1935*. Boston: Northeastern University Press, 1985.

Reagan, Leslie Jean. "When Abortion Was a Crime: The Legal and Medical Regulation of Abortion, Chicago, 1880–1973." Ph.D. diss., University of Wisconsin, Madison, 1991.

Reeves, Margaret. *Training Schools for Delinquent Girls*. New York: Russell Sage Foundation, 1929.

Rippen, Jane Deeter. "Municipal Detention for Women." National Conference of Charities and Correction, *Proceedings* 45 (1918): 132–41.

———. "Social Hygiene and the War." *Social Hygiene* 5 (January 1919): 125–36.

Roberts, Charles. "The Physical Maturity of Women." *Lancet* 2 (July 25, 1885): 149–50.

Rodgers, Daniel T. "In Search of Progressivism." *Reviews in American History* 10 (December 1982): 111–32.

Roe, Clifford G. *The Great War on White Slavery*. New York: n.p., 1911.

Romo, Ricardo. *East Los Angeles: History of a Barrio*. Austin: University of Texas Press, 1983.

Rosen, Ruth. *The Lost Sisterhood: Prostitution in America, 1900–1918*. Baltimore, Md.: Johns Hopkins University Press, 1983.

Rosenbaum, Fred. *Free to Choose: The Making of a Jewish Community in the American West: The Jews of Oakland, California, from the Gold Rush to the Present Day*. Berkeley: Judah L. Magnes Memorial Museum, 1976.

Rosenzweig, Roy. *Eight Hours for What We Will: Workers and Leisure in an Industrial City, 1870–1920*. New York: Cambridge University Press, 1983.

Rothman, David. *Conscience and Convenience: The Asylum and Its Alternatives in Progressive America*. Boston: Little, Brown, 1980.

Rothman, Ellen K. *Hands and Hearts: A History of Courtship in America*. New York: Basic Books, 1984.

Rowles, Burton J. *The Lady at Box 99: The Story of Miriam Van Waters*. Greenwich, Conn.: Seabury Press, 1962.

Rubin, Gayle. "Thinking Sex: Notes for a Radical Theory of the Politics of Sexuality." In *Pleasure and Danger: Exploring Female Sexuality*, edited by Carole S. Vance, pp. 267–319. Boston: Routledge and Kegan Paul, 1984.

Ruiz, Vicki L. *Cannery Women, Cannery Lives: Mexican Women, Unionization, and the California Food Processing Industry, 1930–1950*. Albuquerque: University of New Mexico Press, in association with the Center for Documentary Studies at Duke University, 1987.

Ryan, Mary P. "The Power of Women's Networks: A Case Study of Female Moral Reform in Antebellum America." *Feminist Studies* 5 (Spring 1979): 66–85.

Ryerson, Ellen. *Best-Laid Plans: America's Juvenile Court Experiment*. New York: Hill and Wang, 1978.

Salem, Dorothy. *To Better Our World: Black Women in Organized Reform*. New York: Carlson Publishing, 1990.

Sánchez, George J. *Becoming Mexican American: Ethnicity, Culture, and Identity in Chicano Los Angeles, 1900–1945*. New York: Oxford University Press, 1993.

Saunders, Margaret. "A Study of the Work of the City Mother's Bureau of the

Los Angeles Police Department." Master's thesis, University of Southern California, 1939.

Schlossman, Steven L. *Love and the American Delinquent: The Theory and Practice of "Progressive" Juvenile Justice.* Chicago: University of Chicago Press, 1977.

Schlossman, Steven L., and Stephanie Wallach. "The Crime of Precocious Sexuality: Female Juvenile Delinquency in the Progressive Era." *Harvard Educational Review* 48 (February 1978): 65–95.

Schneider, Eric C. *In the Web of Class: Delinquents and Reformers in Boston, 1810s-1930s.* New York: New York University Press, 1992.

Schneider, Jane. "Of Vigilance and Virgins: Honor, Shame, and Access to Resources in Mediterranean Societies." *Ethnology* 10 (January 1971): 1–24.

Scott, Anne Firor. *Natural Allies: Women's Associations in American History.* Urbana: University of Illinois Press, 1991.

———. *The Southern Lady: From Pedestal to Politics, 1830–1930.* Chicago: University of Chicago Press, 1970.

Sears, Frederick W. "The Wayward Girl." *Vermont Medical Monthly* 18 (January 15, 1912): 7–9.

Sessions, Kenosha. "The Delinquent Girl as a Community Problem." National Conference on the Education of Truant, Backward, Dependent, and Delinquent Children, *Proceedings* (1918): 76–78.

———. "Parole Work under the Superintendent of the Institution." National Conference on the Education of Truant, Backward, Dependent, and Delinquent Children, *Proceedings* (1917): 43–54.

Shaw, Stephanie. "Black Club Women and the Creation of the National Association of Colored Women." *Journal of Women's History* 3 (Fall 1991): 10–25.

Shelden, Randall G. "Sex Discrimination in the Juvenile Justice System, Memphis, Tennessee, 1900–1917." In *Comparing Female and Male Offenders*, edited by Marguerite Q. Warren, pp. 55–72. Beverly Hills, Calif.: Sage Publications, 1981.

Sicherman, Barbara, Carol Hurd Green, Ilene Kantrov, and Harriette Walker, eds. *Notable American Women: The Modern Period.* Cambridge, Mass.: Belknap Press of Harvard University Press, 1980.

Simmons, Christina. "Modern Sexuality and the Myth of Victorian Repression." In *Passion and Power: Sexuality in History*, edited by Kathy Peiss and Christina Simmons, pp. 157–77. Philadelphia, Pa.: Temple University Press, 1989.

Sklar, Kathryn Kish. "The Historical Foundations of Women's Power in the Creation of the American Welfare State, 1830–1930." In *Mothers of a New*

World: Maternalist Politics and the Origins of Welfare States, edited by Seth Koven and Sonya Michel, pp. 43–93. London: Routledge, 1993.

——. "Hull House as a Community of Women Reformers in the 1890s." *Signs* 10 (Summer 1985): 657–77.

Skocpol, Theda. *Protecting Soldiers and Mothers*. Cambridge, Mass.: Belknap Press of Harvard University Press, 1992.

Smith, Daniel Scott. "The Dating of the American Sexual Revolution: Evidence and Interpretation." In *The American Family in Social-Historical Perspective*, edited by Michael Gordon, pp. 321–35. New York: St. Martin's Press, 1973.

Smith, Daniel Scott, and Michael Hindus. "Premarital Pregnancy in America, 1640–1971: An Overview and an Interpretation." *Journal of Interdisciplinary History* 5 (1975): 537–70.

Smith, Jessie Carney, ed. *Notable Black American Women*. Detroit and London: Gale Research, Inc., 1992.

Smith, Judith. *Family Connections: A History of Italian and Jewish Immigrant Lives in Providence, Rhode Island, 1900–1940*. Albany, N.Y.: State University of New York Press, 1985.

Smith-Rosenberg, Carroll. "Beauty, the Beast, and the Militant Woman: A Case Study in Sex Roles and Social Stress in Jacksonian America." In *Disorderly Conduct: Visions of Gender in Victorian America*, pp. 109–28. New York: Knopf, 1985.

Smout, Christopher. "Aspects of Sexual Behavior in Nineteenth-Century Scotland." In *Bastardy and Its Comparative History*, edited by Peter Laslett, Karla Oosterveen, and Richard M. Smith, pp. 192–216. Cambridge, Mass.: Harvard University Press, 1980.

Snitow, Ann, Christine Stansell, and Sharon Thompson, eds. *Powers of Desire: The Politics of Sexuality*. New York: Monthly Review Press, 1983.

Socolow, Jayme. *Eros and Modernization: Sylvester Graham, Health Reform, and the Origins of Victorian Sexuality in America*. Rutherford, N.J.: Fairleigh Dickinson University Press, 1983.

Solomon, Barbara. *In the Company of Educated Women*. New Haven, Conn.: Yale University Press, 1985.

Spencer, Anna Garlin. "The Age of Consent and Its Significance." *Forum* 49 (1913): 406–20.

Spencer, Dorcas James. *A History of the Woman's Christian Temperance Union of Northern and Central California*. Oakland, Calif.: West Coast Printing Company, 1913.

Stansell, Christine. *City of Women: Sex and Class in New York, 1789–1860*. Urbana: University of Illinois Press, 1987.

Stone, Lawrence. *The Family, Sex, and Marriage in England, 1500–1800*. New York: Harper and Row, 1977.

Taylor, Paul S. "Mexican Women in Los Angeles Industry in 1928." *Aztlán* 11 (1980): 99–131.

Tentler, Leslie Woodcock. *Wage-Earning Women: Industrial Work and Family Life in the United States, 1900–1930*. New York: Oxford University Press, 1979.

Thernstrom, Stephan. *The Other Bostonians: Poverty and Progress in the American Metropolis*. Cambridge, Mass.: Harvard University Press, 1973.

——. *Poverty and Progress: Social Mobility in a Nineteenth-Century City*. Cambridge, Mass.: Harvard University Press, 1964.

Thomas, Keith. "The Double Standard." *Journal of the History of Ideas* 20 (April 1959): 195–216.

Thompson, Mildred I. *Ida B. Wells-Barnett: An Exploratory Study of an American Black Woman, 1893–1930*. New York: Carlson Publishing, 1990.

Tiffin, Susan. *In Whose Best Interest?: Child Welfare Reform in the Progressive Era*. Westport, Conn.: Greenwood Press, 1982.

Tilly, Louise A., and Joan W. Scott. *Women, Work, and Family*. New York: Holt, Rinehart and Winston, 1978.

Tilly, Louise A., Joan W. Scott, and Miriam Cohen. "Women's Work and European Fertility Patterns." *Journal of Interdisciplinary History* 6 (Winter 1976): 447–76.

Towne, Arthur W. "The Place of the Juvenile Court Detention Home in the Community." National Conference on the Education of Truant, Backward, Dependent, and Delinquent Children, *Proceedings* (1917): 43–54.

Trattner, Walter I. *Social Welfare in America: An Annotated Bibliography*. Westport, Conn.: Greenwood Press, 1983.

——. *Social Welfare or Social Control?: Some Historical Reflections on Regulating the Poor*. Knoxville: University of Tennessee Press, 1983.

True, Ruth. "The Neglected Girl." In *West Side Studies*, edited by Pauline Goldmark. New York: Russell Sage Foundation, 1914.

Valverde, Mariana. *The Age of Light, Soap, and Water: Moral Reform in English Canada, 1885–1925*. Toronto: McClelland and Stewart, 1991.

——. "When the Mother of the Race Is Free: Race, Reproduction, and Sexuality in First Wave Feminism." In *Gender Conflicts: New Essays in Women's History*, edited by Franca Iacovetta and Mariana Valverde, pp. 3–26. Toronto: University of Toronto Press, 1992.

Vance, Carole S. *Pleasure and Danger: Exploring Female Sexuality*. Boston: Routledge and Kegan Paul, 1984.

Vandepol, Ann. "Dependent Children, Child Custody, and the Mothers' Pensions: The Transformation of State-Family Relations in the Early Twentieth Century." *Social Problems* 29 (February 1982): 221–35.

Van Waters, Miriam. "Juvenile Court Procedure as a Factor in Diagnosis." The American Sociological Society, *Publications* 16 (1921): 209–17.

——. *Parents on Probation*. New York: New Republic, Inc., 1927.

——. "Where Girls Go Right: Some Dynamic Aspects of State Correctional Schools for Girls and Young Women." *Survey* 48 (May 27, 1922): 361–76.

——. *Youth in Conflict*. New York: Republic Publishing Co., 1925.

Van Winkle, Mina. "The Policewoman as a Socializing Agency." *American City* 34 (February 1926): 198–99.

Vice Commission of Philadelphia. *A Report on Existing Conditions with Recommendations to the Honorable Rudolph Blankenburg, Mayor.* Philadelphia, Pa.: N.p., 1913.

Viehe, Fred W. "Black Gold Suburbs: The Influence of the Extractive Industry on the Suburbanization of Los Angeles, 1890–1930." *Journal of Urban History* 8 (November 1981): 3–25.

Vorspan, Max, and Lloyd P. Gartner. *History of the Jews of Los Angeles.* Philadelphia, Pa.: Jewish Publication Society of America, 1970.

Walker, Jean. "Factors Contributing to the Delinquency of Defective Girls." *University of California Publications in Psychology* 3 (April 3, 1925): 147–213.

Walkowitz, Judith R. *City of Dreadful Delight: Narratives of Sexual Danger in Late-Victorian London*. Chicago: University of Chicago Press, 1992.

——. "Male Vice and Female Virtue: Feminism and the Politics of Prostitution in Nineteenth-Century Britain." In *Powers of Desire: The Politics of Sexuality*, edited by Ann Snitow, Christine Stansell, and Sharon Thompson, pp. 419–38. New York: Monthly Review Press, 1983.

——. *Prostitution and Victorian Society: Women, Class, and the State*. 1980. Reprint. Cambridge, Eng.: Cambridge University Press, 1983.

Warshaw, Robin. *I Never Called It Rape*. New York: Harper and Row, 1988.

Watson, Walter Thompson. "The Recreation Problem at Fort MacArthur." Master's thesis, University of Southern California, 1919.

Weeks, Jeffrey. *Sex, Politics, and Society: The Regulation of Sexuality since 1800*. 2d ed. New York: Longman, 1989.

Weiner, Lynn Y. *From Working Girl to Working Mother: The Female Labor Force in the United States, 1820–1980*. Chapel Hill: University of North Carolina Press, 1985.

Weiss, Jessica. "The Feminine Point of View: California Women's Struggle for a Voice in the Legal System." Unpublished paper, Berkeley, Calif., 1986.

Wells, Ida B. *Crusade for Justice: The Autobiography of Ida B. Wells*. Edited by Alfreda Duster. Chicago: University of Chicago Press, 1970.

—— [Wells-Barnett]. "A Red Record: Tabulated Statistics and Alleged Causes of Lynchings in the United States, 1892–1893–1894." In *Selected Works of Ida B. Wells-Barnett*, compiled by Trudier Harris, pp. 138–252. New York: Oxford University Press, 1991.

——. "Southern Horrors: Lynch Law in All Its Phases." In *Selected Works of*

Ida B. Wells-Barnett, compiled by Trudier Harris, pp. 14–45. New York: Oxford University Press, 1991.

Welter, Barbara. "The Cult of True Womanhood, 1820–1860." In *The American Family in Social-Historical Perspective,* edited by Michael Gordon, pp. 224–50. New York: St. Martin's Press, 1973.

White, Deborah Gray. "The Cost of Club Work, the Price of Black Feminism." In *Visible Women: New Essays on American Activism,* edited by Nancy A. Hewitt and Suzanne Lebsock, pp. 247–69. Urbana: University of Illinois Press, 1993.

———. *Ar'n't I a Woman?: Female Slaves in the Plantation South.* New York: Norton, 1987.

Wiebe, Robert. *The Search for Order.* New York: Hill and Wang, 1967.

Wigmore, John H. *A Student's Textbook of the Law of Evidence.* Chicago: Foundation Press, 1935.

———. *A Treatise on the System of Evidence in Trials at Common Law, Including the Statutes and Judicial Decisions of All Jurisdictions of the United States.* 4 vols. Boston: Little, Brown, 1904.

Willard, Frances. *Glimpses of Fifty Years: The Autobiography of an American Woman.* Chicago: Woman's Temperance Publication Association, 1889.

Wilson, Lisa. *Life after Death: Widows in Pennsylvania, 1750–1850.* Philadelphia, Pa.: Temple University Press, 1992.

Wilson, Otto. *Fifty Years' Work with Girls, 1883–1933: A Story of the Florence Crittenton Homes.* Alexandria, Va.: National Florence Crittenton Mission, 1933.

Woods, Robert A., and Albert J. Kennedy, eds. *Young Working Girls: A Summary of Evidence from Two Thousand Social Workers.* Boston: Houghton Mifflin, 1913.

Worrell, Doris Rhoda. "A Study of the Leisure Time Habits of Adolescent Delinquent Girls in Los Angeles County." Master's thesis, University of Southern California, 1931.

Yans-McLaughlin, Virginia. *Family and Community: Italian Immigrants in Buffalo, 1880–1930.* Ithaca, N.Y.: Cornell University Press, 1977.

Yarros, Rachelle S. "Experiences of a Lecturer." *Social Hygiene* 5 (April 1919): 205–22.

Yellin, Jean Fagan. *Women and Sisters: Antislavery Feminists in American Culture.* New Haven, Conn.: Yale University Press, 1990.

INDEX

Abbott, Edith, 104–5, 106, 107, 111; *The Delinquent Child and the Home*, 100, 103, 115
Abortion, 24, 58
Adolescence, 2, 99, 101, 104, 106, 107
Adolescent female sexuality, 2, 100, 101–2, 143, 187–88
African American men, 26; lynching of, 28–29, 30; punishment in rape cases, 80–81, 185–86
African Americans: criminal justice system and, 28, 120; migration to California, 42, 167; attitudes toward sexuality, 46, 47; use of courts to control daughters, 159, 167
African American women: employment opportunities, 2, 47, 48, 171; ignored by social purity reformers, 4, 9–10, 25, 26, 29, 37, 186; Progressive reformers and, 4–5, 105, 186–87; clubs and organizations, 5, 27; sexual exploitation of, 25–26, 29, 30, 33, 47, 186; and age-of-consent campaign, 26, 30, 198 (n. 50); support of social purity campaigns, 26–27; moral protection work of, 26–28, 47, 118–19; antilynching campaign, 29–30; racist stereotypes of, 32–33, 36; and female delinquency, 119–21
Age-of-consent campaign: assumptions and goals of, 3, 4, 8–9, 15, 16–17, 18, 187; racism in, 4, 9–10, 186; in California, 8–9, 36–37, 73; male opposition to, 9, 31–33, 36, 68; as part of social purity move-

ment, 10, 11, 35; in England, 12–13; women suffragists and, 15–16, 20, 73; black women and, 26, 30, 198 (n. 50); in southern states, 32, 35–36, 37; physicians and, 34–35
Age-of-consent laws, 1; enforcement of, 5, 39, 72, 81, 185, 191; prior to reform efforts, 9, 12–13, 14–15; states' passage of reforms to, 9, 30–31, 34, 36–37, 185, 199 (n. 59); Congress and, 30; efforts to undo reforms of, 31, 33–34; effects of, 37, 38, 39, 64–65, 185, 188; working-class parents' use of, 39, 49, 188; criminal justice system and, 64, 65, 67–68, 71, 72, 81, 185–86
Alabama, age-of-consent law, 36
Alabama State Federation of Colored Women's Clubs, 119
Alameda County, Calif.: population growth, 40; sexual morality in, 42–43, 47
Alameda County Superior Court, rape prosecutions: case records, 6, 191, 201 (n. 2); age-of-consent law and, 38, 39; working-class parents and, 39, 43; pregnancies involved in, 51; age of defendants in, 53; consensual sexual relations in, 53; forcible assaults in, 58, 204–5 (n. 74); male court officials and, 63–64, 72; and sexual double standard, 64, 72; pretrial detentions, 65; disposition of cases, 76; sentencing of offenders, 77, 79, 80
Alexander, George, 110

American Purity Alliance, 10, 72
American Woman Suffrage Association, 16
Amusement parks, 23, 48, 88, 104, 142
Anthony, Susan B., 16
Antiprostitution campaign, 2, 96, 97–98, 122
Arena, 34
Arizona, age-of-consent law, 34
Atlanta Exposition (1895), 28
Atlanta University, 120

Baker, Newton, 121
Barrett, Janie Porter, 93 (illus.), 118, 119
Bartelme, Mary M., 112
Bathing costumes, 90 (illus.)
Beaches, 91
Binford, Jessie, 125
Birth control, 141
Blackstone, William, 13
Blackwell, Emily, 10, 13, 20
Blackwell, Henry, 16, 205 (n. 89)
Bogardus, Emory S., 163
Boyer, Paul, 211 (n. 39)
Breckinridge, Sophonisba, 104–5, 106, 107; *The Delinquent Child and the Home*, 100, 103, 115
Brooklyn, N.Y., 45–46
Bullen, Margaret, 132
"Bundling," 44
Burleigh, Edith, 117

California: moral reform movement, 6–7; migration to, 7, 41, 42, 43, 134, 165, 167; age-of-consent law, 8–9, 36–37, 39, 73, 81; women's suffrage, 36, 73; rape prosecutions, 39, 75; immigration to, 41, 42; jury service for women, 73–74; juvenile justice system, 74, 135; probation rules, 77; criminal justice system, 81; reformatories for girls, 147; Board of Charities and Corrections, 147, 148; mothers' pension law, 169–70, 218 (n. 24); Industrial Welfare Commission, 171; minimum wage, 171; child labor law, 171–72
California Civic League, 74
California Federation of Women's Clubs, 73
Capitalism, 2, 46, 99
Catholic Church, 44
Central Pacific Railroad, 40
Chamberlain-Kahn Act (1918), 125
Chant, Mrs. Ormison, 30
Chaperonage, 49
Chastity, 24, 43, 47; social purity campaign and, 11, 36; sexual double standard and, 18, 44, 64, 72; religious strictures, 44; juvenile justice system and, 71, 78; physical examinations for virginity, 144–45
Chicago, Ill.: Protective Agency for Women and Children, 72–73; juvenile court, 115
Child labor laws, 171–72
Children, sexual abuse of, 60
Class bias, 4, 20, 189
Commission on Training Camp Activities (CTCA), 121–22, 123, 124, 125, 126, 127
Committee on Protective Work for Girls (CPWG), 122–23
Connelly, Mark, 50
Cook County, Ill., Juvenile Court, 100, 111
Cooper, Anna Julia, 27
Courtship, 45, 46, 48, 162

Criminology, 103
Crist, Wiley, 73

Dance halls, 85 (illus.), 104, 106–7, 136, 142, 189
Dating, 54, 162, 189
Davis, Katherine Bement, 124, 125
Department stores, 104
Detention homes, 113–14, 126
Dewson, Mary ("Molly"), 118
Domestic servants, 2, 21; sexual vulnerability of, 26, 59–60; reformatories and placement as, 117, 146–47; minimum-wage exemption, 171
Donahue, William, 78
Double standard of morality, 44, 189; reform campaigns against, 4, 8, 9, 18, 37, 57; male court officials and, 64, 72, 74, 75, 81; female court officials and, 153
Dummer, Ethel Sturges, 118, 131; in campaign against venereal disease, 122–23, 125; support of El Retiro reformatory, 133, 217 (n. 15)

Education, 102, 146
Elopement, 163
El Retiro School for Girls (Los Angeles), 133–34, 147–49, 214 (n. 70)
Employment, women's, 197 (n. 32); effects on young women's social autonomy, 2, 24, 160; opportunities for African Americans, 2, 47, 48, 171; labor force participation rates, 21; occupations, 21–22, 23, 42; changes between 1880 and 1920, 21–22, 45, 48, 86–87, 159–60; in Los Angeles, 42, 48, 171,

174–75; wage discrimination, 55, 170–71; Progressive reformers and, 103–4, 146; of mothers, 134, 152–53, 170–71, 174–75; job training, 146–47; children and teenage daughters, 171–73
Environmental explanation of deviancy, 103
Eugenics, 96–97, 98

Factory labor, 21–22, 159–60
Falconer, Martha P., 132; as Sleighton Farm superintendent, 116–17, 118, 133; in campaign against venereal disease, 122–23, 125–26
Families: working-class, 6, 102–3, 105, 106, 150; generational conflict in, 6, 159; sexual abuse in, 39, 58–59, 60–62, 138–39; middle-class reformers' ideal of, 105–7, 149, 150
Family economy, 43–44, 177; role of daughters in, 20–21, 47–48, 159–60
"Feeble-mindedness," 98
Female delinquency: Progressive reformers and, 3–4, 95–96, 99, 103, 104–5, 108; working-class family blamed for, 103, 105, 106–7; judicial system and, 108, 109, 119, 158, 181; women judicial officials and, 110, 121, 123; prevention through institutionalization, 114–15; black reformers and, 119–21. *See also* Sexual delinquency
Female-headed households. *See* Mothers, single
Female victimization, model of, 3–4, 53, 64, 95, 97
Feminism, 5–6, 194 (n. 6)

Fernald, Walter E., 98
Florence Crittenton Home (Los
    Angeles), 148
Florida, age-of-consent campaign,
    36, 37
Flower, Benjamin O., 34
Fosdick, Raymond, 121, 122, 123,
    124, 125
Frankfurter, Felix, 130
Freedman, Estelle, 211 (n. 39)
French, Rose, 72
Freud, Sigmund, 101

Gardener, Helen Hamilton, 19, 20;
    Is This Your Son, My Lord?, 17;
    Pray You, Sir, Whose Daughter?,
    17–18, 20; "The Shame of Amer-
    ica," 34
Gay, Elizabeth, 10
Gender bias, 4, 20, 155–56, 186, 189
General Federation of Women's
    Clubs, 34
Georgia, age-of-consent law, 37
Gibbons, Abby Hopper, 10
Gilbert, Aletha, 111
Goddard, Henry, 98
Gordon, Linda, 60
Great Britain, 11, 12–13

Hall, G. Stanley: *Adolescence*, 101–2
Harper, Frances E. W., 26–27, 28
Harris, Frances, 117
Hartmann, Heidi, 6
Holly, Carrie Clyde, 24, 25
Homosexuality, 2, 178, 189
Hoover, Herbert C., 130
House of the Good Shepherd (Los
    Angeles), 148, 183
Hunt, Mary, 33
Hunter, Jane Edna, 120

Idora Park (Oakland), 48
Immigrants: Progressive reformers
    and, 4–5, 104–5, 186–87; to Cali-
    fornia, 41–42; sexual morality
    codes, 44, 45–46; conflicts with
    courts, 79–80, 81; eugenics move-
    ment and, 97; nativist hostility
    toward, 97, 104–5; parent-daugh-
    ter conflicts among, 159, 160–
    61, 165; use of courts to control
    daughters, 159, 162
Incest, 62, 178
Independent, 26
Industrialization, 1, 20, 103, 105
Infanticide, 19, 24
International Association of Police
    Women, 111
Italian immigrants, 41, 44, 49

Jewish immigrants, 41, 45
Job training: as part of Progressive
    reform efforts, 146–47
Judges: women as, 5, 96, 112–13,
    129, 186; and age-of-consent laws,
    67–68, 69–71; and male sex offend-
    ers, 75, 76, 78, 79, 155
Jury service, for women, 73–74
Juvenile courts: establishment of, 5,
    74, 111–12; women officials in, 5,
    110, 112–13, 129, 143, 156, 186; and
    rape prosecutions, 74; and male
    sex offenders, 75–76, 153–56, 186;
    Progressive reformers and, 109,
    110, 111, 113, 114, 129, 132, 186;
    and female delinquency, 114–15,
    129, 135–36, 143–46, 180–81, 187,
    188; probation and punishments,
    115, 130–31, 146–47, 148, 155–56,
    186; black women and, 119–20,
    187; young women's perceptions
    of, 148–50; critical attitudes

toward working-class parents,
150–53, 182; working-class parents' use of, 158–59, 176, 177–79,
181, 184, 188
Juvenile delinquency, 103; working
mothers and, 107; juvenile court
system and, 111–12, 150; immigrant parents and, 161; gender
double standard of, 176. *See
also* Female delinquency; Sexual
delinquency
Juvenile Hall (Los Angeles), 93
(illus.), 113, 132; sexual history
interrogations, 143–44; physical
examinations for virginity, 144–
45; detention in, 178, 180–81
Juvenile Protective Association, 99

Kansas, age-of-consent law, 30, 31,
33
Kansas Equal Suffrage Association,
33
Kennedy, Albert J., 104, 106, 107;
Young Working Girls, 100–101
Kenney, Jane M., 26–27
Kentucky, age-of-consent campaign,
36
Knights of Labor, 16
Ku Klux Klan, 25

Latin American immigrants, 159
Leisure activities, for youths, 3,
22–23, 48, 91 (illus.), 104
Long Beach, Calif., 90; "the Pike"
amusement park, 88–89 (illus.),
142, 151
Los Angeles, Calif., 6; population
growth, 40; economy of, 40, 42;
immigration to, 41, 42; women's
employment in, 42, 48, 171, 174–
75; migration to, 42, 165, 169, 224

(n. 34); sexual morality in, 47, 49;
leisure activities, 48, 49, 137, 142;
female runaways, 50; women
police officers, 110, 142; juvenile
justice system, 120, 129, 132;
female-headed families in, 167,
168, 169, 224 (n. 26)
Los Angeles County, Calif.: population growth, 40; sexual morality
in, 42–43, 47; single mothers
in, 168, 169–70; Outdoor Relief
Department, 169–70; Charities
Office, 170
Los Angeles County Juvenile Court:
female officials of, 112–13; female
sexual delinquency cases, 118,
128–29, 146–47, 157–58, 191–92;
single-mother assistance, 169, 170,
171, 172, 174
—rape prosecutions: case records, 6,
191, 201 (n. 2); age-of-consent law
and, 39; working-class parents
and, 39, 43; pregnancies involved
in, 51; age of defendants in, 53;
consensual sexual relations in, 53;
male court officials and, 64; and
sexual double standard, 64, 74;
sentencing of offenders, 76;
forcible assaults in, 204–5 (n. 74)
Los Feliz Hospital (Los Angeles),
126
Louisiana, age-of-consent law, 36
Lynching, 28–30

Mann Act (1910), 97–98
Mark, Georgia, 13
Marriage: pregnancy and, 23–24, 45,
46, 47; women's sexual activity
and, 47, 54, 56–57; arranged, 162;
generational conflicts over, 162,
163; companionate, 189

Mathews, Victoria Earle, 27, 28
Medical Age, 31
Memphis race riot (1865), 25
Men: seen as danger to women, 3, 9, 16–17; opposition to age-of-consent reforms, 9, 31–33, 36, 68; moral education of, 11, 28, 75; sexual exploitation of women, 18, 25–26, 59; sexual double standard and, 18–19, 44, 64, 72; lynching of African Americans, 28–29, 30; fear of women's sexuality, 31, 32, 33, 68; sexual assault of relatives, 39, 58–59, 60–62, 138–39; juvenile courts and sex offenses of, 75–76, 153–56, 186; working-class parents' use of courts to control, 176–78
Mexican immigrants, 42; sexual morality codes, 44, 45, 49; parent-daughter conflicts, 163; denial of mothers' pensions to, 169–70
Michigan, age-of-consent law, 34
Middle class: reformers of working-class sexuality, 1, 2, 3, 4, 9, 24–25, 62, 142, 185, 187, 188; moral concerns of, 1, 4, 24–25; sexual ideology of, 4, 24–25, 37, 43, 142, 187, 188; women in justice system, 5, 121, 129, 186, 187; and age-of-consent campaign, 9, 18, 39; mothers and moral education, 19–20; ideal of adolescence, 102, 107; ideal of family life, 105–7, 149, 150; sexual mores of teenagers, 188–89
Migration: to California, 7, 41, 42, 43, 134, 165, 167; to Los Angeles, 42, 165, 169, 224 (n. 34). *See also* Immigrants
Military training camps, 121–22

Miner, Maude E., 113–14, 122–23, 124–25
Minimum wage, 171
Morality: campaigns for protection of women's, 1, 4, 25; middle-class standards of, 4, 24–25; generational conflicts over, 5; working-class standards of, 5, 43, 46–47; single sexual standard of, 10, 19, 28, 64, 75; black social purity reformers and, 26, 27, 28, 47. *See also* Double standard of morality
Morse, Fannie French, 118
Mothers, single, 168–69, 223–24 (n. 25), 224 (n. 26); black community and, 46; reliance on children's labor, 167, 171, 172; conflicts with daughters, 167, 172; use of courts to control children, 167, 176; state pensions, 169–70, 218 (n. 24); charity support of, 170; employment, 170–71; conflicts with courts, 182–83
Mothers' pensions, 107–8, 169–70, 218 (n. 24)
Movies, 104, 189
Murphey, J. D., 79

National Association of Colored Women (NACW), 27, 119, 120–21
National Association of Women Lawyers, 112
National Colored Woman's Congress, 28
National Conference of Social Work, 130
National Conference of Unitarian Churches, 30
National Consumer's League, 99
National Federation of Afro-American Women, 27

National Federation of Settlements, 100, 102, 104, 105, 107

National League of Colored Women, 27

National Woman Suffrage Association, 16

Native-born population, in California, 41, 165, 224 (n. 34)

New Deal, 169, 218 (n. 24)

New Jersey, age-of-consent law, 30

New York (state), age-of-consent law, 13, 30, 31, 33, 34, 35

New York Committee for the Prevention of State Regulation of Vice, 10, 13, 34

New York Probation and Protective Association, 114

New York Society for the Prevention of Cruelty to Children, 72

New York Woman's Loyal League, 27

New York Working Girls' Society, 11

"Nightcourting," 44–45

Oakland, Calif., 6; economy of, 40; population growth, 40; immigration to, 41; migration to, 42; sexual morality in, 47, 49, 72; leisure activities, 48, 49; female runaways, 50

Oakland Tribune, 50

Ogden, Frank B., 68, 71, 79–80, 81

O'Keefe, Paul, 60

Olney, Warren, 122

Pall Mall Gazette, 12

Passionless female, ideal of, 32, 101

Patriarchy, 19, 43–44, 163

Penal reform, 109, 111

Pennsylvania, age-of-consent law, 30

Pensions, mothers', 107–8, 169–70, 218 (n. 24)

Philadelphia New Century Guild of Working Women, 11

Philanthropist, 10, 13

Phillis Wheatley Homes, 28, 120–21

Physicians, 10; and age-of-consent campaign, 34–35; in campaign against venereal disease, 97, 123–24; women as, 123–24, 144–45

Pickney, Merritt, 112

"Pike, the," 88–89 (illus.), 142, 151

Police, 64, 75, 81, 154–55; women officers, 5, 96, 110, 111, 186

Politics, women in, 9, 20, 31, 33

Portuguese immigrants, 41–42, 44

Poverty, 20, 100

Powderly, Terrence, 16

Powell, Aaron Macy, 10, 13

Powell, Anna Rice, 10

Pregnancy: and marriage, 23–24, 45, 46, 47; out-of-wedlock, 24, 51, 52, 57, 59, 140, 188; and abortion, 24, 59; working-class families and, 51, 52; and rape prosecutions, 51–52, 57–58, 141; and judicial proceedings against females, 140

Probation officers, 76, 120; women as, 5, 96, 112, 153, 186

Progressive reformers, 98–100; and women's sexuality, 3–4, 95, 99, 102, 187; female delinquency theories, 3–4, 95–96, 99, 103, 104–5, 108; and sexual regulation, 4, 96, 108; and black and immigrant women, 4–5, 104–5, 186–87; anti-prostitution campaign, 96, 97–98; campaign for women judicial officials, 96, 109, 110, 186; and eugenics movement, 98; and environmental influences, 103, 105, 108;

and women's employment, 103–4, 146; juvenile justice policies, 108–10, 113, 114–16, 118–19, 129, 132, 133, 146, 147, 211 (n. 39); and campaign against venereal disease, 121, 124–26, 186

Prostitution, 136; state regulation of, 10; as "white slavery," 11–12, 50, 84, 97; Progressive campaign against, 96, 97–98; military campaign against, 122

Protective work, 4, 5, 108–9, 129, 185, 187, 189

Protective officers, 123, 125

Protestantism, 1, 43

Punishment: of male sexual offenders, 75–79, 80, 156; race of defendant and, 79, 80–81, 185–86; of female sexual offenders, 130–31, 146–48, 155–56

Quinn, James G., 79

Racism: among women reformers, 4–5, 186; in social purity campaigns, 9–10, 29; in judicial system, 79, 80–81, 185–86; in eugenics movement, 97

Rape, 200 (n. 81); age-of-consent laws and, 8–9, 13; of black women, 25, 32–33; and lynching of black men, 28; parents and prosecution of, 39, 43; pregnancy and prosecution for, 51–52, 57–58, 141; of teenage girls, 58, 78; treatment of females in prosecutions for, 65–72; acquaintance rape, 69; punishment of male offenders, 74–81, 155. See also Alameda County Superior Court; Los Angeles County Juvenile Court; Sexual assault

Reconstruction, 26

Recreation. See Leisure activities

Reeve, Sidney, 74–75, 113, 155, 156

Reformatories, 5, 115–18, 119–20, 121, 126, 133, 147, 179

Reformers. See Age-of-consent campaign; Progressive reformers; Social purity campaigns

Religion, 44

Respectability: working-class standards of, 46–47, 165; middle-class standards of, 142, 187; judicial system and, 185

Ridley, Florida Ruffin, 30

Rippen, Jane Deeter, 125

Ruffin, Josephine, 28

Runaways, 50–51, 56, 138

Samuels, George, 70–71

San Francisco, Calif., 72, 168

Sebastian, Charles, 111

Seduction narratives: purity reformers and, 9, 16–17, 18, 24; female youth and, 20, 24, 53; male officials and, 31, 68

Selective Service Act (1917), 122

Sexual assault, 140, 188; of black women by white men, 25, 26; of domestic servants, 26, 59–60; and lynching of black men, 28; by male relatives, 39, 58–59, 60–62, 138–39; of children, 60; women's resistance of, 61–62, 139; judicial system and, 78, 141. See also Rape

Sexual danger: age-of-consent reformers and, 1, 4, 10, 16, 18, 20, 185; and black women, 4, 9–10, 27; narratives of, 16–17, 18; male relatives and, 39, 58, 60

Sexual delinquency: Progressive reformers and, 4, 95–96, 103; prevention through institutionalization, 114–15; "protective work" for prevention of, 123; women judicial officials and, 129, 131, 134, 143; females arrested for, 134, 136–38, 143; juvenile justice system and, 143–45, 150, 180–81; of young males, 177–78. *See also* Female delinquency

Sexuality: middle-class worries about young working-class women's, 1, 2, 3, 4, 9, 24–25, 62, 142, 185, 187, 188; exploitation of young women, 23, 57, 58–60, 138–39, 140, 185, 188; working-class teenagers' attitudes toward, 24, 39, 53, 54–57, 136–38, 143, 187, 188–89; middle-class reformers' attitudes toward, 24–25, 37, 142, 187, 188; male fears of women's, 31, 32, 33, 68; racist attitudes toward, 32–33, 186; late-nineteenth century ideology of, 43; working-class parents' attitudes toward, 43, 44–46; judicial system and, 67–68, 69–72, 78–79, 143–44, 186; early-twentieth century ideology of, 96, 97; middle-class teenagers' attitudes toward, 188–89

Sexual regulation: state, moral reform campaigns for, 1–2, 3, 96, 109; state enforcement of, 2, 5, 64, 81, 189; Progressive reformers and, 4, 96, 108; traditional methods of, 39, 45–46, 47, 49; parental use of courts for, 39, 49, 184

Shontz, Orfa Jean, 113, 129–30, 131–32, 142, 146

Sisters of the Good Shepherd, 115

Slavery, 25, 26, 27

Sleighton Farm (Glen Mills, Pa.), 116–17, 118, 126, 133

Smith, Carrie Weaver, 118

Smith, Mortimer, 71

Social hygiene campaign, 97, 122, 124–25, 145, 186

Social purity campaigns, 188, 194 (n. 6); and age-of-consent reform, 10, 11, 36, 185; in England, 11–12; black women and, 26–27; physicians and, 34–35; southern women and, 35–36

Social settlements, 99

Social workers, 3–4, 115, 123, 125

South: lynchings, 28–29; age-of-consent campaign, 35–36, 37; legal status of African Americans, 120; rape laws, 200 (n. 81)

South Carolina, age-of-consent law, 36

Southern California Telephone Company, 175

Southern Pacific Railroad, 40

Stansell, Christine, 60

Stanton, Elizabeth Cady, 16

States: age-of-consent laws, 9, 12–13, 14–15, 30–31, 34, 36–37, 185, 199 (n. 59); antiprostitution laws, 97; compulsory sterilization laws, 98; juvenile detention homes, 114; detention for venereal disease, 124; mothers' pension laws, 169, 218 (n. 24)

Stead, William T., 12

Sterilization, compulsory, 98

Stone, Lucy, 16, 205 (n. 89)

Stowe, Harriet Beecher, 17

Survey, 133

Tennessee, age-of-consent law, 36

Terrell, Mary Church, 27

Texas, age-of-consent law, 33, 36

Thurman, Lucy, 26–27

Tompkins, A. C., 32–33, 36

Travelers' aid societies, 11

Treating, 55

True, Ruth, 103; *The Neglected Girl*, 101

Truelove Home (Los Angeles), 148

Union Signal, 13, 73

U.S. Congress: age-of- consent law, 30; Senate prostitution investigation, 97; and campaign against venereal disease, 125

Urbanization, 1, 20, 103, 105, 167

Van Waters, Miriam, 94 (illus.), 217 (n. 15); as juvenile court referee, 113, 129; encouragement of juvenile justice reform, 116, 130, 131–32; management of El Retiro reformatory, 118, 133–34, 142, 144, 147–48, 214 (n. 70); handling of juvenile court cases, 129, 151–52, 153, 154, 155, 161, 178–79, 183; background, 130; *Parents on Probation*, 130; *Youth in Conflict*, 130; "Where Girls Go Right," 133; and domestic service employment, 146

Venereal disease: eugenics movement and, 97; military campaign against, 121, 122, 126, 127; Progressive women reformers and, 121, 124–26, 186; compulsory examination and quarantine for, 124, 125, 126, 145; juvenile court system and, 140, 144, 145, 180–81

Ventura (Calif.) state reformatory, 147

Vermont, age-of-consent law, 32

Victorian morality, 2, 16, 19, 32, 53, 95, 101, 189

Virginia, age-of-consent law, 36

Virginia Industrial School for Colored Girls, 119

Virginia State Federation of Colored Women's Clubs, 119

Virginity. *See* Chastity

Wages, for women, 46–47, 55, 170–71

Waverly House (New York), 113–14

Weeks, Jeffrey, 46

Weller, Charles, 73

Wells, Alice Stebbins, 92 (illus.), 110–11, 123

Wells, Ida B., 29

White Cross Society, 11

White Rose Home (New York), 27

"White slavery," 11–12, 50, 84, 97

White Slavery (Mann) Act (1910), 97–98

White supremacy, 28–29, 35–36

Wigmore, John H., 70

Wilbur, Curtis D., 74

Willard, Frances, 18–19, 24–25, 83 (illus.); as WCTU president, 10; and age-of-consent reform, 16, 35; and antilynching campaign, 29

Williams, Fannie Barrier, 28

Wilson, Woodrow, 125

Woman's Christian Temperance Union (WCTU), 19; and age-of-consent reform, 8–9, 15, 16, 30, 34, 35, 36; social purity campaigns, 10–11, 35; black women and, 26–27; and antilynching campaign, 29–30; and rape prosecutions, 72

Woman's Era, 28, 29, 30

Woman's Era Club (Boston), 28, 29–30

Woman's Journal, 16

Women Lawyers' Journal, 112

Women professionals, 185; police officers, 5, 96, 110, 111, 186; probation officers, 5, 96, 112, 153, 186; judges, 5, 96, 112–13, 129, 186; Progressive campaign for judicial appointment of, 96, 109, 110, 186; and reform of juvenile justice system, 109–10, 129, 131–32, 143, 156; judicial "referees," 113, 129; in campaign against venereal disease, 121, 123–24, 186; "protective officers," 123, 125; physicians, 123–24, 144–45; efforts to reform delinquent girls, 129, 141–42, 143–44, 146, 147, 187; and male moral offenders, 153–55

Women's suffrage, 15–16, 30–31, 73

Women's Trade Union League, 99

Woods, Robert A., 104, 106, 107; *Young Working Girls*, 100–101

Woolwine, Thomas, 132

Working-class parents, 2; use of courts to control daughters, 5, 6, 39, 49, 158–59, 176, 177–79, 181, 184, 188; conflicts over daughters' autonomy, 5, 6, 50, 53, 159, 167, 181, 184; standards of morality, 5, 43, 46–47; and rape prosecutions, 39, 43; and age-of-consent laws, 39, 49, 188; attitudes toward sexuality, 43, 44–46; and pregnancy of daughters, 51, 52; middle-class reformers' criticisms of, 102–3, 105, 106, 107; working mothers, 107–8, 152–53, 170, 174–75; juvenile courts' criticisms of, 150–53, 182; use of courts to control sons, 176–78

Working-class young women: middle-class reformers and sexuality of, 1, 2, 3, 4, 9, 24–25, 62, 142, 185, 187, 188; sexual regulation and, 1, 2, 4, 39, 49, 108, 118, 129, 188, 189; employment, 2, 21–22, 48, 55, 103–4, 106, 135, 172; recreational activities, 3, 22–23, 48, 104, 106–7; parental use of courts to control, 5, 6, 39, 49, 158–59, 176, 177–79, 181, 184, 188; conflicts with parents over autonomy, 5, 6, 50, 53, 159, 167, 181, 184; sexual attitudes and behaviors, 20, 24, 25, 39, 53–57, 68, 136–38, 140–41, 143, 187, 188–89; role in family economy, 20–21, 47–48, 159–60; sexual exploitation of, 23, 57, 58–60, 138–39, 140, 185, 188; out-of-wedlock pregnancies, 24, 51, 52, 57–58, 59, 140, 188; male fears of sexuality of, 31, 32, 33, 68; runaways, 50–51, 56, 138; Progressive social studies of, 100–101, 103. *See also* Female delinquency; Sexual delinquency

World War I, 121, 126, 127, 186

Young Men's Christian Association (YMCA), 34

Young Women's Christian Association (YWCA), 34, 123–24

Youth culture, 3, 5

Delinquent Daughters: Protecting and Policing Adolescent Female Sexuality in the United States, 1885-1920, by Mary E. Odem (1995)

U.S. History as Women's History: New Feminist Essays, edited by Linda K. Kerber, Alice Kessler-Harris, and Kathryn Kish Sklar (1995)

Common Sense and a Little Fire: Women and Working-Class Politics in the United States, 1900–1965, by Annelise Orleck (1995)

How Am I to Be Heard?: Letters of Lillian Smith, edited by Margaret Rose Gladney (1993)

Entitled to Power: Farm Women and Technology, 1913–1963, by Katherine Jellison (1993)

Revising Life: Sylvia Plath's Ariel Poems, by Susan R. Van Dyne (1993)

Made from This Earth: American Women and Nature, by Vera Norwood (1993)

Unruly Women: The Politics of Social and Sexual Control in the Old South, by Victoria E. Bynum (1992)

The Work of Self-Representation: Lyric Poetry in Colonial New England, by Ivy Schweitzer (1991)

Labor and Desire: Women's Revolutionary Novels in Depression America, by Paula Rabinowitz (1991)

Community of Suffering and Struggle: Women, Men, and the Labor Movement in Minneapolis, 1915–1945, by Elizabeth Faue (1991)

All That Hollywood Allows: Re-reading Gender in 1950s Melodrama, by Jackie Byars (1991)

Doing Literary Business: American Women Writers in the Nineteenth Century, by Susan Coultrap-McQuin (1990)

Ladies, Women, and Wenches: Choice and Constraint in Antebellum Charleston and Boston, by Jane H. Pease and William H. Pease (1990)

The Secret Eye: The Journal of Ella Gertrude Clanton Thomas, 1848–1889, edited by Virginia Ingraham Burr, with an introduction by Nell Irvin Painter (1990)

Second Stories: The Politics of Language, Form, and Gender in Early American Fictions, by Cynthia S. Jordan (1989)

Within the Plantation Household: Black and White Women of the Old South, by Elizabeth Fox-Genovese (1988)

*The Limits of Sisterhood: The
Beecher Sisters on Women's Rights
and Woman's Sphere*, by Jeanne
Boydston, Mary Kelley, and Anne
Margolis (1988)